THE LONGS OF LOUISIANA

THE
LONGS
OF LOUISIANA

By Stan Opotowsky

E. P. DUTTON & CO., INC.

New York 1960

The author gratefully acknowledges the permission of the
respective publishers to quote from the following books:

Forerunners of American Fascism, by Raymond Gram Swing
(Julian Messner, Inc., 1935)

Huey Long—A Candid Biography, by Forrest Davis (Dodge
Publishing Co., 1935)

Behind the Ballots, by James A. Farley (Harcourt, Brace Inc.,
1938)

Southern Politics, by V. O. Key, Jr. (Alfred A. Knopf, 1949)

Louisiana Hayride, by Hartnett T. Kane (Wm. Morrow & Co.,
1941)

Library of Congress Catalog Card Number: 60-6001

Manufactured in the United States of America
By American Book-Stratford Press, Inc., New York

DEDICATION
To Martha,
and to Peter and Anne

Contents

5923-19

7

Illustrations
Following page 96

Huey Long as a salesman.

Huey in the Senate.

Huey in New York.

Huey in the statehouse just before his assassination.

Mrs. Huey Long.

Governor Richard W. Leche.

Luncheon at Antoine's.

Abe Shushan.

Seymour Weiss.

Former Governor James A. Noe.

Dr. James Monroe Smith.

Earl Long on the stump.

Mrs. Earl K. Long.

Earl Long in July 1959.

Leander Perez.

Russell Long.

9

Preface

I WAS FIVE YEARS OLD, AND STARTING KINDERGARTEN IN NEW Orleans, when Huey Long became governor of Louisiana to save us all from the depression.

I was twelve years old when a neighbor's middle-of-the-night scream to her husband—"My God, you'll lose your job" —told us Huey Long was dead. (Her husband was a highway commissioner. He would lose his job only if someone killed Huey.)

I was fifteen years old, and writing my first lines for the New Orleans *Times-Picayune,* when suddenly Huey's political heirs began appearing on our front page, adorned in handcuffs, as the Louisiana scandals broke.

I was twenty-five years old when I first became indebted to the Longs; I received a veteran's bonus, courtesy of Governor Earl Long, just in time to furnish my first apartment after I married.

I was thirty-six years old when I sat down to write a book about the Longs of Louisiana.

In brief, I have lived in the shadow of the Longs all my life. And yet when the time came to write this book, I faced an enormous reporting job because I knew many opinions but very few hard facts about this remarkable political family. My father had told me that Huey Long, for all his faults, was trying to help the poor people. My first editors on the *Times-Picayune* told me that Huey Long was just a cheap demagogue hoodwinking all the people. My history and civics teachers didn't tell me much either way because they felt it practical not to mention so controversial a man.

I had to dig, and what follows is the result. I found several good biographies of Huey Long as well as *Louisiana Hay-ride,* Hartnett T. Kane's excellent chronicle of the scandals. But these were all written many years ago, too early to pass full judgment on the lasting good which is as much the Long legacy as the scandals. Too, these seemed to pass off Huey's brother, Earl, as just a hungry relative who blundered into power—but actually Earl subsequently made a record all his own. These books were all written too soon to encompass Russell's record in the United States Senate.

I emerged from my researches with the feeling that those who were willing to sell their freedom were contented with the price they received. The others—those who valued consti-tutional government above all—despised the Longs.

It was easy to be anti-Long as I studied the chronicles of demagoguery and political chicanery. But, I must confess, it was also easy to be pro-Long that day the bonus check arrived in time to pay for our newly bought furniture. It all depends upon your point of view.

There are many points of view cited in this book, and some of them belong to friends who helped so much during the research and writing. I owe particular thanks to Edgar A. Poe, the Washington correspondent, Arthur F. Felt, Jr., the city editor, and Warren Nardelle, the librarian, of the New Orleans *Times-Picayune;* to Warren J. Rogers, Jr., an ex-Louisianian who is now a Washington correspondent of the New York *Herald Tribune;* to Edward W. Stagg, an ex-newspaperman gone right with the Public Affairs Research Council; to Margaret Dixon, whose political savvy shows in every edition of her Baton Rouge *Morning Advocate;* to Mel Opotowsky, for having the good sense to write the college thesis which would be useful six years later; to George S. Trow, Jr., for his nimble fingers and sturdy legs; and to the editors of the New York *Post* who graced the project with kindness and understanding.

There have been many political giants in the history of our country, some selfless leaders and some crass demagogues, but there has been no family like the Longs. They have given

Louisiana what amounts to three generations of government in the thirty-three years normally considered a single generation: Huey was a generation unto himself in Louisiana politics; his brother Earl was certainly his own political generation; and his son, Russell, now is prepared to provide still a third generation of Long politics.

This book is the story of these three generations, told, it is hoped, with full appreciation of all of the good and all of the bad which has been their result.

S.O.

THE LONGS OF LOUISIANA

CHAPTER ONE

"When you have a perfect democracy it is pretty hard to tell it from a dictatorship."

"FIRST YOU COME INTO POWER—THEN YOU DO THINGS," SAID Huey Long. Huey came into great power and did some fantastic things. Next was Earl Long, with new power to do new things. Now Russell Long is on the threshold of authority, and after Russell there surely will come more Longs promising to do more things with more power.

For thirty years, on and off, Huey and Earl Long have run Louisiana. They gave the nation the closest thing it has ever known to absolute dictatorship. They earned the world's scorn and the world's guffaws, and they also earned the pious devotion of a large segment of Louisiana. They have weathered impeachment, scandal, prosecution, Congressional investigation, palace revolt, and psychiatric incarceration. The nation has had other bosses and demagogues, quick flashes like Joe McCarthy and durable types like Harry Byrd. But it has had no other ruling family like the Longs of Louisiana. Virginians may do the Byrd bidding at the polls, but only in Louisiana do the people purchase advertisements in the religious columns of the newspapers offering "grateful thanks to St. Rita and Huey P. Long for favors granted."

The founder of the dynasty was Huey, a crude and comical and brilliant man who cut a wide swath across the nation in the early 1930's. The mention of his name today conjures up visions of a hoary political giant, long entrenched. Yet the truth is that Huey Long served only one term as governor and less than a full term as United States senator before an assassin's bullet cut him down. He grabbed all his power and did all his deeds in that short span.

Upon Huey's death Louisiana fell to those henchmen whose grab into the boodle bag was swiftest and firmest. For several rollicking years they ruled on the strength of Huey's voice: their radio network played recordings of the dead leader's speeches to vouch for their stewardship. The nominal chieftain was the governor, Richard W. Leche, who frankly said that "when I took the oath of office I didn't take any vow of poverty." His income-tax return backed him up on that. In his three years as Louisiana's $7,500-a-year governor he made $450,000.

But whereas Huey had the touch, all these men had was grab; and soon the pretenders to Huey's throne marched in lockstep to the federal penitentiary. This did not sour Louisiana on Longism, however. Instead, the scandal merely convinced the electorate that it had better avoid synthetics and stick to the real thing. It began by installing Huey's brother Earl as governor. "Happy days are here—the Longs are back in the saddle!" he shouted, and he sat as governor three times, the only man in Louisiana history to do so. Another brother, George, was sent to Congress, and before long there came Russell, Huey's oldest son: Russell has been a fixture on campaign platforms since he was fourteen, and he became United States senator the first year he was old enough to run.

The world outside Louisiana often has laughed at the Longs, and indeed at Louisiana itself for tolerating the Longs. Huey seemed the buffoon, a puffy-faced man with a bulbous burlesque-comic's nose, with a passion for controversy. Earl was a profane, horse-playing hick who became world famous as "the crazy governor" after he wiggled loose from the mental institution to which his wife committed him. Newspaper readers even got a few chuckles out of Russell. There was one election day, for example, when the scion of the great political family was turned away from the polls because he had forgotten to register.

But within Louisiana the laughs often brought tears. As Huey said, "You've got to get the power," and he got it. He made the state militia his personal army, and rammed through a law exempting it even from court injunction. He made most of the state legislature his personal rubber stamp, and then urged its re-election because it was "the best money can buy." The judiciary consisted largely of his judges, and when the Bar Association revolted he formed his own bar association. His State Tax Commission was empowered to change any local assessment, so that he could punish rebellious city governments by whittling down their income or so he could leash troublesome businessmen by hiking their taxes ruinously. His bank examiners controlled the banks, his "Civil Service Board" could hire and fire police chiefs, his attorney general could supersede any district attorney, and his School Budget Committee could pass on the appointment of every teacher. His own men could not rebel against him because they signed undated resignations before they collected their first pay check.

When the Baton Rouge parish police jury—Louisiana's equivalent of a county board of supervisors—stood fast against the onslaught of Huey's power, his legislature passed a bill packing the jury so that the anti-Long jurymen were outnumbered. And when the shocked anti-Longites gathered to discuss their plight, the state police broke up their meeting by force.

You couldn't lick Huey's militia, state police, and Criminal Identification Bureau (the latter were secret police with the authority to hold a citizen without charge and without bail). And you couldn't lick his ex-officio goons, either. On several occasions these toughs assaulted political irritants and then presented police-court judges presigned pardons from the governor.

Huey would punish entire cities for political transgressions. When Shreveport balked at accepting Huey's free schoolbooks, because it could afford its own, he blocked construction of a federal airfield by withholding the use of state land. He would relent, he said, only after:

1. Shreveport agreed to accept the textbooks.
2. Mayor L. E. Thomas publicly apologized for his "attacks."
3. The people of Shreveport assured him that henceforth its citizens would "bow to me on the streets and not scowl at me."
4. The elite of Shreveport ceased "ignoring" him at "public functions."

There was no crevice too dark for Huey's sight when he wanted a job done. Dr. V. L. Ray resigned after eighteen years as president of the State Normal College because, he said, "On election day Governor Long called me on the telephone and told me that one of the ballot boxes near the school wasn't going right. He told me to get out and get busy."

Yes, Huey got the power, and he thought no one dared challenge it. When a Senate committee investigated him, he sat in the front row and blandly ordered one witness not to answer questions.

"On what grounds?" sputtered the enraged committee counsel.

"On the authority of the Kingfish of Louisiana," Huey answered. The witness made it plain that he recognized this authority over that of the United States Senate, and the exasperated committee counsel had no choice but to dismiss him.

When Earl Long succeeded to the throne, his power was not so obvious. He did not march the militia through sullen communities and he had no secret police. But many in Louisiana thought Earl was more dangerous because his power was built where it could not be so readily seen. He had absolute hire-and-fire power over some forty state boards which could regulate anything from the liquor industry to the state mental hospitals. These were his strength.

Earl was a browbeater, a man who bawled out legislators

on the floor of the House or Senate, a man who hailed officials into his office for loud dressing downs well salted with threats and curses. He knew he could get away with it. "Anybody who tells you the Louisiana legislature can't be bought doesn't know what he's talking about," Earl said.

Once, when one of his pet bills failed to pass, Earl charged onto the floor of the Senate screaming, "Double cross! I had sixty-nine votes—more than enough." Then he ran a cold eye around the hushed room. First one, then another, and then a third red-faced legislator shuffled up to the clerk to change his vote. When the parade was through, Governor Long did indeed have his sixty-nine votes, and the bill was passed.

Earl was not only a tough governor; he was also a tough man. He bit the finger off one opponent and he sank his teeth into the neck of another. When a committee chairman refused Earl permission to speak, the governor simply gave the man a shove and seized the microphone by force.

Both Huey and Earl used the state's property as their very own. Huey didn't like the executive mansion, and tore it down without bothering to get the legislature's permission. A New Orleans newspaper revealed that a full-time state policeman was the manager of Earl's farm, a circumstance not entirely inappropriate, it developed, because the laborers were state convicts. Earl said he paid the prisoners $25 a week. One complained that he was getting only $10 for his seven-day week. The governor replied that this particular convict was a spendthrift and that the money was being saved for him.

But despite Earl's power, and despite his feat of becoming Louisiana's only three-time governor, many people consider him only a stand-in. Russell is the true heir, they say. Russell is Huey's son and "the spittin' image of Huey." He doesn't have the affinity for the country folk that his father and uncle displayed, but on the speaking platform he can be another Huey when he puts his mind to it and forgets his New Orleans airs. And it is Russell's hand which must grasp the reins of Longism now.

Will his hold be firm? There is no indication of how Russell would handle power. He has served a little more than two terms in the United States Senate, but he has held no position in Louisiana which has made him anyone's boss. Those who know him best say that he would never become a ruthless autocrat like his father or even a domineering overseer like his uncle. Russell will gain power, they say, but he will use it with far more compassion than his predecessors showed their subjects.

As members of this single family succeed one another as Louisiana's rulers, it is natural to talk of the "Long Dynasty" and the "Long Machine." The phrases are proper, however, only by connotation, not by definition. This may be a dynasty, but success is by no means automatic. Each Long has to fight for his place. Earl was frozen out for years after Huey's death.

Certainly Huey did not groom Earl as his heir apparent. Huey said, "One Long in politics is enough," and he continually frustrated his younger brother's political ambitions. The feeling erupted into a bitter family feud, one which led Earl and brother Julius to give damning testimony against Huey to a Senate committee and which once induced Earl to run for office on an anti-Long ticket. Huey was only forty-two when he was killed, and he had given little thought to training his teen-aged sons to follow him onto the throne.

Earl, now sixty-three, has shown more inclination to tolerate the other Longs in politics. He made Russell his protégé and he helped Russell get elected to the United States Senate. Earl is childless, a condition which grieves him deeply, and he tries very hard to heap a father's affection onto nephew Russell. But they are not without their political differences. They backed opposing candidates for governor in 1952, and Earl is quite candid about his doubts that Russell can get the country folk to follow him the way they followed Longs in the past. Brother George, who was a Congressman until he died, sought several times, but always in vain, to get the family to back him for governor. There is considerable evidence that everyone believes in the Long dynasty except the Longs themselves.

Yet in effect there is a dynasty, centered upon the magic memory of Huey. The body of Huey Long reposes not in a cemetery, but in the sunken garden of the state Capitol grounds. From the Capitol tower a light shines eternally (or almost) upon the monument to the Kingfish, and folk from the backwoods still make pilgrimages to his grave. The years of scandal and exposé have not stained Huey's memory for the poor folk, and perhaps their eagerness to vote for someone—anyone—named Long is a form of wishful thinking, a step back to the good old days.

The Longs don't operate a machine in the Tammany Hall sense, with its precinct captains and district leaders. Late in his brief career Huey began organizing along these lines; but, as always, his motives and his techniques were unique. He formed the Louisiana Democratic Association in New Orleans chiefly as a defense against the city's Chocktaw Club, the so-called "Tammany Hall of the South." His real organization was the network of Share-the-Wealth Clubs.

They were his bid for national power, and they stretched from Louisiana to both coasts of the nation. Unlike most organizations built of demagogic premises and oratory, Huey's clubs were not a money-making racket. There were no dues and no contributions. The clubs were designed only to carry the message of Huey Long to the rest of the nation, for Huey was determinedly heading toward the Presidency of the United States when he was shot down in his Capitol in 1935. There were thousands of these Share-the-Wealth Clubs, and they claimed a membership of millions when Huey was killed. Certainly they were the nucleus of a tremendous personal political machine, the likes of which the nation has never seen.

But when Huey died, the Share-the-Wealth organization died with him. A few of the boys tried to convert the clubs into a profitable racket, but they did not get very far. Neither Earl nor Russell has made any attempt to revive the organization, partly because they seem to have no national ambitions and partly because there is no depression to feed upon.

Earl Long's organization of today is simply the state government. The Long people hold the state jobs, and the outsiders don't. It is not unusual in Louisiana for state employees to find portions of their pay checks withheld for campaign contributions. ("De ducts are flying," say the jobholders at such times.) The first order of business for every Long legislature is to wreck any effective civil service which a previous administration may have installed.

This, furthermore, is the only organization which Earl wants. State Senator Charles Deichmann, a Long leader from New Orleans, explains it this way: "Earl doesn't believe in grooming successors. He always busts up his organization and rebuilds after an election. When he's out, he wants the whole bunch out with him. That way everyone stays dependent on him and nobody gets big ideas."

Huey and Earl's strength has not been with the doorbell-ringing precinct workers; it has been with the voters themselves. Why? The newspapers have constantly exposed graft and shakedowns and the boldest kind of political nepotism, yet the voters blithely reaffirmed their devotion to the Longs and Longism. There must be a secret. There is. The secret ingredient is money. Louisiana is The Welfare State. Its poor get three times the national average of welfare benefits in some form or other.

This was Huey's pitch when he started—to "Share the Wealth," to make "every man a king"—and it remains the Long pitch to this day. Let the others dabble in such passing fancies as isolationism, Red-hunting, and even white supremacy. The Longs have something more durable. The poor are always with us—and they vote.

The poor, as much as the Gold Coast politicians with their ostentatious estates, are the direct beneficiaries of Longism. Miles and miles of good paved roads reach out to the most remote farmers. Sturdy Long-built bridges cross the myriad water holes in the swamp country. Thirteen charity hospitals, good ones, treat millions throughout the state for everything from cancer to a toothache. Public schools provide free textbooks, free lunches, free transportation, and even free pencils and erasers. The Louisiana old-age pension is one of the nation's highest, and it goes higher with each new Long administration. Six out of every ten persons over sixty-five draw the pension; this is three times the national average. The Public Affairs Research Council of Louisiana compiled statistics to show that 8.3 per cent of the state's population gets some sort of public aid, and these people, with their large families, may represent as much as 30 to 40 per cent of the vote.

Louisiana's welfare bill is $145,000,000 a year, topped only by the much larger states of California, New York, and Texas. Louisiana leads the nation in old-age assistance and disability assistance, and is third in aid to dependent children. Although Louisiana's per capita income is fortieth in the nation, its per capita public assistance is third. Louisiana is third in the ratio of its income to the amount it spends on its public schools.

Where does the money come from? Huey used to get on the radio and tell the people that it's all very simple—"Share the wealth," cut down the great fortunes, soak the big corporations. Louisiana has cut down on no great fortunes. It has soaked the corporations up to a point: it has severance taxes which bring in $130,000,000 from the oil and sulfur interests. It also draws $117,000,000 in matching federal funds. But if the rich get soaked, the poor get liberally sprinkled. There's a tax on everything in Louisiana from auto parking and laundry to slot machines (even though they're illegal). In 1950 Earl Long refused to exempt even funerals, coffins, and tombstones from the sales tax. Louisiana's per capita income ranks fortieth in the nation, yet its per capita tax ranks fourth.

The "better people," who always oppose Longism, splutter and sputter with indignation because the masses cannot understand that the free ride is not really free. But the country folk don't care. Show them the statistics, and they say: "That may be true, but at least we get something from Long. The others give us nothing."

They're not far wrong. It is true that Longism produced a governor who bragged that he took no vow of poverty, but it is also true that the reformers produced a candidate whose campaign slogan was "Live and let live." As long as there has been a Louisiana there has been someone gobbling at the trough, and leftovers taste better than nothing.

Iberville and Bienville founded New Orleans in 1718, and immediately the city became the center of a vast hoax. The Mississippi Company, chartered by the King of France to exploit the Louisiana territory, began selling stock on promises of great wealth from the gold and silver mines—even though Bienville had informed the company that there was no gold or silver to be had. To create the impression that colonists were rushing to build up the new land, the Mississippi Company rounded up every bum, high-born and low, it could locate in Paris, and these were all but shanghaied onto the waiting ships. Many were actual criminals funneled from the jails. When the first colonists complained of the lack of white women in Louisiana, eighty-eight girls were taken from the Paris house of correction to fill the need.

Bienville, the first governor of the territory, quit in disgust in 1743, and was succeeded by the Marquis de Vaudreuil who brought to New Orleans its first state dinners, its first fancy balls, and its first taste of organized political corruption. He peddled the government's business openly, and sold the provisions France sent him for use by the army.

The Louisianians soon learned to take their territorial government with a grain of salt and a bushel of cynicism. It was just as well. For one period they could hardly tell which nation governed them anyway. As France lost its foothold in the New World, it ceded Louisiana to Spain in 1762—but the colonists were not informed until 1764, and for seven years after that the French continued to administer the territory while waiting for the Spanish to send in forces.

In 1800 Spain, unable to cope with the roistering territory, gave it back to France, but it was three years before any

French arrived to take command. When they did come, it was just in time for the Louisiana Purchase. Thus on November 3, 1803, Louisiana was handed by the Spanish to the French and, scarcely a month later, on December 20th, it was handed by the French to the United States. The colonists by now didn't care who governed them, although there were some tears shed in the streets of New Orleans upon the thought that the American barbarians would destroy the finery of Creole culture.

The Americans did bring their own brand of machine politics, as corrupt as the Mississippi Company. The territory's business was conducted through graft. Every governmental function, even tax collecting, went to the highest bidder on contract. The entire New Orleans police department changed with each new political administration. Bought voters were herded into the polls in full view of the public.

The general disdain for law showed itself in actual piracy. By 1813 Jean Lafitte, captain of the band of pirates and smugglers of Barataria Bay, was the leading supplier of the New Orleans merchants. Lafitte moved about the city unmolested. When Governor Claiborne offered a reward of $500 for his arrest, Lafitte plastered the city with formally worded proclamations offering $1,500 for the governor's arrest. When Lafitte's brother, Pierre, eventually was indicted, the district attorney resigned so that he could become Pierre's defense attorney (at a fee of $20,000).

Louisiana was admitted to the union in 1812. The state legislature immediately became a coalition of the rural planters and the New Orleans businessmen. These people owned eight-ninths of the state's wealth, and showed no inclination to share it. The poor whites either owned the leftover scrub land or else they competed for jobs with the slaves.

Louisiana was a reluctant secessionist when the Civil War came—General Sherman was president of the state university, and resigned only when called to active duty—but it suffered as much as any state during the Reconstruction. General William Butler, in command of the Union occupation forces, was known as "Spoons Butler" because of his fondness for other people's silverware. His brother demanded 50 per cent ownership as the price of operation of any gambling house. The scarlet ladies of New Orleans painted Butler's likeness on the bottom of their chamber pots. Drunken Negroes lounged in the hallway of the state Capitol while carpetbaggers acted in their name to steal the state naked. The old ruling class tried to make political compromises with the Negro, and then gave up. These conditions inspired a bloody riot, and in 1877 the White League managed to throw out the Reconstruction administration and restore the old order with the election of ex-Confederate General Francis T. Nicholls as governor.

The men who ran for office thereafter were caricatures of the Southern gentleman. Their campaigns were confined to exhorting white supremacy and motherhood. Once elected, they did the bidding of the planters and the utilities and the big corporations which paid them far more than the pittance of the state legislature. Never did they hear the mutterings of the poor whites who were kept from revolution only for want of a leader. Never? Well, *once* they did. John M. Parker did run for governor as a "gentleman liberal." He was elected on his promises to induce better things from the big-money boys. They spurned his inducements, and that was that. But his administration was significant for two reasons: he planted the seed of reform, and he convinced a young firebrand named Huey Long that since you can't induce the corporations you must reduce them.

However, it was hard to unite Louisiana for revolution or anything else because of its make-up. To the south the state is Catholic, Creole, free-drinking, easygoing, somewhat liberal, somewhat wealthy with oil in the ground and fish in the sea. To the north it is Baptist, Anglo-Saxon, dry, hard-bitten, uncultured, and mean poor. There are few issues on which the twain might meet.

It took a Huey Long, with his promise to lead the poor out of their misery, to find the common ground. And when he found it, he used it mightily. His successors, Earl and now Russell, use the same pitch. It has been said that the Longs are the only Southern politicians since the Civil War who did not climb to power over the backs of the black man. They climbed up the wells of the Standard Oil Company instead.

The Longs had the voters behind them. They didn't have to steal elections for themselves. But because the Longs did have occasional trouble selling the people on particularly unsavory underlings, Huey's and Earl's administrations have not been free of election shenanigans. Huey once canceled an entire election in the Florida parishes. "Those parishes are too poor to finance an election right now," he explained. Earl met the onslaught of the voting machines with a simple expedient: a law vague enough to allow help to anyone baffled by the machines (and woe to the state jobholder if he or his kin doesn't get a Long poll watcher to help him every time he enters the polling booth).

Since Louisiana is a one-party state, the primary system lends itself to all sorts of shenanigans. The system works like this: There are two primaries. Anyone can enter the first. If no candidate gets 51 per cent of the votes, then the two leading candidates face each other in the second. Any time the anti-Long candidate appears formidable, the Longs can put a fake in the race beside him and split the anti-Long vote while the pro-Long vote remains solid.

Another facet of the system is that every candidate is permitted to appoint his representatives to the Election Commission as soon as he qualifies to run. If he withdraws, his representatives nevertheless remain on the commission. It has been Long practice to put up a number of dummy candidates and then withdraw them as soon as their appointees have packed the Election Commission to control it.

Longism is such a recognizable thing in Louisiana that the state might be said to have a two-party system, pro-Long and anti-Long, except that the opposition can never get together. It always runs through all shades from the pure reformers to the cynical pros who only want to cause enough trouble so that the Longs will buy them off.

The manipulation of elections has made it possible for the Longs to elect not only themselves but also any henchmen they choose. Thus the legislatures assemble and immediately cede their powers to the dictatorship.

Or is it really dictatorship? To be sure, the word is used too loosely, especially by a world which has known Hitler and Stalin. Yet Huey Long certainly was a dictator. He lived in an era of great demagogues—Theodore Bilbo of Mississippi, Eugene Talmadge of Georgia, Ruby Laffoon of Kentucky, to name a few—but these were never his peers in the collection of power. Huey's word was law. A New Orleans woman recalls today, "Even if you had nothing to do with politics you didn't dare criticize Huey in your back yard for fear the neighbors might hear." The man's power cowed all but the most desperate political opponents, and these stood up only because they had nothing left to lose. Furthermore, Huey insisted on complete power for himself alone. He did not permit his lieutenants to appoint even a district road inspector without his personal approval. He personally checked all of the bills passed by the legislature, not only during his term as governor but also after he went to the United States Senate.

Earl Long has not cast such a fearful shadow over the ordinary citizen. However, he has ruled the machinery of the state government just as firmly. Actually, Earl's power was never fully tested, for he used it only to gain immediate goals. Huey, on the other hand, would at times use the power for no reason other than that of showing that the power was there.

Both Longs made certain that there was no competition from parish or city governments. They believed in states' rights, but not in home rule within the state. Their thorn was always New Orleans, and legislatures passed law after law to reduce the unfriendly city government to a façade.

Earl snorts indignantly at any talk about dictatorship. He points out that the Longs spread free education and eliminated the poll tax. "What dictator wants a better educated people and attempts to increase the total vote?" he asks. He has a point: if the people of Louisiana are dictated to, they certainly install the dictator of their own free will, and then return him to office knowing what they will get.

Huey treated the subject more lightly. When he first arrived in Washington to claim his Senate seat, he was asked to describe his position in Louisiana. "Me, I'm the Kingfish of the lodge," he said. Later, when he was bidding for national power and was more sensitive to nation-wide public opinion, he explained: "There is no dictatorship in Louisiana. There is perfect democracy there, and when you have a perfect democracy it is pretty hard to tell it from a dictatorship."

CHAPTER TWO

"I wanted those folks to think I was somebody, and they did."

OLD PAPPY LONG LECTURED HIS SONS OFTEN. "BOYS," HE'D SAY, "there wants to be a revolution. What do the rich folks care for the poor man? Their women don't even comb their own hair." Old Pappy was mean poor at the time. Later he came into better luck, but the Long boys never forgot his words, and for thirty years they've been running Louisiana on a promise to right the wrong of poverty.

Huey said later that everything surrounding his boyhood cried out for the revolution that Pappy proposed. One of his earliest recollections was the pitiful sight of a farmer losing his land at auction. "Before the sale, standing on the steps of the courthouse, this farmer begged the crowd not to bid for his home," Huey said. "He pled that it would be taking it away from his children, that if given time to raise another crop he could pay his debts. No one in the crowd offered a bid. The creditor remained silent until the sheriff was about to declare 'no sale,' when he took courage and made his bid.

"The poor farmer was out. I was horrified. I could not understand. It seemed criminal."

Winn Parish, in northwest Louisiana, is no Garden of Eden even now, but in the days just before the turn of the century it was a grim roll of scrub land producing cotton, hogs, and children, mostly children. There was no railroad and there were few roads. Winn was a bitter land, a desperate land; it was abolitionist and antisecessionist before the Civil War, a feeling born out of hatred for the rich planters rather than sympathy for the slaves.

A visit by Eugene Debs in 1908 prompted the parish to elect a full Socialist ticket to local offices.

It was to miserable Winn Parish that John M. Long brought his family from Virginia in 1859. John's son, Huey, married a Scot, Caledonia Tilson, and on August 30, 1893, she quite unsuspectingly launched a political dynasty when she gave birth to her eighth child, Huey Pierce Long, Jr. (Huey later claimed he was part English, part Dutch, part Welsh, part Irish, part Scotch, and part French. Apparently he was willing to forgo Louisiana's Lithuanian vote.)

Huey, Sr., owned his cotton farm and the log cabin on it, and the family was brought up on hard work and harder praying. Winn was Baptist, so Baptist that an invading Methodist preacher nearly starved to death and had to be rescued by a charitable society. When the railroad came to Winn and brought with it a logging camp, Huey's father sold his farm and moved to another, ten miles from town, so that his family would not be corrupted by the sinful ways of the woodchoppers. The family reading was the Bible. The Longs' only social event was the revival meeting. Young Huey learned the scriptures well, and later recited verse after verse over the radio to vouch for his escapade of the moment. Huey never cursed until he was sixteen, but by the time he was eighteen he had caught up and was forging ahead. Huey told later of backbreaking work in the cotton fields. His brother Julius insisted, however, that "Huey never did a day's work in his life." Old-timers in Winn Parish say the truth is somewhere in between: Huey did work in the fields, but he was also caught stuffing a watermelon in his sack to make it appear he'd picked a lot more cotton than he had.

As a boy he was a thinker. He certainly wasn't a fighter—not then or later. His kid brother, Earl, had to handle the fisticuffs, and often, Earl said, Huey didn't stick around to see how the fight turned out. This distaste for physical battle remained with Huey throughout his lifetime. His greatest victory was scored over an offensive newspaperman whose arms were pinioned back by two bodyguards while Huey rained his swats.

At thirteen Huey was a printer, until the newspaper publisher bought a Linotype machine. At fourteen he was an auctioneer of books. At sixteen he was the high school's champion debater, and he won a scholarship to the state university. His father, by now affluent through land sales to the new railroad, sent six of his nine children to college, but there wasn't enough money left for Huey, even with the scholarship.

Huey early showed a political bent. At fourteen he contracted to manage a man's campaign for election as tick inspector. Huey's deal called for $2.50 to start, and another $2.50 upon the man's election. Young Huey collected his $5.00. He showed early, too, that he thought revenge was part of the game. When the school principal broke up the secret society Huey had formed to run things, Huey circulated a petition among the parents to get the bounder fired. "The school principal was removed," Huey said later, "but I did not go back to school."

He became a traveling salesman, peddling a cooking oil known as Cottolene. He later told reporter Hermann Deutsch, "If I couldn't convince the woman no other way I'd go right into the kitchen and bake a cake for her, or cook supper for the family. I also used the Bible on them, showing where the Lord had forbidden the Israelites to use anything from the flesh of swine food, and how cottonseed oil, seeing it was a vegetable product, was just bound to be pure."

Even when Huey decided to go back to Shreveport High School to complete his education, he continued selling. One day the teacher asked him to define a compound. "Well, Cottolene is a compound," he said, and then he proceeded to give the class a rousing sales talk. He didn't sell any Cottolene in the school but he did get his diploma.

He continued as a salesman and squeezed in a year at the University of Oklahoma, thanks partly to the money he got from kid brother Earl, also a drummer by now. But Huey wanted to be a lawyer. The course was three years, but Huey completed it in one. He worked sixteen hours a day, practically memorizing the texts, and he passed every subject. Nevertheless Tulane would not give him a degree. He never forgave the school for this, and he eventually got his revenge. Not long after he became governor, he decreed one year that the Louisiana automobile license plates be the colors of the state university so that all Tulane people would have to display the purple and gold of their despised football rival.

Finished with law school and yet not able to practice law, Huey was stuck—but not for long. He called upon Frank A. Monroe, chief justice of the state Supreme Court. When Huey finished talking, the chief justice assembled a special meeting of the Bar Association to grant Huey a special examination and then a special meeting of the Supreme Court to conduct that examination. Huey passed, of course, and found himself a lawyer at twenty-one, a lawyer without a college degree.

He went back home to Winn to set up shop. He bought a fifty-cent shingle, "Huey P. Long, Lawyer," and induced the Bank of Winnfield to rent him—on credit—a $4-a-month second-floor room, lighted by a kerosene lamp and equipped with two kitchen chairs and a pine-topped table. The shoestore on the corner let him use the telephone, and Huey was all set, except for clients. Soon one came. Oscar K. Allen, who had the farm next to the Longs, was being sued over an act of kindness that boomeranged. A Winn Parish man had died in Shreveport's Charity Hospital, and the family asked Oscar to arrange to have the body sent home. Bungling Oscar got the name wrong. After the family hauled the pine coffin fourteen miles into the backwoods, they opened it for the wake and found the body of a colored man. The enraged family lugged the coffin fourteen miles back to Winn and announced their intention to sue Oscar. Huey talked them out of it, and thus won his first case.

Still the clients did not come crowding, and Huey went into partnership with his oldest brother. Julius was one of those children Pappy Long had sent to college, and now Julius was Winn's district attorney. His partnership with Huey didn't last. Huey persisted in defending the clients brother Julius was prosecuting; furthermore, Huey was getting them off free with annoying consistency. He developed a special technique to obtain the juries he wanted. Before the trial Huey made it a point to be seen socially with several prospective jurors, even if he had to invite total strangers to dine with him at a restaurant. Naturally the prosecution challenged these "pals" off the jury. In so doing, the prosecution would exhaust its number of challenges. Then Huey could step in and hand-pick his jury from the remaining veniremen.

Eventually Huey found a bonanza—workmen's compensation cases. Most lawyers wouldn't take them because the moneyed people objected. Huey built this specialty into a good business, collecting as much as 50 per cent of the damages awarded as his fee. He furthered his growing reputation as the poor man's lawyer when he forced the Bank of Winnfield to pay off a widow whose funds had been lost to an absconding officer.

In the course of his fight for the widow's funds he met State Senator S. J. Harper, who, though wealthy, grieved much over the misery of Winn's poor whites. Huey spent hours soaking up Harper's Populist philosophy, and it was to Harper that Huey turned when he saw his law practice imperiled. The legislature decided that $300 was the maximum a widow could collect if her husband died as the result of his employer's negligence. Harper promised to try to kill this law, and Huey went to the capital to help.

The legislature he found was by and large a sorry one, typical of the degradation of Louisiana politics in the pre-Long era. The members were for the most part brazen hacks unbashedly serving the special interests which hired them. When Huey tried to testify before the House Ways and Means Committee on behalf of Senator Harper's amendments, the chairman laughed at the unruly upstart from the hills.

"Who do *you* represent?" he asked with obvious scorn.

"Several thousand common laborers," said Huey.

"Are they paying you anything?"

"No."

"They seem to have good sense," said the chairman, and the committee roared with laughter.

Huey reddened and sat down. At midnight the committee prepared to adjourn, still without hearing the fuming little pest from Winn. Huey jumped to his feet and, without being formally recognized, made the speech which launched his political career.

"For twenty years has the Louisiana legislature been dominated by the henchmen and attorneys of the interests," he said. "Those seeking reform have, from necessity, bowed their heads in regret and shame when witnessing the victories of these corrupting influences at this Capitol. But, gentlemen, with all this, not until 1914 did they possess the brazen audacity to command the General Assembly of Louisiana to pass unanimously a law by which a laborer's family should not receive over an average sum of $300 for a life upon whom they depend for education and support, though it be lost while in the honest discharge of duty.

"Yet there are those here representing the combined corporations who declare that they merely seek justice.

"What a subterfuge! Exposure seems to be an irresistible converter. There are hours when the infidel invokes God and the anarchist calls on the government. There are times when the people cling to that which they have repudiated. Can it be that these gentlemen, after exposure seems imminent, soon will attempt to invoke the term 'justice' after their continued practice of such fraud and deceit? We are afraid of such conversions."

World War I came, and Huey showed no inclination to fight. He claimed exemption as a public official; he was a notary public. He didn't get away with that, but he was exempted as the head of a family. In later years it was inevitable that Huey's opponents would taunt him about his war record. He was quite frank about it. He said: "If they'd come and got me I would have grabbed a flag and yelled 'Hurray!' and 'Let's go!' but they didn't come around so I didn't go. I wasn't mad at anybody."

The war gave Huey a chance to settle his debt to Senator Harper. The senator, a pacifist, was indicted for sedition. Huey successfully defended him.

Huey knew now he would go into politics. He tried to become assistant United States attorney in Shreveport; but the corporations, bitter and perhaps frightened over his "rabble rousing" before the legislature, blocked the appointment. Huey said: "Once disappointed over a political undertaking, I could never cast it from my mind. I awaited the opportunity of a political contest."

Huey was only twenty-five. He had to shop around. There weren't many political offices open to a man that young, but finally he found one with no age requirement—railroad commissioner. Brother Earl put up the necessary $125 entry fee, and Huey launched his campaign.

Huey later told Hermann Deutsch: "They told me I'd have to wear slouchy old clothes and chew tobacco and go around with a horse and buggy. Shucks, I got me lots of white linen suits and wore them fresh. I borrowed enough money to buy the newest and shiniest automobile I could get. I wanted those folks to think I was somebody, and they did.

"But where I had my big edge on the other fellows was this: When I was a salesman, I'd never stop in town overnight when I was on the road. I'd drive on beyond town and stop at some farmhouse. They'd always be glad to see somebody that could talk their own language and still had been traveling around. Most times they wouldn't want to take pay for the night's meal and lodging, but I'd always make 'em take a dollar, which was less'n I'd have to pay in town, and made the man my friend. And I'd get his name and address, too, and some time later I'd drop him a letter about crops or something."

Huey kept that file of names, and these were the people he called upon to vote for him for railroad commissioner and maybe get their friends to vote the same way. Brother Earl campaigned house to house. Brother Julius wrote the circulars. Huey tacked up the signs as he went from town to town. "I knocked on an awful lot of doors, selling things the way I used to," he said. He sold Cottolene that way, and he sold Huey Long, too. He was elected railroad commissioner by a scant 636-vote margin.

Huey was a big shot now. He thought his new title so grand that he proposed the commissioners wear gold badges. The Railroad Commission, forerunner of the Public Service Commission, was a perfect sounding board for Huey's fight against the big interests. This fight had picked up real heat now that he had declared a personal vendetta with the Standard Oil Company. (He owned stock in a small oil company, and Standard forced the pipelines to cut off service to all independent companies, making his stock worthless.)

Huey fought the big corporations constantly. He fought them when they were right and he fought them when they were wrong. He blocked one railroad merger that would have cost Louisiana considerable rail traffic, and he blocked another that would have given the state vastly improved service. But he made himself a hero with the voters when he forced cancellation of a telephone rate increase and made it retroactive for two years. Those refund checks were something the people could feel.

Huey also developed into a showboat. When he appeared in the telephone rate case, he cited all the precedents and arguments from memory rather than submit a brief. This was quite a feat, although a pointless one since the judge would give as much attention to a written brief as to Huey's display. Huey began to get rich. His law cases piled up, and he built a $40,000 home in Shreveport; he marched the architect downtown to the Commercial National Bank to show him what kind of grillework he wanted on the front windows.

Huey loved to deflate the big shots. When Louisiana was devastated by a flood, Secretary of Commerce Herbert Hoover rushed to the state with a disaster plan: He told a special gathering of state officials that the federal government would donate millions of cabbage plants to the farmers so that they could recoup their losses. The state officials listened gratefully, all except Huey, who piped, "You ain't gonna turn Louisiana into no cabbage patch." That was the end of the disaster plan.

Huey stepped up his fight against Standard Oil with every fresh breath. In 1920 he backed the "gentleman liberal," John M. Parker, for governor on Parker's promise that he'd do something about Standard's pipeline stranglehold. But after Parker was elected Huey broke with him when the governor refused to adopt Huey's oil program. Huey said later, "He made his own program with the help of the Standard Oil lawyers who had been called in to write some of the laws affecting that corporation." Huey's attacks on Parker got so vitriolic that Parker had him arrested for criminal libel; Huey was convicted but given a suspended sentence and fined one dollar, a fine the judge and the two defense lawyers paid when Huey refused.

There was only one thing left for Huey to do—run for governor himself. Only Huey could save the people from being devoured by Standard Oil and the other vicious corporations. The election of 1924 came due, and Huey entered the race. The Messiah had arrived, he told the awe-struck country folk who flocked to hear him. Speaking in the Cajun country under the famous Evangeline oak, he said:

"And it is here that Evangeline waited for her lover Gabriel, who never came. This oak is an immortal spot, made so by Longfellow's poem. But Evangeline is not the only one who has waited here in disappointment. Where are the schools you have waited for for your children, that have never come? Where are the roads and highways that you spent your money to build, that are no nearer than before? Where are the institutions to care for the sick and disabled? Evangeline wept bitter tears in her disappointment. But they lasted through only one lifetime. Your tears in this country, around this oak, have lasted for generations. Give me a chance to dry the tears of those who still weep here."

There was Huey's program—the schools, the roads, the hospitals. Neither he nor any other Long has ventured from it to this day. But first Huey had to get elected, and here he ran into an unexpected snarl. The Ku Klux Klan became a campaign issue. This is especially ticklish in Louisiana, for the state is divided between the bigoted pro-Klan north and the Catholic anti-Klan south. Of Huey's two opponents, attorney Hewitt Bouanchaud from the Cajun country was bitterly anti-Klan, and hardware merchant Henry Fuqua was lukewarm, with some leanings to the Klan. Huey tried to straddle the issue. In the south he talked anti-Klan; in the north he put his hopes on the acknowledged Klan leader, Swords Lee, for Swords Lee was Huey's uncle.

On election day it rained. When the first box reported in, it was from Clay Parish. The vote was 60 for Huey, 1 for Fuqua. Huey's headquarters cheered. But Huey slumped to his chair in gloom. "I'm beat," he said. "There should have been 100 for me and one against. Forty per cent of my country vote is lost." It was, washed out by the rain. Fuqua was elected.

Huey studied the returns. He found that in the Protestant north he was as strong as he hoped to be. In New Orleans he was trounced, as he had expected. But in south Louisiana he was, to his surprise, quite weak. Obviously this Baptist uplander was suspect, and Huey had to do something to inspire confidence. He shopped around for an idea, and the impending election for United States senator gave it to him. Edwin Broussard, beloved throughout south Louisiana as "Cousin Ed," was running for re-election. Huey would support him.

The choice wasn't difficult. Broussard's opponent was L. E. Thomas, the mayor of Shreveport, and Thomas already was Huey's bitter enemy. Huey's speeches against Thomas became more vulgar by the day. "Ladies and gentlemen," he'd say, "at birth the sugar tit of the state of Louisiana has been in L. E. Thomas' mouth. It's been there ever since."

Although Huey could best help Broussard by campaigning in north Louisiana, he insisted on touring with the senator in the south so that the Cajuns could see him fighting alongside their hero. Broussard was re-elected, but that wasn't important. Huey had won over the Cajuns, and that *was* important.

In 1928 he ran for governor again. This time his opponents were Lieutenant Governor O. H. Simpson and Congressman Riley Wilson. The "better people" were backing Wilson.

It was a hot campaign. There are no accurate reports of Huey's speeches because the newspaper reporters of the time said they simply couldn't print this man's utterances in a family newspaper. Huey campaigned against all the previous administrations Louisiana had known. "There needs to be a revolution," Pappy Long had said, and now here was Huey promising it to Pappy and all the other pappies who had chafed so long under the coalition of the plantation owners and the corporations. Huey made his promises: free textbooks, vocational training for the deaf, dumb, and blind, free bridges, hard-surfaced roads, better marketing facilities for the farmers, draining of the marshes, enforcement of conservation (except that in south Louisiana, where the trappers abound, Huey promised to rout the meddlers on the Conservation Commission). He campaigned twenty hours a day, making as many as eight speeches in eight different towns in a single day. He attacked the "plutocrats" and the "plunderers" without respite.

He denounced former Governor Parker so acidly that Parker, a man then pushing seventy, went hunting Huey and found him in the lobby of New Orleans' Roosevelt Hotel. Two of Huey's henchmen pinioned Parker's hands, and Huey swung a roundhouse right. He missed, and dashed into the elevator. Parker wriggled loose and sprinted after him. Both got in just as the doors closed, and the lift started up. They proceeded to stage the most private public fight on record; the only witness was the elevator boy who later reported it wasn't worth seeing. Both men did more missing than hitting.

Election day dawned clear all over Louisiana. There would be no rain to keep Huey's farmers off the muddy roads this time. And when the returns were in, Huey Long had 126,842 votes, Wilson 81,747, and Simpson 80,326.

Up to now Huey had not been taken seriously by the big city newspapers who had looked on him as just another annoying, loud-mouthed radical who would surely be repudiated by sober and right-thinking voters. Now here he was on the verge of becoming governor.

He lacked a majority of votes, and thus wasn't elected yet. Under Louisiana's two-primary system, he would have to face Congressman Wilson in a runoff. But when Wilson began making the rounds of his supporters, the "better people," he found that they were no longer prepared to make campaign contributions. They had seen the vote and suddenly realized that this was a revolution, a fait accompli. They would be wasting their money to throw it into a second election campaign. Wilson had to withdraw. The second primary was called off, and Huey Long was declared governor of Louisiana.

CHAPTER THREE

"I voted No and the machine showed Yes!"

HUEY SWIRLED INTO THE STATEHOUSE AND HIS PALS IMME-
diately followed to take the lush jobs. Huey had promised
during the campaign to eliminate the fee-rich sinecure of
inheritance-tax attorney and use the money to build a new
tuberculosis hospital, but instead he appointed brother Earl
to continue the job, prompting a New Orleans newspaper to
print Earl's picture with the caption "New Lakefront TB
Hospital." He made Oscar Allen, his old Winn neighbor,
chairman of the Highway Commission. He put a country doctor in charge of the charity-hospital network.

Huey didn't have a majority of the legislature behind him,
but that didn't matter. Those representatives up for sale
were quickly bought, and enough of the others were tricked
or bulldozed. Once, when Huey's patronage and reform bills
were jammed in the legislature, the Long floor leaders suddenly moved for passage of *all* bills without debate. The
stunned opposition had to go along or else vote against its
own bills. All measures passed. Then Governor Long riffled
through them, signing those he wanted and vetoing those he
didn't.

The real floor leader of the Long forces was Huey himself. Not content to remain in the governor's office, he bobbed
up and down the aisles of the Senate and House directing
passage of his legislation. Sometimes during a voice vote he
would call out the "Aye" or "Nay" himself when the clerk

44

reached the name of a bought legislator. Huey publicly castigated the men who weren't voting right. When he was told
that his conduct was offensive, he said, "I'd rather violate
every one of the damn' conventions and see my bills passed
than sit back in my office, all nice and proper, and watch
'em die."

In eight months he accomplished all his objectives. He
ran the Highway Commission, the Board of Health, the New
Orleans Levee Board, the Board of Liquidation (which held
vital purse strings), and the Board of Education, all on a
hire-and-fire basis. He passed the law granting free textbooks
to the public schools, and when the Catholics raised a cry he
supplied the parochial schools, too. The constitution insisted
upon separation of church and state, but Huey got around
that by providing the free books to the children rather than
to the schools. He began building the roads he promised,
and no one seemed to care that the state paid $2 per cubic
yard for the same gravel that cost private contractors 67½
cents a yard.

To make certain that nothing would block his path, Huey
handled everything personally. He promised to build an
"airline highway" from Baton Rouge to New Orleans—with
not a single curve—as a replacement for the old river road that
followed the twistings of the Mississippi. Huey negotiated the
purchase of rights of way himself. He ran into only one hitch:
a property holder was offered $2,500 and held out for more.
Huey blew up. "The road's too straight anyway," he snorted.
"It's getting monotonous. We'll build one curve—around
you." The man surrendered, but Huey would deal with him
no further. The man dropped his price to $1,500, yet Huey
was adamant. The road was built straight—with one curve
to keep it from being too monotonous.

Huey took one look at the drafty old executive mansion,
and refused to inhabit it. He took a suite at the Heidelberg
Hotel and asked the legislature for permission to build a
new mansion. The legislature balked, but as soon as it ad-

journed Huey had the mansion torn down, its furnishings sold, and a new one built.

Huey sent the state militia to smash the gambling dens of New Orleans. He wasn't moralistic about it. The gamblers supplied funds to the city machine, and the machine had opposed Huey's election. He got his revenge via the militia.

As the official proceedings of the state legislature indicate, it was in a nasty mood when it reconvened in 1929. Huey had been going too far, stepping on too many toes, too many well-shod toes. For one thing, he was trying to force through an "occupational tax" on his sworn enemy, Standard Oil, and Standard was threatening to close its refineries throughout the state if the tax went through. Rabbi Walter Piser set the tone of the legislative session when he refused an invitation to deliver the opening prayer because he "could not call down the blessings of God on such a governor."

Representative Lavinius Williams rose at the start of the session and asked that the House enforce its rule forbidding lobbying on the floor. Everyone knew what he meant. The governor was the legislature's most dogged lobbyist. Then the House passed a resolution condemning Huey's new superintendent of education for dragging the schools into politics; the superintendent had led a delegation of teachers into the House gallery clamoring for the new tax on Standard Oil to raise funds for education.

The Shreveport *Times* called editorially for impeachment. Then Charles Manship, publisher of the anti-Long Baton Rouge *State Times,* stunned the legislature. He announced that Huey had threatened to "publish the names of the people who are fighting me who have relatives in insane asylums." He means me, said Manship, whose brother, Douglass, was in the East Louisiana Hospital under observation. The legislators were outraged at this low blow. Huey became frightened. He issued orders to his men to adjourn the legislature quickly before something happened.

The motion to adjourn was made, but in the next moment Representative Cecil Morgan was on his feet. He called out in loud, even tones, "I have in my hand an affidavit from a Baton Rouge citizen that the governor has tried to procure the assassination of a member of the House."

There was a gasp. Long's Speaker, John Fournet, banged his gavel and said, "Mr. Sergeant at Arms, seat the gentleman!"

There was bedlam now. The sergeant at arms and two assistants moved through the aisle toward Morgan. Half a dozen anti-Long legislators charged up and brushed them aside. The legislators then formed a cordon around Representative Morgan and escorted him to the front of the chamber.

"It is charged by Battling Bozeman—you will not shout me down—it is charged by Battling Bozeman that Governor Long wanted to hire him to assassinate J. Y. Sanders, Jr.," Morgan said.

A torrent of shouts rained through the House, and Speaker Fournet called, "A motion to adjourn sine die is recognized. A vote."

The representatives scurried to their seats to press their buttons on the electric voting machine. The red and green lights blinked on the board over the speaker's head. Suddenly there came a cry:

"Fix! Fix! The machine is fixed!"

Representative after representative had punched the button red for no adjournment and then looked up to see the board registering him green—for adjournment.

There was a screech, "I voted No and the machine showed Yes!" There was another cry, and another. Visitors poured down from the gallery and onto the floor. Someone yelled, "Open that machine, you God-damned coward."

One representative leaped to the rostrum, seized the gavel from Speaker Fournet's hand, and began pounding it wildly. Another clambered up the ladder to the voting machine and then leaped down atop a pocket of arguing legislators. There was a flash of brass knuckles, and one representative stumbled bleeding back to his seat.

"Point of order!" came an incongruous cry over the riotous scene. "A motion to adjourn sine die is unconstitutional. No House can adjourn for more than three days without the consent of the other House."

Suddenly there was silence. This was a telling point, the moment of truth, so to speak. The voice continued, "I want to appeal the decision of the Chair."

But the chair was empty. Speaker Fournet had left the hall.

"I call on the clerk to call the role."

But there was no clerk. He, too, had gone.

"Very well, I will call the roll myself."

The roll was called, by voice with no machine used, and the vote was 71 against adjournment, 9 in favor. The House recessed until morning.

Speaker Fournet was there the next day, and apologized. The voting machine registered wrong, he said, because it had not been properly cleared after the previous vote. (Subsequent investigation indicated he was probably correct; for one thing, the voting machine was operated by an anti-Long man.)

That night six thousand attended an impeachment rally in Baton Rouge. Huey, unseen, watched from a nook in the balcony. He noted bitterly the legend on the bass drum of the brass band—"Stancola," the nickname of the employees' band of the Standard Oil Company of Louisiana. Brother Earl rushed up from New Orleans, and he said later that Huey threw himself on his bed that night and wept like a baby.

The House impeached Huey. It made nineteen charges. They were:

1. That he used his appointive power to influence the judiciary.

2. That he was guilty of misuse, misappropriation, and misapplication of state funds.

3. That he bribed and attempted to bribe legislators.

4. That he contracted illegal loans for the state.

5. That he demanded and obtained undated resignations from his appointees.

6. That he removed public-school officials for political purposes.

7. That he made unlawful use of the militia to subordinate military authority.

8. That as governor he attempted to force official bodies in the parishes to follow his dictation in public litigation.

9. That he habitually carried concealed weapons.

10. That he was guilty of violent abuse of citizens and officials who visited him on public business.

11. That he was guilty of gross misconduct in public places.

12. That he publicly flouted the United States and state constitutions and usurped the powers of the legislature.

13. That he caused to be purchased a $20,000 ice machine for the state penitentiary without advertising for bids.

14. That he attempted to intimidate the press through the Manship incident.

15. That he demolished the executive mansion without authority.

16. That he destroyed furniture in the mansion and State House without authority or accounting.

17. That he unlawfully paroled a convict from the penitentiary.

18. That he repeatedly appeared on the floor of the House without authority.

19. That he was guilty of suborning murder in his attempt to hire Battling Bozeman to assassinate J. Y. Sanders, Jr.

The Senate began hearing testimony. The most sensational, of course, came from Bozeman, who had been one of Huey's bodyguards. He testified that one day Huey ranted about the obstructionist tactics of Representative Sanders and then said:

"I've chosen you to do away with the bastard."

"Governor, what do you mean?"

"I mean for you to kill the son of a bitch. Leave him in a ditch where nobody'll know how or where he got there. I'm the governor of this state, and if you're found out I'd give you a full pardon and many gold dollars."

Bozeman said he refused, and was fired.

A parade of legislators testified at the official impeachment proceeding as to how they were browbeaten or bribed or threatened. H. H. Huckaby, of Caddo Parish, said that when he called upon the governor to ask that the parish road maintenance fund be unfrozen he was told: "Caddo Parish has got to get right before it gets a damned thing out of this administration. Before you get anything you will have to see that the schoolbook suit is withdrawn"—Caddo had challenged the legality of the free books—"and that Caddo representatives support me on every damn' thing."

Representative Adolph Gueymard testified that he was told it would be worth his while to support all Long legislation down the line: "The governor asked me how much I owed the banks . . . how much it took me to do business. I told him about $25,000 a year. He told me I would not have to worry as he controlled the bank examiners and the banks were violating the law anyhow. The first position the governor offered me was that of head of the penitentiary at St. Gabriel and then a job on the Highway Commission."

Representative Davis Richane said that he and Representative Felix Delaune were asked to make their votes pro-Long. What followed, he testified, was this:

"I want a job," said Delaune.

"How much education have you got?" asked Huey.

"I have very little but I have some brains."

"Would $150 a month do?"

"Yes, with expenses."

"All right, you start on the payroll March 24th. Good night. That's all."

But that wasn't all, Richane testified. Representative Casagne came in next and was asked his price. He said he wanted to name the registrar of voters in his parish.

Richane testified, "The governor simply called in his secretary and told her to remove the registrar of St. John Parish."

Sheriff C. H. Andrews of East Feliciana Parish then testified that Governor Long told him of one prominent legislator, "I bought and paid for Mr. Bennett like you would a carload of potatoes." Mr. Bennett thereafter was dubbed "Sack of Potatoes Bennett" in the legislature, but his constituents, who apparently liked potatoes, kept returning him to office.

Not all of the testimony at the impeachment proceedings was on such serious issues as bribery. Widowed Mrs. L. W. Lundy, telephone switchboard operator for the Highway Commission, said she was slow in connecting the governor to Chairman Oscar Allen and that she heard the governor tell Allen, "The first thing I want you to do is go out and fire that —— telephone operator." Mrs. Lundy said she was dismissed that afternoon.

One of the charges against the governor was that he was guilty of "gross misconduct in public places." Huey, who hadn't used a cussword until he was sixteen, had become the gayest blade in New Orleans' French Quarter.

Now before the legislature there came a hula dancer. She solemnly testified that she had sat on Huey's lap—she said she was wearing a grass skirt and "something up here and nothing between here and here"—during a Mardi Gras party in New Orleans. She also said she had seen Huey over in the corner on a couch stroking another girl's hair. The House formally demanded—and got—the hula dancer's telephone number before it dismissed her. Then came the owner of "The Frolics" cabaret who testified that in his place Huey was known as the "Singing Fool" because of his performances with the band. "He's not much of a singer but he gets plenty of encores," the man said.

The investigation hit upon some expense funds unaccounted for. Seymour Weiss, the ex-shoe clerk who had become major-domo of the Roosevelt Hotel, testified that some of the money went for a party for visiting governors and that he had better not say exactly how each dollar was spent. Throughout the nation the next day governors who had attended the party howled righteously that they hadn't done anything their most Baptist constituent would disapprove.

The testimony rolled on, but Huey did not sit back without a fight. He could not expect solace from the newspapers, but

the Highway Commission trucks and the state police cars
fanned out through Louisiana delivering his printed circulars to the people. "The Same Fight Again—the Standard Oil
Co. vs Huey Long," screamed the headline. And in the text
Huey said, "I had rather go down to a thousand impeach-
ments than to admit I am the governor of a state that does
not dare call the Standard Oil Co. to account so that we can
educate our children and care for the destitute, sick and
afflicted."

Huey called his own mass meeting at Baton Rouge, and
spoke for two hours. "What's this about bribery?" he cried.
"Yes, bribery so the schoolchildren could have free textbooks.
. . . I proposed a little tax on the Standard Oil Co. They told
me if I put a little tax on oil they would impeach me."

Huey got on a state-wide radio network, and he said:
"They"—Standard Oil, of course—"have turned Baton Rouge
into a lobby today to fight the sick, the blind, the deaf, the
dumb and the insane and every schoolchild in the state of
Louisiana. . . . Oh, you know what I mean, all you financial
agents, you henchmen of the Standard Oil Co. who are listening to me. You know what I mean by the use of money in the
city of Baton Rouge today."

Huey took to the stump next. He toured the state. At one
stop he said, "I fought the Standard Oil Co. to put them pie-
eating members of the old gang out of office. They've got
some two-bit stuff about me cussin' out somebody at some
time or another and about me tearing down the mansion but
them ain't the real reasons for this impeachment." Deep in
the backwoods he said: "I'm tired of taking off my hat when
I go to New Orleans. They said I couldn't remove Dr. Leake
from the New Orleans Charity Hospital Board. I put him out
and I got Dr. Vidrine from Ville Platte to do the job. The
country people can hold the big jobs as well as the city men."

The people rallied. The folks who looked upon Huey as
the Messiah thought naturally he was being crucified. But
this was not the people's decision. The Senate of Louisiana
must pass upon the evidence. Huey returned to the State

House and listened one night to brother Earl's reports. The Senate was adjourned for the weekend.

The next morning fifteen senators awoke to find state limousines at their front doors. They were asked to make a quick trip to see the governor. They all did. And behind closed doors Huey Long blocked his impeachment.

He needed only fourteen senators on his side to prevent a two-thirds vote for conviction. The fifteen summoned agreed to sign a round robin which said that "by reason of legal irregularities" they would not vote for conviction *no matter what the evidence*. Why did these men sign such a paper? None has ever said, of course, but later each popped up in a big-paying state job.

They presented their round robin in form of a demurrer to the Senate. The twenty-four other senators realized they were licked. The Senate adjourned, the impeachment proceeding was dead, and Mrs. Long rushed down from the gallery to grab Huey in a victory hug.

The opposition was stunned, and Huey moved into the vacuum to seize even more power. He was now unchallenged master of the state. He doled out new roads in five-mile strips placed where they would do the most political good. He began openly calling himself the "Kingfish." He said the nickname was old, drawn, of course, from the Amos 'n' Andy radio character. He first used it publicly while personally supervising the sale of highway bonds. One prospective purchaser objected to Huey's running the show, saying the governor had no authority in such matters. Huey replied, "I am participating here anyway, gentlemen. For the present you can call me the Kingfish."

Huey's antics even caused an international incident. That was the case of the green pajamas. On a Sunday morning the German cruiser *Emden* was in port, and, by appointment, Commander Lothar von Arnauld de la Périere, accompanied by German consul Rolff L. Jaeger, paid a formal call upon the governor in his Roosevelt Hotel suite. Ushered in, the commander clicked his heels, bowed—and gasped. There stood Huey, tousel-haired, bleary-eyed, in green silk pajamas topped by a red-and-blue lounging robe. The commander and the consul stamped out: Germany had been affronted.

Weiss, the major-domo of the Roosevelt, followed them, stammering explanations. They want a formal apology, Weiss told Huey.

"What's the matter with 'em?" Huey snorted. "I took the time to put on bedroom slippers and this twenty-five-dollar robe the State Banking Department gave me for Christmas. What more do they want?"

He had a point. He received official callers in less, sometimes in absolutely nothing. But Weiss explained that this was different. Huey said to send the consul back in.

He told Herr Jaeger, "I have not been well," and made arrangements to return the call, properly, the next day. Huey later revealed he borrowed pin-stripe trousers from Weiss, a boiled shirt from a hotel waiter, and a swallow-tailed coat from a preacher to wear when he went aboard the ship to right the wrong.

But Huey's main concern was not Germany but the publicity about the silk pajamas. What would they think in the upcountry? They all believed that Huey slept in his BVD's the way they did. Huey exercised caution thereafter. Once, when the legislature passed an important bill at 4:00 A.M., it was brought to the executive mansion for Huey to sign immediately. He donned a cotton nightshirt and called in the photographers. No one could see the silk pajamas he was wearing under the nightshirt.

Huey cavorted about the state in the company of many bodyguards, and sometimes the steel-helmeted state militia tagged along. The Kingfish brazenly bragged about his power, and he merely laughed when a newspaper revealed that favored convicts under sentence at the state penitentiary were found to be living in Baton Rouge in a special building, wearing civilian clothes, driving cars around town, and staging wild parties on such evenings as they chose to return to their barracks. Westbrook Pegler wrote, "They do not permit a house of prostitution to operate within a prescribed distance of the state university but exempt the state Capitol from the meaning of the act."

In Louisiana the governor cannot succeed himself, and so in 1930 Huey announced he would run for the United States Senate. His term as governor would still have two years to run, but he promised that he would not move to Washington until after his time was up. When someone complained that this would leave one of Louisiana's Senate seats vacant, Huey snorted: "Vacant for a year or two? Why, with Ransdell up there the Louisiana Senate seat has been vacant for many years."

Ransdell, the incumbent Senator Joseph E. Ransdell, was Huey's opponent. The senator was seventy years old, distinguished, pompous, old school. His campaign speeches were stilted and formal, and he was certainly no match for the likes of Huey. Alluding to the senator's goatee, Huey promptly dubbed him "Feather Duster Ransdell." Huey promised his delighted audiences that the good old Kingfish would be "even less dignified" than in the past.

State employees "volunteered" 10 per cent of their pay checks to Huey's campaign fund. In the weeks just before the election some state payrolls actually doubled. Highway Commission surveyors toured the state putting up little red flags to show farmers the site of new roads. (If the farmer wanted the road moved a little to the left, sure, that was O.K.) Convicts painted election signs. Capitol stenographers addressed campaign letters. Highway Department trucks delivered leaflets. Huey got on the radio and even sang for the folks. He always began the same way: "This is Huey P. Long talking, but I ain't gonna say nothing important for the next few minutes so you can go to the telephone and call up four of your friends and tell them to tune in too."

Huey had one fright during the campaign—scandal. His secretary was Alice Lee Grosjean, a twenty-five-year-old brunette who was close to the governor. One of her relatives on the state payroll was Sam Irby, the husband of

Alice's ex-husband's aunt. Irby was fired, and then suddenly announced that he and James Terrell, Alice's ex-husband, would file $50,000 lawsuits against Huey. Terrell was going to charge Huey with "breaking up my home."

They flew to Shreveport to file their suits, and were met at the airport by Senator Ransdell's local campaign manager. That night there was a knock on their hotel room door. In came the men of the state Bureau of Criminal Identification, Huey's plain-clothes police. They took the two men off "for questioning."

For days there was no trace of Irby and Terrell. Their attorney, Pike Hall, filed habeas corpus proceedings. Huey first said he had no idea where the men were, and then announced that they had been arrested for filching state property. Now, Huey didn't believe these two men had done such a thing, but if they were arrested what could a mere governor do? And anyway, Huey added, Pike Hall wasn't their attorney. Right on cue Hall received a telegram: "I renounce your efforts to bring any suit for me. It is unauthorized. James Terrell. This also applies to me. Sam Irby."

Huey promised to produce the two men at a public rally. Twice he failed to do so. Hall filed kidnaping charges against Huey in federal court. Then, lo, here was Sam Irby. On the radio. From Huey's hotel suite. He was now prepared to explain his disappearance, Irby said. He had asked to be taken into custody. He had found $2,500 under his pillow in the hotel room and he was afraid to be alone with all that money. Then Huey took the microphone and said Sam had decided to donate the $2,500 to the Long-for-Senator campaign fund.

As soon as the broadcast began, reporters rushed to Huey's suite. They arrived just in time to see Irby nudged into the freight elevator by two men brandishing pistols. Two days later, Irby was escorted into federal court by the same two men, and he asked that the kidnaping charges against Huey be dismissed because there had been no kidnaping.

Years later, Irby said he had been held for days chained to a tree at remote Grand Isle. He said he was tortured and forced to make the broadcast at gunpoint. Huey replied that it wasn't a gun he pointed at Irby in order to get the broadcast: it was the $2,500. At any rate, Irby and Terrell disappeared from Louisiana, and Alice Grosjean was appointed secretary of state.

The scandal didn't hurt Huey's campaign. He convinced his voters that it was just another trick of the big interests to discredit the friend of the people. "Them pie-eaters say they want peace and quiet," Huey said. "Yes, oh, yes they want peace—they want a piece of that $30,000,000 road pot."

Huey won. He beat Ransdell by 40,000 votes. Now he was Louisiana's senator-elect, but he had to remain its governor, too. He might have reneged on his promise to stay in Baton Rouge except for his bitter feud with Lieutenant Governor Paul Cyr.

A dentist, Cyr had been elected on the Long ticket, but the pair soon split and became the bitterest of enemies. A murder was behind the feud. Two lovers, Dr. T. E. Dreher and Mrs. Ada LeBoeuf, were accused of luring Mrs. LeBoeuf's husband out at night, of murdering him, and of sinking his body into a lake. The case was naturally a sensation and, because no woman had ever been executed in Louisiana, the whole state seemed to take sides. Dr. Dreher and Mrs. LeBoeuf were convicted, and Huey was on the spot: he had to permit execution or commute the sentences. Lieutenant Governor Cyr was a close friend of the Dreher family, and urged Huey to spare the pair from the gallows. But Huey didn't want to show mercy to these rich people after so many of the poor had marched to prison. He refused to commute the sentence. Cyr, enraged, immediately became one of Huey's most persistent critics.

Now that Huey was senator-elect, he didn't dare leave the state for fear that the lieutenant governor would seize power. Once he did cross over into Mississippi for the night, but had to dash back to Baton Rouge when Cyr heard about it. He was just in time: his car and Cyr's pulled up to the Capitol at the same moment. At another time he tried to induce Cyr to accompany him to New York on a state university football trip so they'd both be out of the state, but Cyr refused.

After a year of this, Cyr, on October 13, 1931, announced that since Huey Long was senator he could not possibly be governor and that he, Paul Cyr, had taken the oath of office. Huey rushed the state militia into the Capitol and prevented Cyr from entering the governor's suite. Then he announced that if Cyr took the oath of governor he wasn't lieutenant governor. Huey swore in the president pro-tem of the Senate, A. O. King, as lieutenant governor, and ordered the state payroll changed. Cyr announced that indeed he was governor and that the temporary Capitol was now in the Heidelberg Hotel. Huey telephoned the owner, Roy Heidelberg, and Cyr was evicted. Cyr moved his "Capitol" to his home in Jeanerette. He became a laughingstock. Throughout the state —and even in New York—wags went before notaries public to get themselves sworn in as governor of Louisiana. Huey went along with the various gags, although he warned Secretary of State Grosjean not to accept any of the joke credentials, just in case.

But by now the whole issue was becoming academic. Huey's term was about to expire. Huey announced his candidate for governor, faithful Oscar Allen, head of the Highway Commission. Brother Earl stormed into Huey's office in a rage. *He* wanted to be the candidate for governor. Huey was adamant, as well he could be, for now he even had an alliance with the New Orleans machine which had fought him for so many years. The rest of the Long family sided with Earl and insisted that Huey back his brother at least for lieutenant governor. Huey refused this, too. Earl announced he would run for lieutenant governor against the Long ticket.

Huey said: "It was already being charged that I was a dictator and that I had allowed many relatives to be placed on state payrolls. To have added a family name to the head of the ticket either for governor or lieutenant governor would have been disastrous to the whole ticket. My brothers and sisters, however, could not see the matter in that light."

Brother Julius joined Earl and said later: "Huey Long and Oscar Allen went by my poor father's house at 1:30 in the morning and tried to browbeat that poor old man to fight the candidacy of Earl for lieutenant governor. Huey begged his father to fight his own son."

Earl said it was just a case where Huey "couldn't see his kinfolk get ahead."

Earl ran against John Fournet, who had been Huey's Speaker of the House during the impeachment uproar. Earl cracked jokes about Huey and berated Huey and sneered: "Am I my brother's keeper? No, but he needs one!"

It was to no avail. Oscar Allen collected 56 per cent of the state's vote and carried Fournet in with him. Earl was beaten. Huey could go to Washington now and claim his Senate seat.

"I've done all I can for Louisiana," he said as he departed. "Now I want to help the rest of the country."

CHAPTER FOUR

"I don't believe he could get the Lord's Prayer endorsed in this body."

IT IS CUSTOMARY FOR FRESHMAN SENATORS TO SLIP QUIETLY into Washington and devote their time to learning the rules of the club. Not so Huey Long. He clanged into Washington noisily and began trying to teach the club his rules.

He began on his very first day in the Senate, January 10, 1932. Traditionally a new senator is introduced to the members by the senior senator from his state, but Huey would have none of that. He was feuding with Louisiana's senior senator, Edwin Broussard. This was the same Broussard to whom Huey had clung like a leach when he was trying to win over the south Louisiana Cajuns, but somewhere along the line Broussard had blundered onto Huey's purge list, and Huey refused to walk beside him into the Senate chamber. Democratic floor leader Joe Robinson, of Arkansas, stepped up to pinch hit.

Robinson, however, was left with mouth agape in the Kingfish's wake. Huey, puffing on a cigar in violation of Senate no-smoking rules, bounced happily onto the chamber floor and began introducing himself to the members. He slapped distinguished old Senator Borah on the back. He prodded Senator Watson in the ribs. He darted from one end of the hall to the other making certain that Huey Long's presence was known to all. He announced to the Senate that he had come to Washington "to spread the wealth of the land among all the people," and within two days he was leading the fight against a presidential appointment. He opposed William E. Humphrey for the Federal Trade Commission because, he said, the Hoover administration was "reaching into the back yards of the corporations" for the men who administer the government.

This was to be his program in the Senate—the same program which had captured Louisiana: Share the wealth. Soak the rich. Smash the corporations. The country, in the very depths of the depression, was certainly receptive to such words. It takes more than words, however, to pass a law in the Senate; it takes votes, and there wasn't the slightest inclination to vote Huey's words into law. The Kingfish learned this quickly, and turned his wrath upon the Senate leadership in a series of monumental feuds which blazed throughout his four years in Washington.

He first tangled with the floor leader, Robinson, when Robinson refused to throw his support behind Huey's original Share-the-Wealth resolution. Vengeful Huey read into the *Congressional Record* a list of Robinson's law clients, and then said, "When a man comes into the Senate without enough clients to make up a corporal's guard and winds up representing every big corporate interest, if that does not mean something, what does?" Huey's feud spread to powerful Pat Harrison, of Mississippi. That one grew so bitter that once Harrison and Long exchanged epithets on the Senate floor for six hours; the transcript was so ugly that both agreed to have it stricken from the record.

But Huey could not confine all of his energies to slaying the dragons of Washington. He still had Louisiana to run. Of his first 139 days in the Senate, he spent 81 back home in Louisiana getting the new administration squared away.

He had installed Oscar Allen as governor, but Oscar, the old Long neighbor from Winn Parish, Huey's first law client, the man who loaned Huey $500 to complete his campaign for railroad commissioner, was a figurehead. Huey made no attempt to have the public believe anything else. Once when Huey was explaining to the legislature his newest program, he turned to the governor and said, "Oscar, go get me those Goddam bills we was talking about."

Oscar reddened. He stared straight ahead, pretending not to hear.

"Goddam you, Oscar, don't you stall around with me!" Huey snapped. "I can break you as easy as I made you. Get those Goddam bills and get 'em on the jump."

Oscar got them. Earl Long later said, "A leaf blew off a tree and through the window onto Oscar's desk one day, and Oscar signed it."

But Oscar didn't mind what they said about him. He told Forrest Davis, the author: "I'm mighty proud to be Long's lieutenant. All the brains and energy that go into the running of the state come from him."

And indeed they did. As United States senator, Huey had no official status in the state government; nevertheless he addressed the legislature at will, ran its committees, made all the patronage appointments, and even used the governor's office as the base of his operations. (If he wanted to have a private chat with someone, he sent Governor Allen out into the hall.) Huey told his trained seals little of what was in the bills he wanted passed. "This one's a tax bill," or, "This one relieves the tax collector of the job of hiring a staff"—that's all they got, and they voted "Yea" on Huey's word. Sometimes the bills weren't even printed in time to be read by those legislators who wanted to take the trouble. There was some opposition, to be sure, but it was completely ineffective. For one thing, so many of Huey's bills mixed genuine good with genuine evil. Take the case of the Louisiana State University dental school:

It was a school founded out of spite. Loyola University operated the state's only college of dentistry, but Loyola also owned a large radio station which refused to give Huey all the free time he demanded. So Huey installed a new—and free—dental college at the state university. Though he acted out of pure spite, there was no blinking the fact that henceforth there would be free dental education for Louisiana's youth and seventy-five dental chairs operated without charge by the school at the Charity Hospital in New Orleans.

Watching Huey do this sort of thing in one of his legislative sessions, Raymond Gram Swing wrote, "This is Huey's statehouse, Huey's legislature, Huey's state, his and his alone. . . . He was like a young father on a romp in the nursery. Anyone could see how much fun it was being dictator."

But it wasn't all fun. Huey put up another old crony, John Overton, against Senator Broussard in the election for the senator's seat, and Overton's victory produced immediate cries of fraud. Broussard asked for an investigation, and the Senate granted it. When the subcommittee sat in New Orleans, Huey tried to take over the hearing as he took over everything else. He sat in the front row and traded barracks-room insults with the committee counsel. He ordered some witnesses not to answer questions. He told the subcommittee, "This hearing is the funniest thing I've ever seen, and I'm enjoying it."

The old Long feud erupted on the witness stand. Brother Earl, still smarting over Huey's refusal to make him governor, began to tell where the bodies were buried. Earl testified that he personally saw Huey take ten $1,000 bills from a director of the New Orleans Public Service, one of the utilities Huey continually castigated in his public speeches. Huey blanched at this testimony, and snapped, "I raised the Public Service's taxes, didn't I?"

Earl was quick to reply. "You started out by proposing a big tax on them and ended up with a tax just about what their lobbying was costing them."

"Liar Earl Long!" screeched Huey. "Why didn't you tell the people what a villain I was in the campaign?"

"I couldn't black you without blacking myself," said Earl. "We stand a lot from our kin. I stood with you as long as I could, but you run wild."

Earl testified that Huey told him he had demanded "help" from another of the "hated interests," Arkansas rail and power magnate Harvey C. Couch.

Huey threatened Earl with perjury.

"Yes, you think you're the whole show," said Earl. "You

hire, fire, can, and run everything, even your governor, Oscar Allen."

Two days later it was Julius Long's turn to take the stand. Huey didn't bait Julius. He had learned enough from Earl to keep quiet. This gave Julius the chance to speak without interruption. He testified at the hearing that he saw Mike Moss of the Union Indemnity Company give Huey "such a big roll of bills that when he stuffed them in his pocket it made his pants bag down.

"In 1926," Julius said, "Huey told me that a mysterious agent of a trust had given him ten or twenty $1,000 bills. Huey was then running on a trust-busting platform. When he was running for governor in 1924 on an antitrust ticket, Huey P. Long, Jr., admitted to me that he had taken money from the Southeastern Gas and Electric Company, one of the biggest trusts ever known. . . .

"Huey's forces extracted from $500 to $1,000 from every road contractor in the state to finance his election campaign. They bought two or three shining limousines, packed them with highway police and skull-crushers, and went dashing about the state. If anybody voiced opposition to Huey's candidates they were beaten up. Every state employee is assessed to make up campaign funds, and those who don't contribute are kicked out of their jobs. He makes all candidates sign undated resignations.

"I remember when he made Governor O.K. Allen sign one. The governor broke down and cried."

The Long family feud was the high light of the Senate hearing, but there was other testimony. The Honest Election League charged: "There are only 2,500 white people over the age of 20 in St. Bernard Parish, yet there were 3,189 votes in the parish, Overton receiving 3,176, Broussard 13."

The questioning of Overton's campaign manager, Allen J. Ellender, produced this:

Q. Who chose you to be Overton's campaign manager?

Ellender. I saw it announced in the newspapers, which prompted me to believe I was it.

Q. What is the influence of the Long machine?

Ellender. I resent that. I am a reputable member of the state bar.

Huey. Go ahead. We are used to these insults.

Q. Overton has testified he didn't know you were his campaign manager.

Ellender. I did not say Mr. Overton chose me. He just understood as I did.

Overton did indeed understand. He had testified that Huey told him he "was as good as elected," and not to worry about the details.

On this happy note the subcommittee ran out of money, and adjourned until it could get more from the Senate. It asked for $25,000, and, despite the story it was unraveling, the Senate refused. Powerful Senator Bennett Champ Clark, of Missouri, fought the expenditure. He was the brother-in-law of James Thompson, publisher of the New Orleans *Item*, which had always been anti-Long but which suddenly swung to the Kingfish just about the time the investigation started. The subcommittee returned to New Orleans for its last gasp, but the spirit was gone. The chairman, Senator Tom Connally, ended the hearing with the judgment that Louisiana election practices were "a fraud upon the rights of citizens" but that the anti-Long people were as guilty as the Long people.

Huey went back to Washington, victorious (as he was at the time of impeachment) simply because no one had been able to do anything to him. He ranted anew about his Share-the-Wealth program, and gained added prominence as the nation's Number One political clown. He became known as—among other things—the Bard of the Senate. He loved to insert his poetry in the *Congressional Record*. Quite often it was to the very point he was trying to make on current legislation.

There was the time Pat Harrison was urging the Senate to accept a finance committee recommendation without revision. Huey jumped to his feet to say:

"When the Senator from Mississippi comes here and says

'stand by the committee,' I am reminded of the old man who died up in East Carroll Parish. He put a little poem on his tombstone:

> " 'Remember, men, as you pass by
> So as you are, so once was I.
> So as I am, you must be.
> Prepare to die and follow me.'

"But the wife who put the tombstone up did not want to be bound by what was on it, and so, as a saving grace to herself, she wrote two more lines:

> " 'To follow you I'm not content
> Until I know which way you went.' "

On another occasion, when the debate on repeal bogged down to a wearisome discussion of how much alcohol it takes to make a man drunk, Huey sought to end all the talk with this:

> "Not drunk is he who on the floor
> Can rise again or drink once more.
> But drunk is he who prostrate lies
> And cannot either drink or rise."

Huey himself could do a lot of drinking and a lot of rising to drink again. He even imported his own bartender from the Roosevelt Hotel when he decided that the Washington variety of the famous Ramos gin fizz was too pallid for his tastes. He was unencumbered, for he had left his wife and children back in New Orleans.

One of his exploits got him into serious political trouble. It started the folks in Louisiana laughing at him instead of with him. And, to make matters worse, the incident occurred at the millionaires' Sands Point Bath Club on Long Island, a gilded hall no enemy of the vested interests should ever enter. It was all quite simple: Huey got drunk and Huey got slugged. There were two versions as to what happened. One is that Huey was too explicit in his anatomical compliments to a certain young lady, and her escort followed him into the men's room to do him in. The other is that Huey went to the men's room alone, aimed between another chap's legs, and missed. At any rate, Huey came out of the men's room bloody and bowed. As soon as the story hit the newspapers, Huey placed the blame on hirelings of the House of Morgan, and wired to Al Capone in the Atlanta federal penitentiary to 'fess up that his agents had done the dastardly deed for Wall Street gold.

There was no reply from Capone, but there was considerable correspondence from the more strait-laced folks back home. And when Huey returned to Louisiana he found that the trouble was serious: He was due to address twenty thousand at the Donaldsonville fair but only eight hundred showed up, many of them hecklers. At a Shreveport bridge dedication there were hoots from the audience. At Alexandria he was the target of rotten eggs. But it all blew over, thanks partly to a diversionary special session of the state legislature, and Huey went back to his Senate seat in Washington.

There he fought constantly for some cure to the depression. In his very first session in the Senate he battled mightily for three income-tax amendments which would have shifted more of the burden to the wealthy. He staged the first of his many filibusters in a play for time during this fight, but he could never muster the votes.

Huey was something of a pioneer in calling for specific federal spending programs to check the depression. Even before he went to the Senate, and a good two years before Franklin D. Roosevelt became President, Long called for federal control of farm surplus. He opposed cutting the federal payroll, for this would only throw people out of work, and he opposed cutting congressmen's pay because this would make Congress a rich man's club.

In the lame-duck session of 1932, after Hoover had been defeated by Roosevelt, Huey advocated high inheritance taxes, a high income tax on the upper brackets, government control of farm surplus, limitation of industrial working hours to balance consumption, inflation of the currency—all the things that later came to pass. But, it must be said, he merely advocated these things; he did not introduce any bills or resolutions to make them reality. In 1933 he did draw up a formal Share-the-Wealth Plan for the Senate, but it got only fourteen votes.

His Senate speeches almost always were on the same subject. "We want something for the poor people of this country," he said. He waged his battle on nonpartisan lines. He castigated his fellow Democrats for "making long-winded political speeches about Hooverism and coming back and voting for everything that Hooverism stands for."

Naturally Huey was a states'-righter. He had to be. He could brook no interference with the duchy he operated in Louisiana. But he did not oppose federal administration of relief in principle at a time when many federal depression cures were delayed by those in the Senate who fought for state control of the program. Huey did, however, become opposed to the federal administration of relief when it put patronage in the hands of his political enemies back in Louisiana.

Frequently Huey's deeds belied his words. He made speeches against tariffs because, he said, they favored the rich industrialist at the expense of the poor consumer. But he made certain that the barriers remained high on Louisiana's products, particularly lumber, oil, and sugar.

Too, Long's motives were often suspect. He fought the Glass Banking bill, calling for sounder banking procedures. He opposed it, he said, because it would hurt the small banks. Senator Glass revealed on the floor of the Senate, however, that Huey had found a strange ally in his devotion to the small banks: he had spent the weekend in conference with an official of the Chase National Bank in New York. The official subsequently testified before the Senate Banking Committee that he had "done some favors" for Huey. Long just laughed this off and continued his fight against the Glass bill. On January 9, 1933, seeing his cause doomed, he began to filibuster. No one helped him. The resentful Senate even refused to permit the clerk to read the long documents Huey introduced, and Huey had to read them himself. On January 12th he had to give up, and the Glass bill passed.

For all his pleas on behalf of the suffering, Huey was uninterested in depression cures he did not originate. He fought many reforms not because he was against the reforms, but because he felt they did not go far enough. His vote against them counted just as much, of course, as the vote of those who wanted no reforms at all.

This attitude eventually made Huey a full-time obstructionist in the Senate. There was no way to predict his vote, for often, as in the case of the Emergency Banking bill, he fought a bill just for the hell of it and then, in the end, voted for it. He criticized the first New Deal relief measures as "too modest," but he voted for them. The only thing he seemed to favor was a veterans' bonus, and the administration was against that.

In 1934 he supported a nuisance investigation of NRA personnel and opposed the appointment of Henry Morgenthau as Secretary of the Treasury. He was so committed to being an "agin'er" by now that he even lined up with the Republicans to demand publication of a secret treaty with Colombia; there was nothing to be gained except that Huey could annoy the administration which refused to follow *his* path to prosperity. He staged five filibusters during the 1935 session, one of them, lasting fifteen and a half hours, designed to hamstring attempts to reorganize the NRA after it had been ruled unconstitutional by the Supreme Court. Others delayed independence for the Philippines and enactment of the Social Security program.

Nevertheless, Huey considered himself a true liberal. The senators he admired most were Norris and Wheeler. He insisted that they alone, along with one or two others, were sincere in their efforts to combat the depression and that the rest of the senators acted from sham.

But when Huey was being playful or comical, the senators

could laugh with him instead of at him. Once, for example, they engaged him in a running debate on the care and feeding of potlikker, that poor Southerner's delicacy which is the juice remaining from cooked vegetables. They could easily endure his lessons on how to make a Ramos gin fizz. And they could only chuckle when Huey formally announced his decision to outdress the Senate's stylist, J. Hamilton Lewis. Huey appeared on the floor in a natty blue suit for the official challenge, but found Lewis so impeccable that he circled the Illinois senator three times with cocked eye and then conceded, "Lord, I ain't even close. I give up."

Yes, the laughs came. But they became gradually more widely spaced as Huey the comedian imperiled serious legislation. Huey made many personal enemies in the process. He drove Senator Bingham, of Maine, from the floor in a torrent of accusations. He was censured by the presiding officer when he lambasted Senator Dill, of Indiana, as one who comes "from a state which can hardly keep a Republican governor out of the penitentiary." He was asked to leave the floor of the Senate when a tirade against Senator Reed, of Pennsylvania, became too personal.

Huey didn't see anything wrong with the way he operated. Hell, he called those bums down in Louisiana much worse, didn't he? Huey thought the formalities of the Senate were unjustified quibbling at a time when breadlines stretched across the nation. "We want to bring the government closer to the people," he said. And he left little doubt about which people he meant. "We have 400,000 qualified voters in the state of Louisiana, and we have to take care of them," he said.

But through the years history has shown that no member conquers the traditions of the Senate. The snubs to Huey Long became ever more pointed. He found the chamber emptying as soon as he began a speech.

And in 1935 Senator McKellar, of Tennessee, summed up Huey's influence in the Senate by saying, "I don't believe he could get the Lord's Prayer endorsed in this body."

CHAPTER FIVE

"I'm going to organize the country like I organized Louisiana."

THERE WAS NEVER ANY DOUBT ABOUT HUEY LONG'S GOAL. HE told T. Semmes Walmsley, mayor of New Orleans, "There's going to be a revolution in this country and I'm going to lead it." When he rebuilt the governor's mansion in Baton Rouge, he made it a replica of the White House, "so I'll be used to living in it." He met former President Coolidge, and devoted the entire conversation to inquiries about White House housekeeping; he was especially concerned over whether the Hoovers were keeping the property up.

Of course, greater men have aspired to the Presidency in vain. But Huey had a gimmick that was captivating millions. He offered his Share-the-Wealth Plan as the pot at the end of the rainbow, and he offered it during the dismal 1930's when most people didn't have a pot.

The Share-the-Wealth Plan was an idea Huey had cooking for a long time. As early as March 1, 1918, he advocated something of the sort in a letter to the editor of the New Orleans *Item.* He complained then that "68 per cent of the people living in the United States own but 2 per cent of its wealth." He concluded that "this is the problem the good people of the country must consider."

And he offered his solution: break up the great fortunes and divide the money among the poor people. "They tell us we are faced with Communism," he cried. "Why not, when one per cent of the people control 59 per cent of the national

71

wealth? Rockefeller and Morgan would sleep much safer tonight if they had $100,000,000 each under their pillowcase instead of a billion or two."

Huey changed his plan as often as he changed his silk shirts, and it got better with each change. But when he finally put it in the form of a Senate bill, it boiled down to this:

He would limit personal fortunes to $8,000,000 a year and confiscate everything over that.

He would limit inheritances to $5,000,000 and confiscate everything over that.

And from these confiscations, Huey promised, he would provide every family head in America with a $5,000 debt-free homestead, a car and a radio (which could be sold only through court order) plus a guaranteed annual income of $2,500. But wait. That wasn't all. There'd be enough left over, he said, for an "adequate" old-age pension, a soldiers' bonus, a public works program, and free college education.

This was good politics but poor arithmetic. He said his capital tax was based on a national wealth of $40,000,000,000; he didn't explain where he got the figure or how he'd split up such portions of the national wealth as were represented by rivers, forests, and unmined natural resources. Furthermore, he said his income tax would bring in $50,000,000,000 a year; but the entire national income at the time was only $58,000,000,000.

But who would listen to quibblers when Huey was promising to lead America out of the depression? Huey and his men certainly didn't quibble. His chief Share-the-Wealth organizer, the Reverend Gerald L. K. Smith (the same Smith now in the anti-Semitism business), explained once why the program didn't specify the amount of the old-age pension: "We originally promised a $30-a-month pension but we discovered we were running afoul of the $40 pension advocates and the Townsend $200 pension advocates, so we decided to use the word 'adequate' and let every man name his own figure."

Huey himself was consistent about only one thing in his

Share-the-Wealth speeches: in each speech he limited himself to mentioning only five points of the panacea because he felt the average man couldn't remember more than five. He always stressed what the poor man would get and not where it would come from. He didn't want the problem to seem intricate. Licking the depression, he said, was "as simple as the sun rising in the morning." Just follow Huey.

Millions did. At first Huey used the Share-the-Wealth Plan only as a rallying point for his supporters in Louisiana. But as he prepared to leave the governor's chair for his Senate seat, he began a national organization. Any two persons could form a Share-the-Wealth Club, and there were no dues and no contributions: the only function of each club was to distribute Huey's Share-the-Wealth literature throughout the community.

Huey made no bones about his objectives. He told Forrest Davis:

"I'm going to organize the country like I organized Louisiana. I am going to have twenty-five men to a precinct, organized all over the country. Right from the ground up we're going at it. We ain't depending on anybody else or any political party. Where do you think the old parties are going to get off when they find out that Huey P. Long has got a majority of the voters in the country organized? I got millions of voters signed up now to Share-the-Wealth Clubs, and when a man signs up for that it's now like these other things that's going around. He signs up with Share-the-Wealth because he wants a $5,000 homestead and a car and a radio and $2,500 cash coming to the family every year and a pension in his withered old age."

Huey provided everything for his Share-the-Wealth movement—a slogan, "Every man a king" (taken from Bryan's Cross of Gold speech: "Let every man be a king yet no man wear a crown"), and even a hymn which Huey helped write:

> "Every man a king,
> Every man a king,

include

For you can be a millionaire.
There's something belonging to others.
There's enough for all people to share.
Be it sunny June or December, too,
In the wintertime or spring:
There'll be peace without end,
Every neighbor a friend,
With every man a king."

Huey knew what the people wanted, and he knew how to organize them, too. He hired a minister who would preach Share-the-Wealth like the gospel. Gerald L. K. Smith, the pastor of a well-to-do Shreveport church, had acquired a considerable reputation as a fund raiser for charities. Huey hired him at straight salary to set up the national network of Share-the-Wealth Clubs.

Smith was the perfect choice. He was a good organizer, but, more than that, he was the ideal showman for Share-the-Wealth rallies. He was a minister of the Disciples of Christ, yet he could quote the pope in Catholic south Louisiana as fluently as he could quote his Bible in Protestant north Louisiana. He made the Share-the-Wealth rallies old-fashioned revival meetings, and the rednecks who flocked to hear him would shout with glee. Harnett T. Kane wrote of one particularly effective bit of audience-participation showmanship which Smith developed. Whipping up the poor folk with tears for their want, he'd shout:

"How many of you have five suits? Hold up your hands."
No show of hands.
"Four."
None.
"How many got three?"
One or two hands rise, wavering.
"Two suits?"
A few more hands.
"One suit?"
Still more hands.

Finally, "How many got just one pair of pants?"

Hundreds of hands would shoot up, and hundreds of voices would roar with indignation. That was the cue. Gerald would burst into the screeching, thundering, threatening, demanding litany of Share-the-Wealth. He was a wow. Huey's lieutenants all hated him, and some feared him, but they had to concede that he was great at these rallies. In a sense Huey was the brain and Smith was the brawn behind the overnight success of the Share-the-Wealth movement throughout the nation.

They had their rivals, of course, but the rivals lacked universal appeal. The Townsend Plan was of interest primarily to the aged; Governor Floyd Olsen and Milo Reno appealed to farmers; Upton Sinclair's idea of putting the idle to work in profit-sharing factories was too specific and sounded too much like work; Father Coughlin's prattling about "social justice" was not specific enough. These men all had big followings, but they never matched Huey Long's strength. Too, they didn't have Huey's forum. They bellowed from their little nooks while Huey Long pranced about the chamber of the United States Senate.

Perhaps the best judges of Huey's increasing popularity were the guides who escorted tourists through the Capitol. They reported that the visitors to the Senate gallery always seemed primarily interested in seeing Huey Long. Fellow senators frequently walked out on Huey's speeches, but the galleries remained packed down to the last echo. Newspapermen flocked around Huey to lap up his colorful quotes, and the radio networks were delighted to give him free time because he was, as one executive put it, "as funny as Will Rogers, and much cheaper." On the day that Huey was invited to address the Georgia legislature, ten thousand showed up to hear him.

Huey's suite in the Senate Office Building was a beehive. He occupied five rooms instead of the usual three. His clerks worked on two shifts to handle his mail, twenty-one on the day shift and fourteen on the night. His executive secretary,

Earle Christenberry, bossed all this with assembly-line efficiency.

Huey himself worked constantly. For one thing, he had no personal friends. Those senators who might have enjoyed his booze and highjinks dared not get too close to him lest they too be ostracized by their colleagues. So when other senators were spending their nights with friend or family, Huey was seducing newspapermen into one more interview about the Long expressway to eternal prosperity.

Did Huey really believe in his Share-the-Wealth Plan? His views must have come from the heart because they couldn't have come from the head. His knowledge of economics was extremely limited. He did not study the subject at any time during the two years he attended college, and his principal experience on the practical side came during his term as governor; his state-house strategy was to pull out of every hole with a bond issue and let future governors worry about paying it off. As virtual dictator of Louisiana he made no attempt to put Share-the-Wealth's key points into law: he proposed no confiscatory taxes; indeed, his state income tax was rather easy on the rich and, of course, he never did get around to distributing the free homesteads, automobiles, and radios.

Nevertheless, Share-the-Wealth captivated millions, and Huey was certain there eventually would be millions more to push him into the White House. Before he would become King, however, he would become Kingmaker. On the eve of the 1932 political conventions he picked Franklin D. Roosevelt as his man.

Not that he was always enamored of Roosevelt. He arrived in Washington to claim his Senate seat in January, 1932, with the pronouncement: "We are for Pat Harrison, Joe Robinson or John Garner, and, after them, Al Smith, for the nomination. We are not going to be for Roosevelt. He ran too poorly with Cox in 1920 and he would be certain to be beat."

In a few weeks Robinson and Harrison were eliminated, for they failed to recognize Huey as the new Democratic leader in the Senate. Huey began plumping for Roosevelt. He said that Senator Norris had a lot to do with his switch. Norris convinced him that Roosevelt was the "only hope for the country," and so Huey took it upon himself to make certain that FDR got the nomination.

But first Huey had to get himself seated in the convention. His dictatorial tactics in Louisiana had led a rump delegation to appear at Chicago claiming it should be seated. Huey's delegation was only a hand-picked collection of satraps, the mavericks contended. Huey didn't deny this. "I *am* the Democratic party in Louisiana," he said. "Who's got a better right to pick out a delegation?" He was enraged when the convention Credentials Committee decided to hear both sides. And when he found several women on the subcommittee assigned to the squabble, Huey snapped, "No bunch of damned skirts is going to decide anything concerning me." The ladies of the subcommittee denounced him as being no gentleman. Huey sent a special plane down to Louisiana to fetch his wife, and then paraded her about Chicago on his arm "to show these damned skirts I know how to treat a lady."

Despite all this, the case was decided on its merits. Jim Farley later said: "On this occasion he showed what a shrewd fellow he was. He sensed the fact that it was time to cut out the horseplay and the oratorical nonsense. He delivered a reasoned, common-sense argument for his side that some thought was the best in the entire debate. His behavior won him considerable support." Huey's delegation was seated, and he turned his attentions to getting Roosevelt nominated.

He tried to take over the whole show. He was invited to a caucus of Roosevelt backers to hear the convention strategy, and soon induced the delegates to switch to Huey Long's strategy. He worked night and day to buttonhole delegates. He caught Alfalfa Bill Murray of Oklahoma in bed at 7:00 A.M.—"a helluva hour for a farmer's representative to still be asleep"—and refused to let the poor man touch breakfast until he heard the merits of Roosevelt.

Huey thought only his genius could carry the day. In the middle of the first ballot he telephoned to Roosevelt and said, "I think you should issue a statement immediately saying you are in favor of a soldiers' bonus to be paid as soon as you become President."

"Well, I'm afraid I can't do it because I'm not in favor of a soldiers' bonus," said Roosevelt.

"Well, you're a gone goose," said Huey, and hung up.

But "gone goose" Roosevelt got the nomination. Unfazed, Huey immediately proceeded to plot the campaign. He demanded a special train to tour the forty-eight states in Roosevelt's behalf. Farley refused to provide this facility.

Huey snapped: "I hate to tell you, Jim, but you're gonna get licked. Yessir, you're gonna get licked. Hoover is going back to the White House and that's all there is to it. I tried to save you, but if you don't want to be saved it's all right with me."

Farley decided to be saved just a little. He let Huey campaign where he thought the Kingfish would do the most good and/or the least harm. Huey took it in good grace. "I think I'd like to campaign in Vermont," he said. Actually, Huey campaigned in the Dakotas and Nebraska. Although considered a political hick, he bypassed the rural centers and concentrated on the cities. The Democratic National Committee received glowing reports about his effectiveness, and Farley said, "We never underestimated him again." Roosevelt carried these states—which had not gone Democratic since 1916—but the national landslide makes it impossible to tell just how much credit Huey could claim for the votes.

Huey tried to swing Roosevelt over to his policies, but failed, and within a month after FDR's inauguration Huey Long was as opposed to the New Deal as the most staunch Vermont Republican. There were several reasons advanced for the quick break. Huey himself said it was because Roosevelt refused to back the Share-the-Wealth Plan. Others said it was a case of general disagreement on how far the New Deal plans should go. Still others said the Roosevelt administration deliberately cut itself loose from Huey because it did not want to be allied with such a demagogic clown. At any rate, Huey himself formally announced the break as differences on farm, banking, and reforestation policies.

The fight became both bitter and petty. Huey was stripped of his patronage, and rose on the floor of the Senate to say, "They can take my patronage and go." Then an Internal Revenue Department investigation of Huey's income-tax returns, begun halfheartedly during the Hoover administration, was stepped up. In late 1933 a number of Huey's top aides were indicted for income-tax evasion. By 1934 the federal patronage in Louisiana was going pointedly to Huey's political enemies. Harold Ickes put a stop order on $10,000,-000 in PWA projects in Louisiana, saying, "No public works money is going to build up any Share-the-Wealth political machine." Harry Hopkins announced that federal employees would take over state administration of NRA funds in Louisiana, and these federal employees turned out to be more of Huey's enemies, suddenly transplanted to Uncle Sam's payroll. Huey denounced the "blue buzzard administration," and said, "It's not Roosevelt or ruin—it's Roosevelt's ruin." He suggested that Ickes "go to hell."

Huey did more than talk. He fought. On February 11, 1935, he set after the patronage boss of the administration, Jim Farley. He demanded that Farley resign as Postmaster General and Democratic National Chairman. On the floor of the Senate he charged that Farley was involved in a racing wire service, that he gave away $80,000 in stamps to his friends, and that he let federal contracts that were, to use the current vernacular, in conflict of interest. Huey presented some Scripps-Howard newspaper stories to back up his charges—and a Scripps-Howard executive found *his* income tax coming under sudden scrutiny.

The administration rallied behind Farley—even Ickes backed him. Nevertheless, Huey blandly announced that Farley would resign: he had it from "the highest authority."

Floor leader Joe Robinson said Farley was not resigning— he had it from "*the* highest authority."

"Who do you mean?" asked Huey.

National Recovery Act

"The President of the United States," thundered Robinson.

Huey laughed. "The President is sometimes mistaken," he said.

But Farley couldn't laugh. The charges were serious, and there was much talk about smoke and fire. He sent a 1,500-word telegram to the Senate denying the charges. Then General Hugh Johnson took to the radio to lump Huey and Father Coughlin as "rash and murderous." He denounced Huey as "the Hitler of one of our sovereign states."

This was a mistake. Huey asked for and got his equal time to reply. When he went on the air he didn't waste that vast audience on Hugh Johnson. He proceeded to make a speech on *his* program and why it was so much better than the administration's program. Huey's answer to Johnson was simply a long commercial for Share-the-Wealth.

"Hitler?" Huey scoffed. "Let's look at this NRA. They had parades and Fascist signs just like Hitler and Mussolini." And the people weren't getting their due out of it, either, Huey said. He then gave out the current version of Share-the-Wealth—that night it happened to be a $5,000 patrimony and a $2,500 guaranteed annual income—to one of the largest radio audiences in history.

The Senate refused, by a 62-20 vote, to grant Huey an investigation of the charges against Farley. Huey crowed: "I'm as big as Roosevelt. Why, he's copying my Share-the-Wealth speeches now—the ones I was writing when I was fourteen years old. So he's just now getting as smart as I was when I was in knee britches."

Huey's bellowing did force some revisions in the New Deal. Congress passed the veterans' bonus. And, after considerable resistance, Roosevelt proposed the inheritance tax Huey had demanded. When the inheritance-tax bill was introduced in the Senate, Huey rose and uttered the only one-word speech of his career: "Amen."

Huey was quite serious about spreading his influence throughout the states. He told Paul Y. Anderson, of the St.

Louis *Post-Dispatch,* "I already have Louisiana, Mississippi, and Arkansas and I'll take Alabama when I get ready."

He had "captured" Arkansas in a single whirlwind campaign. One of his few faithful followers in the Senate was Hattie Caraway, who had been appointed to complete her late husband's term on her promise that she would not run for election when it expired. Huey wanted her to remain in the Senate, and induced her to enter the primary. When she was reminded of her promise not to run, she said, "My sons wanted it, and I just can't go against their wishes."

There were five men running against Mrs. Caraway, who had no political backing, and she seemed certain of finishing sixth. But up from Louisiana came Huey Long, riding not a white charger but a white sound truck, to rescue the damsel in distress. He announced, "I'm here to get a bunch of pot-bellied politicians off a little woman's neck." He made a whirlwind tour of the state, making thirty-nine speeches in a week. He gave advice on the care of babies—"When they cry, give 'em a drink of water"—he lambasted the foe—"I ain't gonna mention his name. My parents taught me to speak well of the dead even if they're politically dead"—and he drew the issue—"Wall Street versus the people."

Arkansas was astounded by Huey Long's style of campaigning. The other candidates orated flowery nothings, but Huey gave the people this:

"I'm reminded of the time my wicked uncle went to get baptized. As the preacher led him into the water an ace of spades floated from his pocket, then the king of spades, then the queen, the jack, then the ten. It was too much for my aunt. 'Oh, Lawd, Preacher,' she cried, 'you can't save him. He's lost.' But her son yelled, 'No, Ma, Pa ain't lost. If he can't win with that hand he can't win at all.'

"And I'm here to tell you, my good friends, that if we can't win with Mrs. Caraway's record of standing by you people through thick and thin then we can't win at all and we might as well admit Wall Street is too strong for us."

Hattie Caraway, who expected to run last in the election,

ran first, with more votes than all of her opponents combined. There was no doubt about who swung the election. She scored a landslide in the counties Huey Long hit; she got scarcely a vote in the others. Huey, the "Kingfish" in Louisiana, began calling himself the "King of the Ozarks" in Arkansas. He backed the winning candidate for governor in Mississippi and announced that "Mississippi is just a province of Louisiana."

As early as 1932 the Farmer-Labor party named Huey its presidential candidate. He chose to ignore this because he wasn't ready. But as the 1936 campaign neared, Huey was forging his Share-the-Wealth Clubs into a third party. "There positively will be a Share-the-Wealth ticket in the field in the 1936 campaign—no doubt about that," he said. "That ticket will be headed by a man who won't go back on his word. He will be a man who is honorable enough to commit suicide if we win and he doesn't make good on his promises."

A reporter asked, "Senator, are you honorable enough to commit suicide under such circumstances?"

Huey laughed. "You may say that my modesty prohibits me from answering that question."

There is considerable question as to whether Huey meant to keep Share-the-Wealth a third party or whether he intended to use it as a club to get what he wanted from the Democratic party. The Democrats certainly took him seriously. Farley revealed that the Democratic National Committee, in anticipation of the 1936 campaign, ran a "secret poll on a national scale" to determine just how much strength Huey really had. The results pollsters decided were:

Huey could get between 3,000,000 and 4,000,000 votes for President.

He had as much strength in the North as in the South—it was estimated he could take 100,000 votes in New York—and showed special strength in Colorado, Washington, Idaho and West Virginia. This was not enough, not nearly enough, to elect a man President. But it was proof that Huey Long was not a phenomenon confined to Louisiana. His Share-the-

Wealth idea was spreading. Huey himself claimed six to seven million signed-up members in the Share-the-Wealth Clubs.

Certainly he knew what he wanted to do. He said, "No man has ever been President of the United States more than two terms." (This was during Roosevelt's first term, of course.) "You know that. Everyone knows that. But when I get in I'm going to abolish the Electoral College, have universal suffrage, and I defy any sonofabitch to get me out under four terms."

Had he lived beyond 1935, could Huey Long have been elected President? It is easy today, with the benefit of hindsight, to say No. But perhaps that answer is too categorical. Perhaps it should be softened to "Probably not." In his favor, it must be remembered, was the fact that he was moving up not in a prosperous post-World War II America but in a hungry 1935. The depression was at its worst. The economic medicine of World War II was not in sight. And Huey was offering a panacea far more appetizing than the nibbles off the New Deal's public works projects. Share-the-Wealth was just beginning its wildfire growth. On the other hand, Huey was fighting no ordinary man, but Franklin D. Roosevelt. Huey's regime in Louisiana was vulnerable to all kinds of federal criminal prosecution. And eventually war in Europe did haul prosperity from its hiding place around the corner.

Huey himself was so certain he'd become President that he wrote a book about it. He called it *My First Days in the White House*. It was written in the past tense: it starts out with the inauguration ceremony and rummages through Huey's cures for every one of the nation's ills.

Today it reads like satire. Huey's Cabinet contained Franklin Roosevelt as Secretary of the Navy ("That's the job you're suited for, Frank."), Herbert Hoover as Secretary of Commerce, William E. Borah as Secretary of State, and Al Smith as Director of the Budget. Huey summoned the Mayo Brothers to Washington to assign to them the job of supervising the health and hospital care of every American, free of charge. The Army put down its guns and got to work on flood control in the East and water conservation in the West. John D. Rockefeller announced he was giving away everything except the $5,000,000 allotted him by the Share-the-Wealth Plan. Attorney General Frank Murphy turned loose all the prisoners who didn't belong in jail. Even the White House correspondents shared in this Utopia; they, not the President, decided when and where press conferences would be held.

Was all of this so fantastic? Men had to dream in 1935, and Huey offered them plenty to dream about. Why not? Didn't he have a special dream of his own?

CHAPTER SIX

"There may be smarter men than me, but they ain't in Louisiana."

THE NEWSPAPER EDITOR LEANS EARNESTLY ACROSS HIS DESK AND says, "Huey Long was all bad—all evil." The Cajun shrimp fisherman gazes wistfully across the water and says, "Huey was good for us—he gave us what none of the others did." Today, as thirty years ago, there is no middle ground in Louisiana: Huey was a devil or Huey was a saint. Yet a study of the record shows both extremes in error, as extremes often are. It is obvious that Huey did much for Louisiana while making a mockery of its constitution.

In the seven years of his reign, this is what Long accomplished: He doubled the bed capacity of the great charity hospitals in New Orleans and Shreveport. He installed major medical and dental schools at the state university. He increased the capacity and instituted sorely needed reforms at the state mental institutions. He cut the tuition at the state university to a token and increased the student body from 1,500 to 4,000. He distributed free textbooks to every schoolchild, and added 15,000 to the school attendance. He established night schools which taught over 200,000 of the state's illiterates to read and write. He greatly improved the ports of Lake Charles and New Orleans. He piped natural gas into New Orleans. He built a seven-mile seawall on Lake Pontchartrain. He paved 3,000 miles of roads. He replaced rickety toll bridges with modern free bridges. He attracted considerable industry to the state. And, in doing all this, he exempted half of Louisiana's homeowners from property taxes by making the first $2,000 in assessments tax free.

Who paid for Huey's largesse? He told the people he was soaking the rich to help the poor, but this was not true. The income tax did not rise sharply in the upper brackets, and the inheritance tax was low. Instead, Huey levied thirty-five new taxes, most of them consumer taxes. Nothing was overlooked, not even insurance premiums. When cigarettes cost fifteen cents a pack, the state tax was four cents. (Huey assigned one hundred police to the borders to prevent cigarette smuggling but warned them not to interfere with the liquor bootleggers.) Yet even as the tax money cascaded into the treasury, it was not enough. Louisiana's indebtedness leaped from $46,000,000 to $143,000,000. Huey said he was soaking the rich, but actually he was soaking every consumer, rich or poor, and then giving a rebate in the form of roads, bridges, and schools.

Huey's devotion to the poor was questionable in other ways. He said he "didn't like to fool with relief," and passed no state unemployment compensation law during the depth of the depression. His legislature wouldn't adopt the federal child labor amendment. And he told a labor group quite frankly, "The prevailing wage is as low as we can get men to take it."

Yet he was loved and admired by the poor. His ruthless methods were considered wildly comic or wonderfully efficient. When the state university lacked funds to rebuild its campus, he said, "Go ahead—I'll get the money," and he did. He bought the land for his new state Capitol from the university at a ludicrously high price. When his engineers told him they couldn't possibly build the skyscraper Capitol on marshland, he ordered them to find a way. And, to Huey's credit, the university did get its rebuilding money and the engineers did find a way to build on the marsh.

Huey kept his eye on every job in the government. He could recite entire payrolls. He knew which men were political fops and which were adroit performers. He always went to the right man for the right job. Sometimes the blind followers of

Huey Long might have seen his weaknesses had they peeked out of only one eye. His roads were scattered throughout the state in short stretches, and served to whet appetites rather than provide for continuity of journey. His money always went for building new roads, not for maintaining the old ones. Yes, the folks could have seen this had they looked— but they didn't want to look. They had waited too long for a Messiah.

The Reverend Gerald L. K. Smith once told a reporter that the people didn't mind Huey's dictatorship because they knew it was necessary. He said: "It is the dictatorship of the surgical theater. The surgeon is recognized as being in charge because he knows. Everyone defers to him for that reason only. The nurses and assistants do what he tells them, asking no question. They jump at his commands. They are not servile. They believe in the surgeon. They realize he is working for the welfare of the patient."

Huey likened himself to his idol, Frederick the Great: "He was the greatest son of a bitch who ever lived. 'You can't take Vienna, your Majesty. The world won't stand for it,' his nitwit ambassadors said. 'The hell I can't,' said old Fred. 'My soldiers will take Vienna and my professors at Heidelberg will explain the reason why.' Hell, I've got a university down in Louisiana that cost me $15,000,000 that can tell you why I do like I do."

Everybody in Louisiana knows the score, Huey said. They like it this way. We get things done.

In elections he went to the people and told them what they were getting at the measly cost of a little democracy. He said: "They tell you that you've got to tear up Longism in this state. All right, my friends—get you a bomb or some dynamite and blow up that new state Capitol. Then go out and tear up the concrete roads I've built. Get your spades and your shovels and scrape the gravel off them roads we graveled and let a rain come in on 'em. That'll put 'em back like they was before I come. Tear down all the new buildings I've built at the university. And when your child starts to school tomorrow morning snatch the free textbooks out of his hands. Then, my friends, you'll be rid of Longism in this state—and not before."

The pinched-face farmers in the crowd would nod at this and then go home convinced that everything said against Huey was the poison of the corporations and the trusts and the utilities.

Huey's wars against the utilities were loud, but often the peace terms had to be whispered. As railroad commissioner he boisterously prevented the Southeastern Gas and Electric Company from getting a small electric rate increase, but later quietly granted the same company a 38 per cent gas rate increase. It was this company, Brother Julius told the Senate Subcommittee investigation, which stuffed the roll of thousand-dollar bills into Huey's sagging pockets. As governor, Huey forced New Orleans Public Service, Incorporated, into serving the people with cheap natural gas as a replacement for electricity, but he gave NOPSI the franchise at a 90-cent rate when another company was offering to serve the public for 65 cents. And Brother Earl told the same Senate investigation he saw a Public Service official hand Huey $10,000.

Huey's career as a trust buster was not all fake. He forced a rebate in telephone rates, blocked a Shreveport streetcar fare rise, won a case against discriminatory freight rates—and he did wage his classic war against Standard Oil.

As mentioned earlier, Huey's fight with Standard began as a personal vendetta. Its control of the pipelines in Louisiana made his own stock in a small independent company worthless. But Huey soon saw that Standard made a magnificent whipping boy, and he continued his public battle against the company for years after the pipeline fight was won. The dispute was over complicated tax formulas, but Huey quickly simplified it for the man in the street. He said: "What the good Lord put into the ground for the people of Louisiana ain't going to come out unless something is paid on it. When these fellows suck an oil well dry, we want a new schoolhouse somewhere to educate the future citizens of this state."

Huey proposed two taxes on Standard. One was for drilling oil; this easily passed the legislature and financed a good part of his education improvements. The other was an "occupational tax" on barrels produced at the refinery. Standard fought it bitterly, and got considerable support from other manufacturers who feared that an "occupational tax" on oil could be spread to cover any other occupation. Standard felt this was double taxation: one tax for drilling the oil and a second for being in the oil business.

Standard sometimes fought Huey with tactics no more admirable than his. Huey twice tried to put through the occupational tax. The first attempt ended with his impeachment as governor. The second ended with a compromise. Standard agreed to a five-cent-per-barrel tax, and Huey agreed to refund four cents per barrel. Standard officials insisted publicly that—despite Huey's loud claims—they did not inspire or finance the impeachment. However, years later, when a high Standard official died in New York, the obituary which his family telephoned to the newspapers mentioned that he was the man Standard sent to Louisiana to work for Huey Long's impeachment. In the end the compromise seemed to make everyone in the state happy—everyone except the owners of the small newspapers. The Standard advertisements which had flooded their pages throughout the years of the fight suddenly were reduced to a trickle.

Huey made much of his control of the banks in Louisiana. He often said that most of them were run in such fashion that any bank examiner could find gross irregularities any time they chose. Often these banks had given him the whip he held in his hands. When his free-textbooks law was challenged in the courts, Huey went to the banks to borrow $435,000 so that he could buy the books and distribute them while the state's funds were held up by litigation. Huey summoned three New Orleans bankers to his hotel suite and presented them his proposition. They balked. The interests fighting the free schoolbooks were powerful, and the banks dared not cross them. Gingerly, the bankers told Huey their lawyers said the schoolbook loan would be illegal.

"I'll be guided by your attorneys' advice," said Huey coldly. "You know the state owes you $935,000 on Board of Liquidation loans now?"

The men gasped. They knew what was coming.

"But that's been ordered paid by the legislature," one banker stammered.

"Ain't been paid yet," said Huey blandly. "And what's more it ain't gonna be paid. If it's illegal to make loans, it's illegal to pay 'em. We'll just keep the $935,000 for the schoolbooks and have $500,000 to spare."

The bankers excused themselves to hold a caucus in the hotel coffee shop downstairs. Presently they returned.

"Governor, we voted to give you the loan," said one.

Huey leaped with glee. He pushed away the sandwich he had just ordered and told the room-service waiter, "Take back this ham and cheese and bring me a steak."

But Huey was by no means an enemy of the banks. He did much to keep them open in the grim days when banks were failing daily throughout the nation. Told that a Lafayette bank was about to go under, he dashed to the scene in the middle of the night. The state had $200,000 in the bank, and Governor Long said he had to protect Louisiana's interests.

When the bank opened in the morning the first depositor in line presented a check for $17,000—he was pulling out while the pulling was good. Huey called him into the president's office. "This bank here has $190,000 on hand," Huey said, "and I was here first with my check for $200,000. If you'll go home and leave your money in here, I'll do the same. If you don't, I'll present my check and there'll be nothing left for you."

The man had no choice. He went. The other depositors, bent on withdrawals, were forced to do the same. Huey saved the bank.

On another occasion a New Orleans bank was about to go under. Huey, by then in the Senate, needed to shut the bank for a day so that funds could be raised. He ordered Governor Allen to declare a legal holiday. Oscar was always ready to do the master's bidding, but what was the excuse? This was February 4th. It seems that nobody who is anybody was born on February 4th. Finally someone searching through the almanacs noted that on February 3, 1917, the United States had severed diplomatic relations with Germany.

"That'll do," Huey shouted. "It just ain't possible that Woodrow Wilson could have finished anything as important as that in one day. If he did it on February 3rd he must have still been busy with it on February 4th. Let's go."

The proclamation was issued: "Whereas the great American people have turned their eyes back to the lofty ideals of human uplift and new freedom as propounded by Woodrow Wilson" the banks of Louisiana were closed.

Thus did Huey Long work. Was it for money or for the sheer love of being boss? Huey died leaving a net estate of $100,000, considerable but not excessive for a good lawyer back in those days of humane income taxes. However, it was whispered that Huey's real wealth was held by political pals so that it could never be traced to him.

Huey openly collected big fees from the state for his legal services even while he drew salary as governor or senator. The various commissions were always hiring him at fees of $5,000 to $20,000 to fight their cases. He actually fought them, and many of his opponents grudgingly conceded he was worth the money the state paid him. He also popped up as advisory counsel for some of the big monied interests he purported to oppose. "Why not?" he once conceded. "I'm the best damn' lawyer in Louisiana, ain't I?"

There were other financial shenanigans pinned on Huey, some big and some small. He was part owner of a Winn Parish rock quarry whose product was rejected by highway and railroad engineers as being too soft. As soon as he became governor, the state began buying this rock at $1.65 per cubic yard instead of the 62½ cents which was the going rate. And brother Julius said even this was watered before shipment to increase the weight of the sealed bags. Thus the roads Huey so grandly gave Louisiana cost $15,000 per mile more than the national average. In 1940 gambler Frank Costello testified at his income-tax trial that he operated his slot machines in Louisiana by arrangement with Huey Long. He said Huey sought him out and proposed the deal originally.

United States Secret Service chief Frank J. Wilson, writing in *Collier's* magazine after his retirement, said he had an air-tight income-tax-evasion case against Huey ready for the grand jury when Huey was killed. Wilson said he was sent to Louisiana from Washington in 1933 with the specific assignment of "bagging" Huey. He said a truck manufacturer who supplied the Highway Department admitted making a $75,000 payoff to a Long lieutenant "with the Kingfish himself overseeing the deal." Wilson wrote that an insurance agent said Huey charged him a 20 per cent fee on the state's bonding business. Wilson also told of discovering that hotel man Seymour Weiss, often described as the treasurer of the regime, paid many of Huey's personal bills—some as large as a $25,000 house mortgage and some as small as $73 for two pairs of silk pajamas at A. Sulka & Company.

Wilson wrote: "I reported to Washington that the case against Huey Long was ready for the grand jury; we had a clear case of tax evasion on some $100,000 in unreported income." Wilson's boss, Internal Revenue Service chief Elmer P. Irey, wrote in his autobiography that the investigation proved that Huey "took plenty and he took it for Huey Pierce Long."

Huey's opponents had always insisted that he was getting wealthy on the people, and Huey had always given a stock answer: "Look what the people are getting." The newspapers attacked him and played up any charges against him, but he had his avenues of reply: He was on the radio frequently; he began his own weekly political newspaper; and his circulars could be distributed overnight to every home in Louisiana (by courtesy of the Highway Department and the state police).

He could outcampaign anyone in Louisiana, even the United States government.

Every dictator knows he must supply bread and circuses. Huey promised the bread—with butter on it—through Share-the-Wealth. His circus was the state university. Governor John M. Parker actually was the first to propose building the school into prominence; but Huey, not yet in power, scoffed at the time. "Our kind don't need college," he told his redneck following. But when he got into office Huey soon recognized the circus value of the university.

First he took complete control. He forced out the president and replaced him with James Monroe Smith, a country school-teacher. Huey said, "There ain't a straight bone in Jim's body, but he does what I want him to and he's a good president." The students called their president "Jimmy Moron." Faculty members who objected to Huey's domination were fired; rebellious students were expelled.

Huey adopted the football team as his special sideshow. He sat on the players' bench when he wasn't racing up the sidelines shouting advice to the quarterback. He gave pep talks between the halves—"What do you care if they break your legs if you break their neck?"—and he fired Coach Biff Jones when Jones objected to these speeches. After Abe Mickal threw the winning pass in a big game, Huey offered to appoint him to the state Senate even though Mickal was a resident of Mississippi and not of voting age anyhow. When LSU lost a game, seven to six, a bill was introduced in the legislature outlawing the point after touchdown. Students could make the out-of-town trips for only seven dollars, a special rate Huey's Public Service Commission secured from the railroads, and they could even borrow the seven dollars from Huey if they couldn't get it elsewhere.

The purple-jacketed band was part of the show, and Huey loved to march down the streets between the drum majors, with the full ROTC cadet corps in formation behind him. Once he planned to make such a march down the streets of Knoxville on the day of the Tennessee game, but ran afoul of an old political feud. The vengeful governor of Tennessee called long-distance to say, "Huey, you can't bring those cadets into Knoxville—they carry guns, and guns are illegal."

Huey only snorted. Came Saturday morning and his cadet corps, unperturbed, marched down the streets of Knoxville on schedule. Each man carried a rifle on his shoulder and a State of Tennessee hunting license in his pocket.

Huey also built a field house—with living quarters for the football players—and the nation's longest swimming pool. He built a new girls' dormitory and a music school with eighty-seven ("Count 'em," he would plead to visitors) grand pianos. In a single year he created a fully accredited medical school. He opened a dental school, and its students gave free treatment to the poor in the charity hospitals.

Huey loved everything about LSU—except its excursion into freedom of the press. When the student *Daily Reveille* printed a letter to the editor decrying Huey's tactics as "a mockery of free political institutions," Huey burst into a rage. He demanded to know the name of the editor. "That little ———!" he shouted. "I'll fire him and all his family. I'll have a new editor by tomorrow. This is my university. Nobody's going to criticize Huey Long. Get me Jim Smith."

Smith called in the student editors and told them that henceforth they must work under a university censor. They refused. Smith said, "We're living under a dictatorship, and the best thing to do is submit to those in authority."

The students asked Smith if he wouldn't help them fight for student freedom. He replied that he'd fire the whole student body and the whole faculty before he'd "offend" Senator Long. The student body called a mass meeting. It was dispersed by campus cops. The *Reveille* editors were expelled. A co-ed who had relatives on the state payroll was appointed the new editor. A few faculty members threatened to resign, and that was the end of the incident—for a while.

Whenever Huey was caught up in an embarrassing fight like this, he simply began campaigning against the vested interests and their hirelings who persisted in libeling Huey

Long. The opposition was "thieves, bugs, and lice." It was "philandering highbinders." It was "that rattin' old gang, shoving to get back at the trough." Huey's knowledge of the Bible held him in good stead. There was a verse to support everything, from the expulsion of the student editors to Share-the-Wealth.

Huey paid off well for loyalty, and for that reason he could expect most of his lieutenants to see him through any crisis. His reward for the early support of Oscar Allen was the governorship. John Fournet, who as Speaker of the House sought to cut off Huey's impeachment with adjournment of the legislature, became—and still is—chief justice of the state Supreme Court. John Overton, who defended Huey against Governor Parker's libel suit, was Huey's hand-picked candidate for the United States Senate, and he remained there until his death in 1952. Allen Ellender, who was campaign manager for Long candidates the year Overton was elected, wound up in the Senate, too, and is still there.

These people were not to be disturbed by some professor's cry for academic freedom or by the ridicule which newspapers heaped upon the legislature when it permitted Huey to run its sessions like a lodge meeting.

Huey said this had to be. He told Raymond Daniell of the New York *Times:* "They say they don't like my methods. Well, I don't like them either. I'll be frank with you. I really don't like to do things the way I do. I'd much rather get up before a legislature and say, 'Now this is a good law; it's for the benefit of the people, and I'd like you to vote for it in the interest of public welfare.' Only, I know that laws ain't made that way."

So Huey made them his way instead. All the while he played the clown. He knew and could speak the king's English fluently and well, yet he persisted in using a hick dialect freely laced with profanity. He boozed it up in public places and he dearly loved a nation-wide squabble over nonsensical issues such as how to mix a cocktail and how to win a football game.

Huey Long was such a fool that many close students of his

career came to the conclusion he wasn't a fool at all: he was taking the sting out of the dictatorship by being a clown. He always ridiculed the enemy. His arch-rival from New Orleans, T. Semmes Walmsley, was always "Turkey Head Walmsley." Henry Wallace of the despised New Deal was "Lord Corn Wallace, the Honorable Lord Destroyer, the Ignoramus of Iowa." Jim Farley was the "Nabob of New York." And when the Imperial Wizard of the Ku Klux Klan, dentist Hiram W. Evans, ran afoul of Huey, the Kingfish told reporters: "You tell that toothpuller he's a lying sonofabitch. That ain't secondhand information and it ain't confidential."

Huey was asked by author Forrest Davis if these burlesque-show antics were considered good politics. Huey's reply was frank: "It cuts both ways. It helps and it hurts, that kind of a reputation. Some of them stab at me for making light of my enemies, but a lot of them wouldn't have heard of Huey Long to stab at him if it hadn't been for the Kingfish and some tomfoolery. I like to have a good time and I figure that most of the people would rather laugh than weep. I don't see any harm in lightening up the tragedy of politics for the people."

In a way this bit of candor seemed to support another pet theory of Huey's.

"There may be smarter men than me," he said often, "but they ain't in Louisiana."

Right. Huey Long in the days when he was selling Cottolene. (*Wide World Photos*) *Below.* Huey in the Senate. Here he has just finished one of his filibusters. (*Wide World Photos*)

Above. Huey in New York supervising the making of a Ramos Gin Fizz. He imported the bartender from New Orleans for just that purpose. (*Wide World Photos*) *Below.* Huey and Allen Ellender in the State House in Baton Rouge in a picture taken just fifteen minutes before Huey was shot. (*Wide World Photos*)

Left. Mrs. Huey Long. This picture
was taken at the time she was
named to serve out Huey's unexpired term in the Senate. (*Wide
World Photos*) *Below*. Governor
Richard W. Leche under whose
administration The Louisiana Scandals blossomed. (*Wide World
Photos*)

Above. The famous luncheon at Antoine's. FDR has finished his "ersters" and is enjoying his coffee. Governor Leche is on his right and the redoubtable Mayor Robert Maestri of New Orleans is on his left. (*Wide World Photos*) *Right.* Abe Shushan shown just after having been questioned by postal inspectors as a result of The Scandals. (*Wide World Photo*)

Above. Seymour Weiss shown in New York in 1935 emulating his friend Huey Long by receiving the press in his lounging robe. (*Daily News Photo*) *Below.* Former Governor James A. Noe (*left*) who ran for Governor again in 1959 with Earl as his running mate, for Lieutenant Governor, shown in 1942 with Mayor Maestri. (*Wide World Photos*)

This is what Dr. James Monroe Smith did after he stopped being President of Louisiana State University. This was after a jury had found him guilty of embezzlement and obtaining money under false pretenses. (*Wide World Photos*)

Earl Long on the stump in his bid for election as Lieutenant Governor in 1959. (*Wide World Photos*)

Right. Mrs. Earl K. Long. (*Wide World Photos*) *Below.* Earl Long at the airport in Fort Worth in July, 1959, at the beginning of his "vacation trip" following his hospitalization in Texas and Louisiana. (*Wide World Photos*)

Left. Leander Perez, Louisiana's leading segregationist, a former Long ally who fought Earl bitterly on the segregation issue (*Wide World Photos*) *Below.* Russell Long, Huey's son, shown here in 1948 campaigning for the Senate seat he won then and still holds. (*Wide World Photos*)

CHAPTER SEVEN

"I wonder why he shot me."

IT WAS SEPTEMBER 8, 1935, AND HUEY WAS MAKING HIS BOLDEST stroke yet. He knew he could outshout FDR's minions in the Senate, but he also knew that they could outspend him with the public dole. Furthermore, Ickes and Hopkins were channeling the money through his enemies. Very well, then: they'd not spread their PWA payrolls across the breadth of Louisiana because Huey Long would forbid them to do so.

It was quite simple. He called the legislature into yet another special session, the seventh of the year, and proposed a series of statutes that would block federal spending in Louisiana. The opposition shrieked with rage. This was the last straw (Huey was a porcupine of last straws). Long promised to Share-the-Wealth, they cried, but he was not willing to share the bread which the federal government extended to Louisiana's hungry.

Huey was confident he could pull his coup. After all, they were *his* bills, going before *his* legislature. But he was not without worry. His bodyguard was increased before he left Washington, and the huskies seemed more surly and maybe a little jittery as they bulldozed their charge through the crowded corridors of the Capitol. As he left for Baton Rouge, Huey told his wife, "I may not be back, but I'll die fighting." One of the bodyguards said: "We were warned to expect trouble. We were told a bunch was planning to storm the statehouse Saturday night."

But it was Sunday morning now, Sunday, September 8th, and no bunch had stormed the statehouse. The legislature traditionally opened on the Sabbath, and so, at 10:00 A.M., the House Ways and Means Committee was assembled to pass on Huey's new bills. This was important business, and Huey conducted the show himself. The Ways and Means Committee Chairman sat solemnly as Huey stood beside him and bubbled with efficiency. He glanced at the first bill. His explanation was simple: "Now this is an enabling act to carry out the principles of the Constitution of the United States."

Up jumped Representative Jack Williams, the only vocal opposition in the room. "Does it intend to block the expenditure of federal funds in Louisiana?"

Huey glared, and replied, "It intends to block the violation of the federal constitution."

"What have you in mind by the bill?"

"We have in mind the preservation of the Constitution of the United States."

"Does this mean keeping vast sums of federal money out of the state?"

"At any cost, the Constitution of the United States must be preserved," said Huey, and moved on to the next bill.

"This one is to preserve the integrity of states' rights," said Huey. And bill Number 3? That was to "prevent the rights of the state from being infringed upon."

Thus it went, for nearly an hour, until all of Huey's bills—with their noble titles and their ignoble aims—were passed by the committee and sent to the House. They passed with only one Nay vote, that of the pesky Representative Williams, and everybody knocked off for lunch.

Just a few blocks away from the statehouse, on Lakeview Drive, the Sunday morning was much more serene.

This was the home of Dr. Carl Austin Weiss, a thirty-year-old undersized, bespectacled, and innocuous-looking man who was becoming one of the city's best ear, eye, nose, and throat specialists, like his father before him.

Dr. Weiss talked a lot about the dictatorship of Huey Long, and the very thought of it seemed to infuriate him. Of course, this was the standard attitude of the upper middle class and the special attitude of the medical profession because of the way that Huey juggled state hospital appointments for political purposes. Yet young Dr. Weiss would get more worked up than most. His mother said it was because he "took all living too seriously." His friends said it was because of Europe: Dr. Weiss had been studying in Vienna when the Nazis grabbed power, and he had seen how a people could be strangled.

Only last week, at one of the hospitals, a group of doctors was gabbing between operations, and the subject inevitably reached Huey Long. The talk became heated. Through it all, young Dr. Weiss sat on an operating table, one leg tucked under him. He didn't say anything, but suddenly he bolted from the room. And as he did so, a surgeon noticed that big tears roamed down Dr. Weiss' face.

It was probably The Trouble, they thought. Dr. Weiss had just been touched directly by Huey Long. Dr. Weiss, two years married and with a ten-month-old son, was probably worried about his father-in-law, Judge Benjamin F. Pavy. The judge, on the bench in the town of Opelousas for thirty years, was an anti-Long man, and Huey's legislature was about to gerrymander him out of office. What's more, Huey had said, "If Pavy screams I'll go on the radio and tell 'em how he's got nigger blood."

Dr. Weiss brooded over this, but no more, apparently, than any other Long victims—and maybe a little less, for Judge Pavy would not go hungry, bench or no bench.

Certainly this Sunday morning was not for brooding. The sun shone, and although it still seared with the heat of August, the Weiss family would soon be in the cooling waters of their camp on the Amite River.

Before Huey's Ways and Means Committee assembled to save the United States Constitution, Dr. Weiss and his wife were up for church. They took the baby to his father's home, and then went to mass. They stopped by a florist to send flowers to a patient—this young Dr. Weiss was developing quite a bedside manner—and the florist gave Mrs. Weiss a bouquet. "For the baby," he said. "It's ten months old, and I still haven't sent you anything."

At the Weiss home the lunch was hearty. It was dinner, really, and the leftover fried chicken would do for an afternoon picnic at the camp.

Huey Long left the Ways and Means Committee meeting and went to his suite on the twenty-fourth floor of the skyscraper Capitol on his private elevator.

The faithful, and those who would be glad to be faithful for just this one little favor, clamored to see him. Most did. There was talk of the bills before the legislature, and no one foresaw any trouble getting them passed. Huey grinned a lot. In his private office there was talk about the next Long candidate for governor. Oscar Allen was going out; he'd done well, and it would be hard to find a man as easy to handle as Oscar.

There were a number of names mentioned. Huey casually dropped one which surprised the gathering, Richard W. Leche, now a district judge, but before that, Oscar Allen's secretary. Leche, who wasn't present now, and who was far down in the hierarchy, had an inkling something was up a few weeks before. Huey had called and asked just one question, "Dick, what's your religion?" Dick had replied that this was a particularly interesting question because he happened to be something of a student of theology and a great lover of the outdoors as well; he found that he best liked the concept of the American Indian, "the Happy Hunting Ground."

Now the question came up again. Someone told Huey, "I think Leche's a Catholic."

"Naw," said Huey. "He's not a Catholic. He's an Indian. Told me so himself."

Other names were mentioned, but no decision was made. There was plenty of time for that. The boys were just chewing the rag until the House of Representatives convened at eighty-thirty that night to pass Huey's bills.

It was a pleasant afternoon, a Bourbony one but not a drunken one, and Huey told some funny stories about Washington.

It was a pleasant afternoon for the Weiss family, too. They picnicked, and young Dr. Weiss and his pretty wife swam while the grandparents played perhaps a little too much with their grandson on the shore.

The senior Mrs. Weiss saw her son cavorting in the water, and said: "Look at him. Skin and bones. You can see his ribs. He ought to do something."

"He works too hard," said Dr. Weiss. "He ought to rest more."

It was all so nice that the Weisses didn't get home to Baton Rouge until seven-thirty. Young Dr. Weiss had to haul the dead weight of the snoozing baby to its bed, and then there were supper and feeding the dog and a telephone call to the hospital to make sure everyone knew about tomorrow morning's operation.

Doting Grandma Weiss, not satisfied with spending a full day with the family, had to call up twice about trivialities; she spoke once with her son and once with her daughter-in-law.

Just before nine o'clock that night, young Dr. Weiss said he had to go on a sick call. He kissed his wife, said he'd not be long, and left the house.

The Louisiana House of Representatives had convened on time. Still no bunch stormed the statehouse, but the uniformed state cops were everywhere and so were the plainclothesmen of the Bureau of Criminal Identification. The sergeant at arms ordered two of the three doors to the House closed, and state cops bunched about the third, permitting only legislators to come onto the floor. They shooed the milling spectators up to the visitors' balcony.

The gavel rapped, and the session began. The bills were going through with scarcely a whimper from the opposition. Wait'll Ickes reads about this in the morning. The House was at work for about fifteen minutes when all heads craned. Huey was coming in.

He was wearing a linen suit and black-and-white shoes.

His hair was touseled as usual. He walked up and down the aisles, and stopped several times to talk with legislators at their desks. Then he went up and sat next to Speaker Allen J. Ellender on the dais.

The House picked up speed. Soon all of the bills were passed. It was 9:20 now. It had taken only an hour and twenty minutes to vote Uncle Sam out of Louisiana. Speaker Ellender rapped adjournment until ten o'clock the next morning.

Huey walked quickly out of the House and into the short corridor which led to Governor Allen's office. Chief Justice of the Supreme Court John Fournet was with him. Public Service Commissioner Jimmy O'Connor was right behind him. Share-the-Wealth organizer Gerald L. K. Smith chased, but became entwined in the mesh of bodyguards trying to keep up.

Huey ducked into the governor's office, spun around, and walked right out again. Chief Bodyguard Murphy Rhoden followed him in and had to back right out, so swift was Huey's turnabout. A couple of people chuckled at Rhoden's awkwardness—"He looked like he was goose-stepping backward."

Huey called to representatives in the hall: "Tell everybody to be here in the morning. Remember, everybody here in the morning."

A slight young man in a white linen suit, who had been standing against the wall of the corridor to avoid the throng, stepped forward and extended his hand, seemingly for a shake.

There was a gunshot.

Fournet shoved the young man, who stumbled. Rhoden lunged forward and grappled for the gun. They wrestled, upright, and Rhoden let out a scream. The man had fired again. The gun was faulty; it didn't go off, but the hammer caught the web between Rhoden's thumb and index finger and tore the skin.

Huey clutched his stomach and staggered two or three paces to O'Connor. He gasped, "Jimmy, I've been shot!"

There was a trickle of blood from Huey's lip, and a small

crimson splotch had appeared on his white shirt. Huey and O'Connor started off, down the hall, to a rear stairway.

Rhoden pulled himself free from the young man in white and fired his gun. One shot. The man quivered, then pitched forward, and down, on his face.

The other bodyguards unlimbered. They began pumping shots, from both directions. The body on the floor bounced convulsively with each blast. And still the guns barked. Bullets ricocheted from the corridor walls.

Then there was silence in the hall, and then a woman's scream, and then panic. Men and women clawed and shoved their way out of the narrow hall. They tried to pour into the House, and the state cops pushed them back.

Governor Allen burst out of his office screaming: "Give me a gun! Somebody give me a gun!" He ran up the hall, then down, then back into his office. "Close the door." A state cop closed it and bolted it.

A young reporter dashed down into the basement press room. "They're shooting upstairs," he cried. "They're killing everybody!"

One of the bodyguards, Joe Messina, ran puffing down the stairs. "Where's Huey?" he cried, "God, where's Huey? Where's Huey?"

Downstairs, Huey and Jimmy O'Connor got into O'Connor's car unnoticed in the parking lot. They started off, around the Capitol drive, to Our Lady of the Lake Sanitarium, within eyesight of the Capitol.

Huey breathed heavily. He pushed his hands against the wound, and breathed heavily. Just before the car pulled up to the hospital, he spoke his only words of the short drive: "I wonder why he shot me."

Back at the Capitol the bedlam roared. The state police cleared the hall, and then the entire building. They blocked off the drives. The coroner came, and in an hour he announced the name of the assailant: Dr. Carl Austin Weiss, Baton Rouge.

Who was he? What was he? No one had ever heard of him.

Huey was propelled into a three-room suite in the hospital. Dr. Arthur Vidrine, the country doctor Huey had appointed superintendent of Charity Hospital, arrived and found that the bullet had gone through three loops of the intestine and nicked part of the kidney. Huey was hemorrhaging.

An operation was needed, and quickly. Send for the surgeons. Two of the best were called at New Orleans. Someone called the Mayos. The superintendent of the Shreveport Charity Hospital was summoned.

Lieutenant Governor Jimmy Noe arrived. He talked to Vidrine and then telephoned to Mrs. Long in New Orleans. He told her that Huey was shot, that Dr. Vidrine said it was not critical, but that maybe she'd better come to Baton Rouge anyway. He called Seymour Weiss to tell him the same.

Huey was losing blood. A transfusion was performed immediately, and it was faithful Jimmy Noe's blood they used.

The surgeons in New Orleans tried to charter an airplane, but none was available. They started up Huey's airline highway by car, but they drove too fast, and crashed. Dr. Vidrine had to take Huey into the operating room. Just as he did, Huey looked up and said, "Nobody is to give any statements." In the operating room he clutched a doctor's hand tightly. He mumbled inaudibly; he seemed to be praying.

The word was out throughout Baton Rouge now. Knots of people buzzed on street corners. Thousands leaped into their cars for a drive past the Capitol and the hospital, and it took the traffic cops an hour to clear the resultant jam. They sealed off the one road to the hospital: no cars, no pedestrians, and if you live past this roadblock, mister, you'll have to leave your car here and walk home up the back street.

At 12:30 A.M. on Monday they operated on Huey, and then wheeled him to his room. He fought to breathe. First they pumped oxygen to him; then they put him in a tent.

The big shots of the regime gathered at the hospital. Mrs. Long arrived, walking down the hall red-eyed but composed, with the three children following her. They went into Huey's room, then left. The children were sent to the Heidelberg Hotel. Mrs. Long stayed on a while, then went to the hotel to sleep.

A cub reporter on the Baton Rouge *State Times* got the cub's traditional big-story assignment. He knocked on the door of the senior Weiss and roused Mrs. Weiss. "Please, ma'am, do you have a picture of your son I could borrow?"

"My son? Why? At this hour of the night?"

"Don't you know? He shot Huey Long. The bodyguards killed him."

Mrs. Weiss screamed. "No, not my son! Oh, my God, we've been opposed to Long, but I didn't think he'd do a thing like that."

The senior Doctor Weiss arose. Sure, his son carried a gun, that Spanish gun, but he always did on night calls, ever since the night he went to the garage and found a drunk sleeping one off in his car. But kill Huey Long? Why? "Something else must have happened."

Dawn brought a bulletin from Dr. Vidrine. Huey's condition was "satisfactory." The next seventy-two hours will tell. The National Guard was assembled, helmeted and bayonets fixed, at Jackson Barracks. The big shots of the regime gathered on the gallery of Huey's hospital suite. The Reverend Gerald Smith issued a call to "all 10,000,000 members of the Share-the-Wealth Society in Louisiana and throughout America" to spend "at least five minutes in prayer" for Long. The telegrams from the well-wishers came from all over, including the White House, and even brother Julius was ready to end the family fued and rush to the bedside. But Governor Bilbo of Mississippi, fearful that Huey would make good his boast of capturing the state, would say only "No comment" because "the shooting is strictly Louisiana's affair."

The vigil went on. There was another blood transfusion, then another. At times Huey was lucid, and at other times he babbled incoherently, seemingly about his forthcoming book, *My First Days in the White House,* and what a big seller it would be. Once he looked up and recognized the fearful Governor Allen. He said, "Step back, Oscar, and give me some air." Oscar stared unbelievingly. Huey was in the oxygen tent.

The coroner released Dr. Weiss' body. He said he found two bullets in the head and sixty-eight bullet holes in the body. Huey's bodyguards had pumped plenty of lead. They had emptied their guns until they had almost shredded the assassin's carcass.

On Monday afternoon Dr. Weiss was buried in a driving rainstorm. Thousands attended the funeral. Some, like former Governor John M. Parker, Congressman J. Y. Sanders, Jr., and Baton Rouge District Attorney Fred Odom were bitter Long foes; they didn't know Dr. Weiss, but they wanted the world to know how they felt. They stood ankle-deep in mud and rainwater at the cemetery as the doctor, his coffin sealed, was buried with brief ceremony.

About the time the coffin was lowered, Dr. E. L. Sanderson worriedly told the Shreveport *Times* by telephone: "Senator Long is not responding to treatment. The next twelve hours will tell."

There were more transfusions, up to three now, and Long continued to roam in and out of consciousness. Once he looked up at his friend Seymour Weiss, and said, "Seymour," but no more.

Shortly before midnight the Long children, who had spent the day at the hospital, were sent back to their suite at the Heidelberg. Mrs. Long went with them. At 2:45 A.M. Tuesday, there was a fifth blood transfusion, and now the end was near. At 3:00 A.M. Dr. Sanderson told the Shreveport *Times:* "Senator Long is dying. We have given up hope for him." At 3:15 Mrs. Long rushed back to the hospital, bringing the bleary-eyed children. At 4:10 A.M., with his family at his bedside, Huey P. Long died at the age of forty-two.

What were the Kingfish's last words? To hear it told in Louisiana, he did everything in that last breath from naming his successor to appointing parish dogcatchers. But Earl Long, who was there, insists that Huey died thinking of his boys and girls at LSU: "What'll happen to my poor boys and girls?"

Medical men say Huey probably died unable to say anything.

Within twenty minutes after his death Huey's body was at the Rabenhorst Funeral Home, the same one that had ministered to the shredded Dr. Weiss just a few hours earlier. And Seymour Weiss, Earl Long, secretary Earle Christenberry, and Governor Allen went to the Capitol to make funeral arrangements. The family wanted Huey buried back home in Winnfield, but the committee said No, let's bury him here, right on the Capitol grounds, in the sunken garden. The family agreed.

Huey lay in state in his Capitol from Tuesday afternoon until Thursday morning. Thousands, uncountable thousands, poured in to see him. They wept, whether they were in the dusty khakis of the north country or the ill-fitting suits of the south or the matronly dresses of the city. The guards called out, "Step lively, please; thousands more waiting."

From the governor's office Christenberry announced that Dr. Weiss had pulled the short straw. It was a murder plot, Christenberry said, and Dr. Weiss had to kill Huey or be killed himself. How did he know all this? Christenberry said the plot was hatched in a New Orleans hotel on August 20th and 21st. Could he prove it? Christenberry said he had "some evidence."

Thursday morning Huey was buried. More than fifty persons fainted, and more than a hundred soft-drink peddlers got rich as thousands stood in the heat for the services. Just before the ceremony sixty state cops rushed out with masses of new wreaths to add to the mountain which already banked the graveside. As they hurried down the Capitol stairs, women reached out and plucked for souvenirs.

Then, promptly at 11:00 A.M., the Reverend Gerald Smith appeared at the top step of the Capitol, looked out at the mass, and started down the steps. Behind him came the bronze casket, Huey in it dressed in a tuxedo, and then Mrs. Long, weeping, and her children.

Smith delivered the funeral oration: "This untimely death makes restless the souls of we who adored him. We cannot be appeased by flattery, we cannot be put at ease by superficial consolation. The ideals which he planted in our hearts have created a gnawing hunger for a new order. This hunger pain, this parching search for better things, can only be healed and satisfied by the completion of that victory toward which he led us."

They lowered Huey into the grave to the roll of drums, and suddenly the police line broke. Thousands trampled to the grave, seized flowers and ribbons and cards, and broke free with their prizes. And the heirs of Huey Long had to fight their way back into their Capitol building.

On Monday the coroner held a formal inquest. It produced nothing more than the quite obvious cause of death. The Reverend Gerald Smith refused to testify. After all, he said, District Attorney Odom, who conducted the questioning, was "one of the co-plotters of this assassination." Odom replied by calling Smith a "willful, malicious, and deliberate liar."

No one dug too deeply into Dr. Weiss' true motives. No one wanted to know them. It was much more convenient to supply your own motives. If you were for Long, then Dr. Weiss was the gunman in an organized political plot. If you were against Long, then you could pass on the whispers that —despite the dozens of eyewitnesses and their remarkably consistent stories—Dr. Weiss didn't kill Long at all; some of the bodyguards did the deed (by hysteria in one version, by design in another). The senior Dr. Weiss preferred to think that his son was temporarily insane unless, he suggested, there were words exchanged, words that no one would admit to hearing. The witnesses all agreed that Dr. Weiss said nothing to Huey before that first muffled shot.

But even the Long men knew that the "why" didn't matter. Huey was dead. Huey was buried—in good style, too—and where do we go from here?

CHAPTER EIGHT

"When I took the oath of governor, I didn't take any vow of poverty."

SUDDENLY THE PALACE WAS OVERRUN WITH CROWN PRINCES. Someone suggested they wear numbers so the public could tell them apart—this was not the first or last time it was suggested that they wear numbers. A gubernatorial election was due. The man elected would inherit Huey's power.

There was no logical heir. Huey had seen to that. The chief lieutenants realized that each was a rival of all the others, and yet to avoid disaster they must all stick together. They began a series of meetings while their anxious subjects waited for the white smoke to appear over the hotel-room transom. These were the Kingfish's ministers who dominated the discussions:

ROBERT MAESTRI, a corpulent and unlettered New Orleans furniture man who had bankrolled Huey back in the days when Huey desperately needed bankrolling;

SEYMOUR WEISS, the ex-shoe clerk who had become commandant of the Roosevelt Hotel and treasurer of the Long machine;

ABE SHUSHAN, the Longs' quartermaster and also the Number One Long man on the lucrative Levee Board;

JULES FISHER, the Long leader in the state Senate and the political boss of lush Jefferson Parish, the commuter and gambling-den parish just north of New Orleans;

JOHN FOURNET, Huey's Speaker of the House during the impeachment days and later lieutenant governor and chief justice of the state Supreme Court;

OSCAR ALLEN, Huey's governor, now leaving office because the law prevented him from succeeding himself;

GERALD L. K. SMITH, the Share-the-Wealth preacher who was regarded as Huey's Number One disciple by the public but who was just another hired hand to the insiders;

EARLE CHRISTENBERRY, Huey's executive secretary, a man who could not be abused because he knew many of the machine's innermost secrets;

JAMES A. NOE, an oil man who had become president pro tempore of the state Senate and, upon Fournet's promotion to the Supreme Court, lieutenant governor;

ALLEN J. ELLENDER, Speaker of the House;

WADE O. MARTIN, chairman of the Public Service Commission, and thus key man in Huey's continuous war against the utilities;

EARL LONG, last and at the time probably least, with no authority and no position, but nevertheless the bearer of the magic name of Long.

Of these, Smith, Christenberry, and Noe were primarily Share-the-Wealth organization men. The others were professional politicians, far more interested in the spoils that Share-the-Wealth could deliver. The difference between the two factions was administrative, not ideological.

As the clan gathered to elect a new chief, Governor Allen said, "Fortunately, there was no doubt in the mind of Senator Long as to who his candidate for governor would be." Everyone agreed. "He picked me," said Martin. "He picked me," said Noe. "He picked me," said Ellender. Actually, it appears that Long hadn't picked anyone. But, on the other hand, it's quite likely he promised the job to these three—and probably to thirty-three others. Huey did a lot of promising to the boys, sometimes in the process of persuading them to perform a particularly unsavory task and sometimes as a reward for services rendered. He never worried about promising two men the same thing because no one dared challenge his final decision.

Earl Long demanded the governor's job. He had squirmed back into Huey's good graces—"He's on probation," Huey had said—just a few months before the assassination and he was at Huey's side when the Kingfish breathed his last. Earl insisted that he was the natural heir because he was Huey's brother, and that he was a sensible heir because he knew the poor country folk just as Huey knew them.

Today, in retrospect, it is easy to call Huey's lieutenant foolish for not using Earl to front their organization. But at the time they balked. For the most part they considered Earl just another of Huey's scrounging relatives, and they also thought him a real political liability because of the years he had spent assailing his brother both in private and in public places.

Earl had support from only one corner: Maestri. They had been friends for years; furthermore, Maestri wanted the name "Long" on the ballot.

The arguments went on behind closed doors for weeks. Then one morning, at 4:00 A.M., the press was handed this announcement: The Long ticket for the forthcoming election would consist of Noe for governor and Martin for United States senator. It looked as if the Share-the-Wealth contingent had pulled a coup. But Maestri and Weiss rushed up to Baton Rouge from New Orleans, and within a few days the Noe-Martin ticket was withdrawn and there was a new Long ticket: Richard W. Leche for governor, Earl Long for lieutenant governor, and Ellender for the Senate.

Richard W. Leche? Who was he? Leche had been Governor Allen's secretary and now he was a state judge. He was regarded as strictly a lightweight. Yet the Long heirs were now announcing that Leche had been chosen governor by the Kingfish just before the assassination. Huey had indeed asked Leche his religion, a sure sign that the man was under consideration for some office or other. But for governor? Huey had mentioned him only casually. Furthermore, Leche wasn't overly anxious to run. He liked his sinecure as a judge. He was a big, easygoing man, hardly a logical successor to so adroit and tireless a performer as Huey Long.

Leche obviously was a compromise. And Baton Rouge whispered that he wouldn't be around long. The insiders told this story: Allen proposed Leche and Maestri held out for Earl. They decided to split the difference: Leche would remain governor only until a federal judgeship could be wangled for him; then he would resign and Earl would step up from lieutenant governor.

Not everyone was satisfied with the compromise. Noe shouted that he had been double-crossed. He also said Gerald Smith had demanded $10,000 as the price of his support, and "I told him to go to hell." Smith headed for a Noe-for-governor rally in Noe's home town of Monroe, in all likelihood bent on capturing it for Leche with one of his silver-tongued Share-the-Wealth speeches. Noe headed him off just in time and gave Smith five minutes to get out of town. Smith beat the deadline.

For a brief while it looked as though the machine would be wrecked by the only thing that could wreck it—internal feuding. But, largely through Maestri's efforts, the angry talk was cooled and the boys pledged loyalty to one another in the name of the dead Kingfish.

The election campaign began, and it was just like the old days. At every rally the principal speaker was Huey, or, to be exact, a recording of an old Huey Long address. His portrait looked down from the wall of every meeting hall. Leche warned the people not to show Huey "ingratitude" by voting for his enemies. Every opposition candidate was accused of being a conspirator in the assassination of the Kingfish. Gerald Smith explained, "The martyr's blood is the seed of victory."

Congressman Cleveland Dear was the anti-Long candidate for governor, and he assailed the rise of Maestri in the Long hierarchy. He called him "The King of the Tenderloin."

Earl led the fight in defense of his benefactor. "If you loved Huey you should love Bob Maestri," he told one crowd.

"Did you love Huey?" rasped a voice from the crowd.

Earl blushed. "Well, I didn't agree with everything he said."

"We did," the voice shot back.

Congressman Dear had one strong point: He was a funnel

through which the federal government had been sending its relief funds in order to keep Huey's hands off the cash and patronage. Dear was able to promise as many new jobs and new highways and new bridges as Leche and Earl. But, alas, the poor folk believed Leche and Earl, and they didn't believe Dear. Or, as Hodding Carter put it, "The poor jobless devils took the work orders readily enough but they didn't vote WPA."

For one thing, the old Share-the-Wealth dream was much rosier than a few days' work digging ditches. The Leche campaigners belittled the vast federal relief projects as a drop in the bucket. Wade Martin, in one speech, called the federal old-age pension "a joke." He said: "You got to be so old as even not to be able to dream, and you have got to sign affidavits that are not worth a damn before you can get an old-age pension. The federal government set aside $49,000,000 for all the states, and after you take out the administrative expenses you haven't got enough left to pay thirty cents a month pension."

That wasn't exactly true, but the truth has seldom invaded Louisiana political campaigns.

In the end, the people showed Huey none of the ingratitude Leche feared. He polled 362,502 votes, 67 per cent of the total; he even carried New Orleans, something Huey could never do. Earl went into office with him, although Earl trailed the ticket by 12,000 votes, apparently a final assessment for his nasty testimony against Huey in the Senate investigation years before.

Now the rulers of Louisiana were Leche, Maestri, and Weiss, and they set out to make things all right with the world.

They had one nagging worry. Fighting back at Huey, the federal government had indicted the top lieutenants—Weiss, Shushan, Fisher, Mike Moss, Joe Haspel, to name a few—for income-tax evasion. Huey had screamed at this persecution; but, as Wilson and Irey said, he was going to be next.

Shushan's trial was first, shortly after the Kingfish's assassination. He was charged with failing to declare $500,000 in income. The prosecution's case set forth evidence of shake-downs involving companies which did business with the Levee Board. Attorney Hugh Wilkinson produced a unique defense: This sounds like an extortion, he said, and extortion is illegal, and if extortion is illegal then the money was not rightfully Abe's, and if the money was not rightfully Abe's then it wasn't income, and if it wasn't income then there's no tax due.

Wilkinson also said that actually the money collected from these firms was not for Shushan. It was a political contribution. "The government calls it graft," he said. "It is a contribution to the welfare of a political party in which they are all interested."

The jury voted not guilty. The Long claque which packed the courtroom cheered, and Huey's ex-bodyguards suddenly appeared from out of the past to usher Shushan out of the courtroom. They left a few smashed cameras in their wake.

The government didn't appear to be discouraged. It continued to produce indictments. But now, after Leche's election, Congressman Paul Maloney went to Washington to make peace with the feds. The result was soon known far and wide as the Second Louisiana Purchase.

The Long boys promised to forget about Huey's proposed opposition to Roosevelt at the forthcoming 1936 Democratic National Convention. They promised to repeal Huey's anti-federal relief laws. They promised to scrap the Share-the-Wealth hoopla which was such a diversion to the New Deal. In return, they asked only one thing: Don't send us to jail.

In any event the United States Attorney René Viosca asked for dismissal of the remaining indictments. The Shushan case was his strongest and he lost it, he said. There was no point to going on. The grand jury which voted the indictments issued a statement saying that this was not true and that the cases should go to trial. Internal Revenue chief Irey said he had the evidence "for successful prosecution." But these were whispers amid bedlam, and the criminal cases against the Long boys were dropped. (The government nevertheless collected $2,000,000 in back taxes from them.)

The regime kept its promises to the federal administration. Soon everyone loved everyone else. Louisiana, far from balking at Roosevelt's renomination, seconded the motion at the convention. FDR himself visited New Orleans to be feted by the state regime. Jim Farley, the man Huey wanted investigated by Congress, delivered the commencement address at the state university. Gaston L. Porterie, who had been expelled from the Bar Association for performing some of Huey's legal shenanigans, was nominated to the federal bench by FDR. And when Roosevelt attended the Texas Centennial at Dallas, the Louisiana legislature officially transferred its session to Texas to act as a cheering claque for his address; it is the only known instance in American history where a legislature met in another state.

Ditching Share-the-Wealth wasn't so easy. Gerald Smith and Earle Christenberry objected strenuously. It had never been a money-making racket, but if Leche and Maestri and Weiss didn't want the Share-the-Wealth Clubs as a political organization Gerald certainly knew what to do with them. He began courting the Townsend Plan people but learned to his chagrin that he was a little late: Christenberry already had sold them the Share-the-Wealth membership rolls and now was going to Washington as Louisiana's liaison to the federal relief agencies. Smith demanded that the boys take care of him, too. He was told to get out of Louisiana under his own power or be carried out. He fled, and soon was devoting that silver tongue (some said it was flannel) and his organizing abilities to the causes of anti-Semitism and white supremacy, a trade he plies to this day.

Leche's legislative program must have started Huey whirling in his grave. The anti-federal relief laws were repealed. Huey's secret police, the Criminal Investigation Bureau, was eliminated. A $100,000 investigation into the plot to assassinate Huey, promised so determinedly during the election campaign, was quietly forgotten.

Leche even agreed to kill the "occupational tax" against Standard Oil. However, here Earl stepped in and threatened to revolt. The memory of Huey's war against Standard was too fresh in the public mind, Earl maintained. Leche gave in. The tax remained but was cut from five cents to one cent a barrel. This had no actual effect since, by private agreement with Huey, Standard had been getting a four-cent rebate on the five-cent tax right along. Earl worked in the legislature to put over the reduced tax.

Huey always had been opposed to a sales tax. Now Leche put one across. He called it a "luxury tax," but it applied to everything from food and medicine to funerals and automobiles. The boys had the public pay the 2 per cent tax in aluminum tokens—ten to the penny—in the hope that the voters would not realize they were shelling out anything of value. It was a good idea; and besides, somebody turned a neat profit selling the tokens to the state.

Leche's administration eliminated the more conspicuous forms of dictatorship. No longer was the state militia paraded as a private army. The state cops stopped delivering campaign literature. The governor still maintained control, by power of appointment, over the election commissions, the judiciary, the bank examiners, and the tax assessors, but the emphasis was different: No longer was there power for power's sake, but only power with which to make a deal. Many of the so-called "better people," who were horrified at the crudities of Huey Long, were quite willing to do business with the Leche administration.

An example in the shift of emphasis was the Long newspaper, originally the *Louisiana Progress* and converted by Huey into the *American Progress* when he moved into the national arena. Under Huey this newspaper was a propaganda organ. Leche inherited it and made it strictly business. State employees had to sell five to ten subscriptions a year in order to keep their jobs. Charity Hospital employees had their subscription fees deducted directly from their pay checks. Contractors who did business with the state kept the paper crammed with ads. The *Progress* advertising salesmen carried letters of introduction from the heads of state departments—and sometimes they also carried photostats of a letter from Roosevelt to Leche celebrating the glory of a free press as represented by the *Progress*.

State employees had to contribute 5 to 10 per cent of their salaries to the machine. No one waited for them to deliver the money; it was deducted automatically from their pay checks. There was no attempt to hide the practice. Earl called it "a legitimate and honorable way of raising funds from people who owe their jobs to the administration." A new phrase entered the lexicon of Louisiana politics—"double dip." It referred to the state employees considered worthy of more than one job at a time. A check showed, for example, that thirteen of the twenty-eight Orleans Parish legislators were on the city payroll.

The Leche administration continued Huey's good work, but now it operated with the federal relief funds which were unfrozen as part of the Louisiana Purchase. The roads reached out even into areas Huey left untouched. More bridges were added. Charity Hospital in New Orleans was enlarged until it looked like Rockefeller Center. Tourists were flabbergasted at this sprawling, supermodern plant; and well they should be, for Longism has always paid its dividend to the poor in grandiose style.

As with Huey, Louisiana State University was a focal point. But while Huey used it for show and as a private plaything, now it, like the *American Progress,* became a money-maker. The new buildings were going up so fast on the campus that the university was forced to hire a full-time construction superintendent, one George Caldwell who soon was making a flat 2 per cent on every job.

Sometimes the buildings went up too fast. Reporters lolling in the Capitol press room one day were told a fantastic tale. Caldwell had just completed a building out at LSU, but nobody knew what it was for. It hadn't been ordered. He just built it to get his 2 per cent.

A fantastic rumor, but it had to be checked. The reporters dashed out to the campus.

They found the university president, James Monroe Smith, in his office, and told him the tale they'd heard.

"Ridiculous!" he snorted.

"Very well, then, Dr. Smith. What *is* the new building for?"

Smith leaned back in his swivel chair and raised his eyes to the heavens for an answer. And, lo, the heavens provided the answer. An airplane flew over.

"Why," said Smith, suddenly brightening, "it's our new school of aeronautics."

And thus, although not a soul had proposed it before, did LSU's faculty immediately sanction a school of aeronautics, hire a staff, purchase the equipment, and recruit the student body in a matter of weeks.

LSU provided such lush pickings that the boys stopped trying to cover up. If you wanted something and you rated high enough down at the Capitol, you bought it and charged it to LSU. There on the LSU books one could find such entries as "Copper pot for governor's summer house, $7.50." There was little or no attempt at subterfuge.

The boys used LSU as an assembly plant. They built prefabricated buildings for their estates on the LSU campus with LSU materials and LSU workmen and then trucked them to the estates in LSU trucks.

A Gold Coast grew outside the fashionable spa of Covington, Louisiana. There was Leche's estate, two hundred acres, with its private hunting preserve. There was Shushan's estate, with its private barber shop. George Caldwell actually had gold bathroom fixtures on his place. Leche was chided about his ostentatious tastes, and reporters asked him how he could manage so well on the governor's $7,500-a-year salary. His classic reply: "When I took the oath as governor, I didn't take any vow of poverty."

Everything turned into money. Huey used to charge a token five cents for an apointment as honorary colonel on the governor's staff. Under Leche the price jumped to twenty dollars.

The boys forgot all about Longism. They never mentioned Share-the-Wealth. The holy crusades against the trusts and the utility corporations were abandoned. They invoked the name of Huey at the slightest provocation, always implying that he had personally ordered their latest caper from That Great Pork Barrel Up Yonder, but this was only lip service. They no longer supplied the poor whites with a cause.

Furthermore, some of Huey's favorite people were jostled out of line in the scramble at the trough. The Kingfish's ex-secretary, Alice Lee Grosjean, was booted off the public payroll and her kinfolk went with her. Dr. Arthur Vidrine was demoted from his job as head of Charity Hospital and the LSU medical school. Attorney Hugh Wilkinson, who was Huey's law partner in the firm which garnered the most lucrative of the state's cases, lost this business. Noe continued to rankle at the manner in which the Leche-Maestri-Weiss clique snatched the gubernatorial nomination from him.

Earl, although lieutenant governor, was strictly an outsider. He fought some of the more blatant deviations from Longism, such as the attempt to repeal the Standard Oil tax, but mostly he remained a sullen outcast at his home in New Orleans or at his farm in Winnfield. It became apparent that, federal judgeship or no, Leche would not resign now that he had discovered the true glories of being governor. He was talking of hand-picking Attorney General David Allison as his successor, leaving Earl even further behind.

Earl could have been put to good use by the boys, touring the back parishes and preaching Longism so the folks would feel Baton Rouge hadn't forgotten them. But they didn't do so. They were having too much fun to be bothered.

Earl hated his obscurity. He hated it under Huey and he hated it even more under Huey's heirs. But the day was to come when he would be deeply grateful for these snubs he was now enduring.

CHAPTER NINE

"If those fellows ever try to use the powers I've given them without me to hold them down, they'll all land in the penitentiary."

WHILE HUEY WAS ALIVE, LSU PRESIDENT JAMES MONROE SMITH was the very model of a satrap, keeping his mouth shut, grabbing only the crumbs which fell off the table, and enduring the Kingfish's public ridicule with a sheepish smile and a subservient nod. But after Huey died Smith forgot all the proprieties as he stuffed his pockets with everything within reach.

Scribner's Magazine investigated Smith's stewardship, and reported:

"Smith's basic policy was to work with Long. It meant personal and academic humiliation. It meant being abused in statehouse corridors and being hanged in effigy. It meant being called to Huey's bedroom at all hours of the night ('Hey, Jim, I've got an idea'). It meant clamping censorship on the student paper and expelling six editors who offended Long. It meant having his university investigated by a number of organizations, it meant becoming the butt of anecdotes which, true or false, were usually in character.

"One revolves around the riding academy set up at LSU. There was a report that Mrs. Smith was using the horses, and a news story about a student being killed while riding. When these items came to Huey's attention he was campaigning upstate, telling backwoodsmen about the thrifty use of tax money. Immediately, according to the story, Huey telegraphed Smith: 'Sell them plugs.'

"Smith understood Huey. He knew that Huey's first question about any university matter was whether it was politically advisable. Smith knew that Huey had boundless energy, ambition, egotism and power. He knew that here were springs to tap, not dam, and that part of the secret was letting Huey talk, encouraging his expansive moods, feeding his vanity. He didn't mind providing Huey with a dazzling school band when it meant that Huey would provide the university with millions of dollars."

And Huey did provide. He tripled the enrollment. He spent $9,000,000 on the plant alone, and he increased its faculty from 180 to 400.

Smith was content to ride with Huey's punches. He docilely accepted the only accolade the Kingfish ever awarded him publicly: "Jim has a hide as thick as a rhinoceros."

Mrs. Smith—Thelma—was wildly ambitious. She had been manager of the Southeastern College cafeteria when her husband became president of LSU, and she longed to show the ladies of Baton Rouge how a grand dame should entertain. Sometimes her snooty parties were left a shambles when Huey showed up to humiliate her sadistically. He'd wander among the guests cursing and ridiculing the hosts as he swilled, while bodyguard Joe Messina greedily picked his way through the delicacies trucked up from New Orleans by a fancy caterer.

James Smith endured these humiliations as the price of admission to the Kingfish's inner circle. When the Kingfish died he took over Huey's university as though he now owned it. Smith fired an employee of the university cafeteria who billed him $3,000 for the food and drink he drew from the commisary to use in his home. He drove LSU cars, lived in an LSU house, was ministered to by LSU servants, and wore LSU clothes. He even billed the university for his life-insurance premiums, and he awarded his daughter an all-expense-paid "study tour" of Mexico.

He took care of the other boys in the regime, of course.

There seldom was competitive bidding for university purchases, and thousands of items were bought at retail. A building listed as a dormitory turned out to be a luxurious house for which few rents were ever collected. Unpaid "student loans" reached $210,000 (and some of the students listed said later they never had borrowed the money in the first place).

Jim Smith was carried by the momentum of the thing. He couldn't stop. He began rewriting the minutes of the Board of Trustees. He gave himself a $3,000 pay raise with forged minutes and doubled Construction Superintendent George Caldwell's 1 per cent rakeoff with forged minutes.

Smith went into the market. He wasn't very bright. He bought a thousand cases of a year-old Kentucky bourbon in a warehouse, figuring it would get more valuable as it aged. But whisky bottled green stays green, and he took a big loss. Then the eminent Dr. Smith went in for something big: reasoning in 1937 that war was near, he began speculating in grain. He presented himself to a New Orleans broker and announced that he headed a big syndicate out to do big things.

"It filled me with joy when he said this," the broker said later. "Smith belonged to the political crowd. They had all the money these days. And he talked economics so masterfully that I could hardly restrain myself from asking him to take me into the group."

Smith started by putting up $300,000 of LSU bonds for collateral in buying 2,000,000 bushels of wheat. Perhaps he knew his economics; but, alas, he didn't know his world politics. There came Munich—and no war. The bottom fell out of the grain market. Smith was in trouble. He walked into a Baton Rouge print shop, dropped off a $1,000 LSU bond, and blandly ordered, "Rush me three hundred of these."

He took these phony bonds to his broker as collateral for more speculation. He was desperate to get out of the hole. The broker, a little wary now, wouldn't take the bonds because he lacked a legal opinion on their validity. Smith came up then with a $300,000 cashier's check. He simply told the New Orleans bank that the LSU Board of Supervisors had authorized him to borrow it. The bank didn't investigate; nobody was investigating anything in Louisiana any more.

When word of Smith's $300,000 loan reached a Baton Rouge banker, he telephoned the Doc and chided him for giving all that business to the New Orleans crowd. "You're right," said the Doc. "I wasn't thinking. Just to be fair I'll take $100,000 from you."

Then one night Dr. Arthur Vidrine, the demoted head of the LSU medical school, dropped into New Orleans' famous all-night French Quarter coffee shop. He met a broker friend he hadn't seen for years. "Say," said the friend, "I wanted to tell you I think it's shameful the way Smith treated you. And you know what he's up to now? He's in the market big."

Dr. Vidrine passed the gossip on to another friend, who passed it on to another, until it reached the ears of Rufus Fontenot, district collector for the Internal Revenue Department. Fontenot was one of those career men who still writhed with indignation over the Second Louisiana Purchase which killed their old income-tax cases against the Long crowd. Now here was a hotter prospect. Fontenot induced Washington to give him its top men for a major investigation of Dr. Smith. The first thing these agents noted was major trading activity by a "James Monroe," trading which followed the pattern they suspected of James Monroe Smith. Furthermore, they could find no affluent James Monroe living in New Orleans.

Meanwhile, a pesky newspaper exposé was bedeviling the administration. Jimmy Noe, another of the Long stalwarts ousted by the Leche regime, had been supplying the papers with hundreds of affidavits (the total eventually reached 980) claiming theft in the state government. Acting on a Noe tip, the New Orleans *States* obtained photographs of LSU window frames being installed at the new home of a Leche aide.

The *States* and the *Times-Picayune* had been printing exposés like this for years, and they seldom caused any real consternation. But this time Leche, jittery over the federal investigation of Dr. Smith, tried to emulate the crafty Huey: Leche announced that the state government would conduct a massive investigation of itself. Leche assigned himself to be the chief investigator.

Just before the hearing, however, he lost his nerve. He called off the investigation because, he announced, he had learned that all of the LSU materials, and the LSU workmen who installed them, had been paid for. Could any citizen avail himself of this cut-rate LSU construction service? Well, no, said Dr. Smith. The same day Drew Pearson's column appeared with the charge—again supported by Jimmy Noe affidavits—that WPA labor had been used to build the barn on Leche's estate and that WPA materials went into the homes of LSU's business manager Jackson and construction superintendent Caldwell.

Leche announced he was resigning the next week. For reasons of health, of course.

Four days later, on Sunday, June 25, 1939, all hell broke loose.

At 11:00 A.M. Dr. Smith telephoned to Leche from New Orleans and asked for an appointment "this very day." He didn't say why, but he insisted the matter was urgent. Leche told him to come along. At 1:30 P.M. Smith arrived at the executive mansion. He told Leche he had borrowed $200,000 from the LSU treasury without the Board of Supervisors' approval. As Leche told it later: "He wanted to know what I thought about it and if I could get the board to approve it now. I told him I'd see what could be done and to get in touch with me later in the day."

Smith left, and Leche sent for Attorney General Ellison and Supreme Court Chief Justice Fournet, who was on the LSU Board of Supervisors.

At 6:00 P.M. Smith returned to the mansion. He told his story again, but now the $200,000 he had borrowed illegally became $400,000. He asked that the board okay the loans retroactively. Leche and Fournet told him the board wouldn't go along. Leche said: "Well, Doc, do you want it the hard way or the easy way? I think you ought to resign and let the board look into it."

Smith said he'd sign a resignation—but not a confession. Leche wrote it out, and Smith signed it. Smith knew then the boys wouldn't cover for him. He went home and started packing. His wife helped him in the scramble. She left evidence of how frantic she was. She began with her expensive flat silverware, abandoned that and turned to her custom-made gowns, quit and switched to her jewelry—until finally she and the Doc had stuffed a smattering of everything into their bags, and left the rest in violent disarray.

Even as the Smiths packed, the state police, under Leche's orders, were rummaging through Smith's office on the LSU campus. The cops quickly found mutilated LSU bonds. They went to a judge's home to get a search warrant for Smith's house. They didn't get there until 10:30 P.M., and the Smiths were gone. The unpacked shambles remained, valuables strewn from one end of the mansion to the other.

Leche called in the newspaper reporters. The governor was in bed—from the "illness" which was causing his resignation —and he announced he had ordered the arrest of Dr. Smith for questioning about "financial irregularities which may total several hundred thousand dollars." Dr. Smith was missing at the moment, and Leche would not resign until all of this was cleared up. Someone changed his mind fast. He resigned the next morning.

The great manhunt was on, not for a Dillinger or a Pretty Boy Floyd, but for the president of Louisiana State University. "I didn't order his arrest right away," Leche said. "I certainly didn't expect him to run away. A Dillinger, a Capone—they might have had some chance. But an amateur like the Doc—he was known from one end of the state to the other."

The Doc had fled Baton Rouge just after dusk. He had ordered the private airplane which LSU maintained for its football coaches to recruit talent, but, oddly enough, the plane was being used elsewhere by a football coach recruiting talent.

So Smith, his wife, and her nephew, J. Emory Adams, who had been awarded the LSU bookstore monopoly as his private domain, had taken off by automobile. The FBI entered the search on orders of Attorney General Frank Murphy, who only a month previously had received an honorary degree from Dr. Smith.

Two days later nephew Adams suddenly returned to Baton Rouge. He revealed he had driven the Smiths as far as Memphis, where they had registered as "Mr. and Mrs. J. M. Southern," and then left them. He had no idea where they were going. The search was pressed from Memphis. Clues popped up in every cranny of the United States. They were all false.

Just when it appeared that the absconding college president had got away, he turned himself in. That was a week after he disappeared. He was in Canada. He had been vacationing in a remote fishing village and was shocked, he said, to learn that the police were looking for him. Smith had $315 on him, and Thelma had $9,400 in her purse. As she stood amid milling police in a country post office, she wailed to a woman bystander, "My husband's in an awful lot of trouble."

Dr. Smith said he would waive extradition. "I won't be made a goat," he said. The Louisiana police set out after him, but only after a jurisdictional dispute over whether state police or parish officers would make the junket. They compromised. The delegation was composed of both. They flew to Canada in that LSU football plane Smith had sought in vain. When they arrived Dr. Smith refused to enter it. He was afraid he'd be pushed out of the window high over some mountain range, he said. The party booked space on a commercial airliner.

And on July 4th, amid holiday trimmings, the once-haughty Smiths arrived at New Orleans Airport. A tremendous crowd was there to witness the spectacle. Among the newspaper reporters covering the story were five of the six student editors Smith had expelled from the university a couple of years earlier. The great event was even broadcast by radio, and Dr.

Smith said a few words over the microphone which was thrust into his face:

"Hello, folks. I'm back. I'm glad to be back. I was ill advised."

With that he got into a police car for the ninety-mile trip to Baton Rouge. Here more crowds greeted them. Women pushed at the straining police lines for a better look at the snooty Thelma Smith. "She's crying!" shrieked one woman with glee as Mrs. Smith daubed a handkerchief at her eyes. The police chauffeur turned on his siren as the car pulled into the courthouse driveway. "Can't we do without that?" Thelma pleaded.

Dr. and Mrs. Smith were both fingerprinted, and then the Doc was locked into a cell for the night.

And, back at New Orleans Airport, there was another arrival. This one was greeted by no crowds. The man was O. John Rogge, a young federal attorney sent into Louisiana as special prosecutor. His orders were not to stop at Smith: go all the way. The Second Louisiana Purchase was dead. The boys had overstepped the bounds and, worse, they'd got their extravagances into the newspapers. The federal government was out to convict.

It wasn't long before Rogge, reportedly with some aid from the now-bitter Dr. Smith, began reaching deep into the administration for a series of indictments that grew with each passing day. The total was to hit 250. It wasn't easy to catch the boys. They had learned from previous frights to pay their income taxes. They knew about the postal laws, so they delivered their checks to the banks in person. But, alas, Rogge finally hooked them on the most technical of technicalities. True, the boys delivered the checks to the banks by hand, he conceded. But the banks in turn sent them to the clearinghouse by mail. And thus the mails were used to defraud. It was the flimsiest pretext imaginable, but it worked. This was the key charge in the Louisiana Scandals. It permitted federal prosecution of cases which ordinarily belonged in the prostituted state courts.

Amid the turmoil Earl Long realized his ambition. He was governor at last. Even under these tumultuous circumstances he considered it too good to be true. The day Leche first announced his intention of quitting, a reporter addressed Earl as "Governor," and Earl replied: "Don't call me that. That man may change his mind tomorrow. He gave me absolute assurance he would resign in the presence of twenty-five people. But I'm like the crapshooter that refused to pick up the money before he'd won it."

But Leche had resigned, under stern insistence from Maestri. Earl immediately set out to salvage the good name of Longism. He pinned all of the blame for the growing scandal on Leche. "I begged O.K. Allen not to make Leche the candidate," Earl said, "but Allen would not listen to me. They made Leche the candidate, and I just went along with them."

Earl himself was investigated thoroughly by Rogge's men. They never found a thing on him. His friends said it proved that Earl was honest. His enemies said Earl simply was too much of an outsider to get his hands on anything. Earl was quoted as saying, "I ain't against stealing, but it takes two of us to steal and the other one might squeal." At any rate Earl never was implicated in any of the myriad of thefts and half-thefts exposed in the scandals.

He said: "I know better. I was brought up in the country, and my mother was a God-fearing woman. When Leche used to say he didn't take the vow of poverty when he took the oath of governor, I used to cringe. I felt like telling him to shut up."

Earl offered full federal-state police cooperation in the investigations. The federal government refused to share its information with him. Earl ignored this barb and blew hot and cold on the scandals: when things were quiet he would minimize the whole thing, and when things got noisy with new exposés he would vow unstinting state prosecution. To many observers he seemed to be trying to make up his mind which direction to take.

Suddenly he had no choice. The investigations turned to

the matter of "hot oil." (Each oil company is permitted to draw only so many barrels per year from a well. Anything over the quota is "hot oil," or illegal oil. If the "hot oil" is shipped by interstate commerce, the violation becomes a federal case.) The Conservation Commission was in charge of enforcing the hot-oil laws, and Earl's patron saint, Bob Maestri, had been chairman of the commission. Furthermore, Maestri, by now mayor of New Orleans, had hand-picked his successor, William Rankin.

The investigations turned up evidence that the Conservation Commission itself had been approving illegal hot-oil deals. Under heavy pressure from the newspapers, Earl fired Dr. J. A. Shaw, a former dentist who was head of the commission's oil proration division. Dr. Shaw refused to be fired. He kept reporting to his office and collecting his pay checks. Shaw said that he was being made a scapegoat and that he'd not go down without taking a few others with him. Earl, the governor, was summoned to New Orleans for a conference with Maestri. As he emerged he announced that firing Shaw was all a mistake. He fired Shaw's boss, Rankin, instead.

The grand juries kept calling for Shaw, and finally he told one of them that he had signed hot-oil permits on instructions from Governor Leche and Maestri. "That's the only way I hold my position," he said. "I do what they tell me to. I would sign anything they stuck in front of me except an order to hang me." Two nights later Shaw went into the bathroom of his home and fired a bullet into his brain.

All of the exposés were coming from federal grand juries. Under new pressure Earl released an old audit which had uncovered shortages at LSU well before Leche announced Smith's resignation. But the state courts were becoming more and more conspicuous by their lack of activity on the scandals.

New Orleans should have been the center of the investigations, but District Attorney Charles Byrne, a Long man, said he had "only rumors" to go on. He stuck to that tune until suddenly his serenity was jolted by a runaway grand jury.

The foreman of the grand jury, H. H. Powell, rose in court

and began to read a petition. Judge George Platt, also a Long man, interrupted immediately. "I'm ordering you not to read that!" he barked.

Powell read a few more words.

"Mr. Sheriff, take this man and lock him up."

Deputies grabbed Powell, but he hurled his petition away and a newspaper reporter caught it. The petition was out, Judge Platt notwithstanding. It accused the district attorney's staff of stalling and even of whisking witnesses out of the reach of the grand jury.

DA Byrne said of the jurymen, "They're God-damned liars." Judge Platt ruled Powell and one other juror in contempt and threw them off the jury. The remaining jurymen appealed to Governor Long to supersede Byrne, and Long appointed Assistant Attorney General O'Connor to investigate. It was hardly an apt choice because O'Connor himself had been mentioned indirectly in a hot-oil investigation.

O'Connor did start a hearing on the jury's charges against the DA. The grand jurymen testified that they wanted to investigate all crime, including the city's wide-open gambling, and that the DA told them this was "too burdensome." When they named specific cases which interested them, the DA's office brought in completed cases against small-fry defendants, vindicating without testimony the administration big shots involved.

The jury said it now wanted to look into padding of the state's payroll. O'Connor said he would permit this. Earl objected. He didn't want the payroll raided of its loyal Longites. He ordered Attorney General Ellison to call off O'Connor. The attorney general refused. Earl fired him and sent the militia to bar Ellison from his own office. Ellison was an elective official, but Long said he had discovered—three years after Ellison's election—that the attorney general held office illegally. Ellison arranged a peace conference with Long and then mysteriously decided not to fight his ouster.

Earl then went to New Orleans to talk with DA Byrne. After the meeting Byrne resigned "for reasons of health."

The investigation of the grand jury's charges was called off. It was obvious now that Earl Long did not intend to prosecute the scandals, although he did go so far as to cancel an order to place 145 Richard Leche plaques on the state's bridges and highways.

The federal cases droned on, and Louisiana learned just how fantastic an operation the Leche regime was. The boys took what they wanted. And what they didn't want they sold to the state.

Seymour Weiss and Monte Hart had been stuck for years with a white elephant, the Bienville Hotel, in New Orleans, a money loser because it was out of the city's business and tourist districts. They had paid $541,000 for it. Despairing of ever breaking even, they sold it to LSU, completely furnished, for $575,000, for use as a temporary nurses' home. Then, amazed at how easy this was, they sold the furnishings a second time for an additional $75,000. Along with Dr. Smith, who got $25,000 of the money as a "loan," they were convicted of defrauding LSU of the $75,000 and sentenced to prison, but Hart committed suicide before serving his term.

This was just one case of double-dealing. A Charity Hospital building had been moved to one spot, then back to its original location at a cost of $500,000. An LSU architect had been paid a $24,000 fee for a campus job, and then, a few years later, was paid $24,000 all over again for the same job. The contractor's bid on an LSU building was $101,000; the final cost was $202,000.

The scandals even touched New Orleans high society. Stockbrokers Bobby Newman and Norvin Harris of the country-club set made a deal with Abe Shushan, president of the Levee Board, to rewrite all of the state's bond issues at a cost of $500,000 to the state. Shushan got $132,000 of it and Herbert Waguespack, chairman of the board's finance committee, got $46,000.

It developed that the boys even arranged their own testimonials. A group of reputable New Orleans businessmen had presented Governor Leche with a yacht in appreciation of his fine administration. Now a grand jury discovered that the yacht, equipped down to the bedspreads at a cost of $12,000, had been paid for by the Conservation Department on Commission Chairman Rankin's orders. Each of the businessmen on the Presentation Committee had been led to believe that he was the only member of the group who hadn't kicked in for the boat; by the time the fund collectors got to him they were "oversubscribed."

In the end, they went to jail, these men who had taken the state for an estimated $100,000,000—LSU President Smith, who was later photographed cutting sugar cane while wearing stripes; Seymour Weiss, Architect Leon Weiss, for overcharging on LSU buildings; LSU's construction superintendent George Caldwell, Dr. Clarence Lorio, who held so many state jobs he had to farm one out to a young physician; Conservation Commission Chairman Rankin, Emory Adams, Levee Board President Abe Shushan, Levee Board Finance Chairman Herbert Waguespack, Stockbrokers Bobby Newman and Norvin Harris, and a host of lesser lights. In addition, there were four suicides—Dr. Shaw and Monte Hart, plus Dr. Smith's financial adviser and LSU's National Youth Administration director.

There were other results of the scandals. The newly built New Orleans Airport had been named Shushan Airport, apparently, it has been said, in honor of the fact that Abe collected only 2½ cents on each yard of gravel used. The state naturally elected to strip the airport of this dishonored name. But everywhere it looked there were epaulets. Shushan had put his name any place it would fit, and where it wouldn't fit —the doorknobs, the light standards—he left his initial "S."

They renamed it New Orleans Airport, but they never were able to eradicate all the Shushan signatures. This soon ceased to matter. Within a few years the airport was obsolete, and the city had to build a new one on the other side of town.

It was easier to pry mementos from the state's property. Down came the plaques "Smith Dormitory" and "Leche Hall" from the LSU campus. The likenesses of the administration demigods were pried from hundreds of bridges and highway markers. But no one dared tamper with the plaque on the Huey P. Long Bridge.

It became *déclassé* in Louisiana to use the low-numbered automobile license plates. These 2's and 3's are cherished as status symbols in most states, but in Louisiana they became status symbols in reverse. They were an invitation to jibes about grand juries and double dips and striped suits. The surviving members of the administration began to drive incognito. They eliminated the low-numbered license plates as a mark of shame.

Naturally, the old enemies of Huey Long tried to trace all of the scandals back to him, and, indeed, the roots had been his. But the redneck worshipers of Huey showed no disenchantment. They followed Earl's lead: "It was the Leche crowd." Actually, Huey had frequently warned his underlings about being too greedy or too careless. He once said, "If those fellows ever try to use the powers I've given them without me to hold them down, they'll all land in the penitentiary."

And they did. They certainly did.

CHAPTER TEN

"There's a difference between character and reputation. Reputation is what people think you are and character is what you are inside."

"SURE I WANT TO BE GOVERNOR," SAID EARL KEMP LONG. "ONLY one person in more'n 2,000,000 people can be governor of this state. Think about that. Ain't that an honor? And every time you go to the door of the mansion somebody's bringing you a turkey or a ham or a basket of something. I like that free stuff. "

Earl was elected governor twice after that gloomy Monday morning when he took Richard Leche's office by default. On three other occasions he tried to slip into power through the back door. The man is infatuated with the office.

Yet Earl Long is a most ungovernor-appearing person. With straw hat perched on the back of his head and stomach protruding arrogantly over his ever-slipping trousers, he talks the lingo of the field hand and displays the manners of the mule skinner. His only concern with elegance is to scorn it from the speaker's platform. His only concern with statesmanship is to circumvent it in the smoke-filled room.

Earl Long has seldom been fettered with inhibitions. At four o'clock one morning, when he was staying with his wife at the Roosevelt Hotel in New Orleans, he got a telephone call revealing an unexpected political development. He had to take action immediately. Because he didn't want to disturb his sleeping wife by his side, he went down the hall, clad only in his shorts, to use the pay telephone. A late-arriving tourist couple was startled to come upon the unclad governor of Louisiana shouting at the top of his lungs in a public phone booth.

But if his crudities make Earl Long something less than a model statesman, they also ensure the voters an unretouched picture of the man they elect. It is a trite American tradition that the governor must be a man of the soil. Even a dandy like Thomas E. Dewey felt compelled to be photographed at his "gentleman's farm" in upstate New York. With Earl this love of the soil is sincere. He talks happily of his "little shack" in Winnfield, Louisiana, and that's exactly what it is—a little shack, without living room, with linoleum on the floor, with calendar pictures on the wall.

Earl's simplicity as a man of the soil is the source of many anecdotes involving his more citified subordinates. They have often suffered because Earl frequently decides without warning to make a pilgrimage to his "pea patch" and invariably orders every underling in sight to accompany him. A Long legislature leader, Senator B. B. Rayburn (nicknamed "Sixty" in memory, it is said, of the highest grade he attained in school), tells of one such midnight foray.

On the way Long decided to stop at a farmhouse to pick up some chickens he had bought. It was 2:00 A.M. "No need to wake anybody up," he said. "We'll just take 'em." He led the reluctant band of state officials through the night's blackness into the henhouse to round up the squawking fowl. Suddenly the lights blazed on in the farmhouse and the farmer appeared on his porch brandishing a shotgun. The cream of Louisiana's state government went scrambling back to the station wagon in terror while Earl shouted frantically: "Don't shoot! It's me. Earl K. Long. The governor of Louisiana. Don't shoot!"

Luckily the farmer recognized Earl's voice, and held his fire.

Earl was a frugal man most of his life. Those neighbors in the vicinity of the executive mansion in Baton Rouge used to sniff with disdain when they saw him loading his station wagon for a weekend visit to the farm. He'd pack aboard all the hams and turkeys and baskets of something which had been delivered to the mansion by admirers, and last he would strap onto the rear two huge garbage cans laden with the week's leavings: he made the cooks save the garbage so he could cart it to the hogs at Winnfield. Whether at Baton Rouge, Winnfield, or out of the state, Earl did the family grocery shopping with a canny eye on prices. He always ordered a hotel suite with a kitchenette so that he could prepare his own meals.

He put on fancy airs for no one. Attorney General Jack Gremillion, like all the others, was shocked on his first visit to the farmhouse. He knew Earl referred to it as "the shack," but Gremillion assumed this to be a figure of speech. He actually was expecting something along the plantation "big house" line. He found, instead, the four-room shack—and when he awoke at 8:30 A.M. he discovered that Earl actually did go tend the hogs at 5:00 A.M.

"What do you want Nannie to cook you for breakfast?" Earl asked solicitously.

"Eggs," said Gremillion.

"O.K.," said the governor to the attorney general. "Go out to the henhouse and get 'em and she'll cook 'em."

Gremillion stepped ever so gingerly out to the henhouse to fetch his own breakfast.

Earl did not mend his ways even in the stately executive mansion in Baton Rouge. Washington correspondent Warren Rogers, Jr., had once covered the Louisiana statehouse and, upon a return visit, was invited by Governor Long to bring his family to Sunday dinner. The Rogerses arrived to find Mrs. Long expecting them but the governor nowhere in sight. They sat about uneasily for more than an hour while Mrs. Long three times sent a state policeman upstairs to summon the obviously indisposed governor.

Finally Mrs. Long escorted the Rogerses into the dining room without the governor. After dinner Earl was summoned again, and this time he lurched downstairs sleepily, stuffing his shirt into his pants, his face still wet from the water he had just splashed upon it.

He sat in the delicately appointed East Room of the mansion and chatted. Once he attempted to spit fifteen feet into the fireplace; he didn't come close. He sent a state cop out to the yard to bring in a hunting dog he wanted to show the Rogers children. (The Longs are childless, and the governor has a deep love for any and all children.) The dog came in and promptly relieved himself on the pale gray rug. The governor snickered. Mrs. Long turned her head away in embarrassment.

Many of the visitors at the executive mansion were, of course, shocked at such crudities. One Long supporter, a man who earnestly believed in the wisdom of Earl Long's political policies, came away from such an experience saying: "Is this the man I support for governor? How can I face my children now?"

On another occasion, just after an election victory, Earl entertained visitors in his hotel suite by spitting all afternoon at a copy of the opposition New Orleans *Item* he had spread out on the floor.

These habits of Earl Long were sober habits. Until he was well past sixty he drank only sparingly, and he certainly was no wencher. His one major vice was horse playing. He was such a compulsive bettor that, in an emergency, the ponies could draw him close to his bitterest enemies. These emergencies did arise. There was the occasion when Long became embroiled in a particularly newsworthy political scrap, and yet he disappeared from the reach of reporters. The one exception was the New Orleans *Times-Picayune,* the paper which Earl hates with unreasoning fury. Yet while all other reporters sought the governor's whereabouts fruitlessly for days, the despised *Times-Picayune* published an exclusive interview with him every morning.

How? Why? It seems that Earl was traveling around the country to keep out of the reporters' reach. But every night he simply had to call the *Times-Picayune* sports department to get the last race results which did not appear in the afternoon papers. The sports desk was supplied with a list of political questions, and refused to give Earl the racing information until he answered the questions.

Earl is a man with a fearful temper. During the impeachment of brother Huey he ran upon anti-Long leader Harney S. Bogan in the statehouse corridor and immediately began trading punches. "Long bit me on the face and neck and scratched me. He also stuck his finger in my mouth and attempted to tear my cheek," Bogan said.

Later, when Huey was running for the United States Senate, Earl came upon anti-Long attorney Frank P. Krieger on New Orleans' Royal Street. Earl's friends said Krieger was given "an awful beating." Krieger said Earl almost bit off one of his fingers and scratched and clawed his face.

Earl, born on August 26, 1895, was the next to the youngest of the Long children. Like Huey, he quit school to become a traveling salesman, selling shoe polish, "never-fail" oilcans, and a patent medicine. At one time he was division manager for a St. Louis dye firm. He helped Huey through a year at the University of Oklahoma, and, still working his route as a salesman in north Louisiana, campaigned for Huey for railroad commissioner. After Huey was elected in 1924, Earl went to law school at Tulane and Loyola. It took him two years to complete the course and, like Huey, he passed the bar examination without getting a college degree. He met Blanche Revere of Covington at her post at the Monteleone Hotel cigar stand and they were married in 1932.

Earl had spent most of his life in Huey's shadow. He said that he, of the nine Long children, was closest to Huey. "When we were children we slept together," he said. "We grew up together and, I would imagine, as in all families, children near the same age as that would probably know more about each other and be more closely connected than older and younger members of the family. I think that condition existed throughout our lifetime to a large extent."

Earl had claimed credit for inspiring and engineering the round robin which saved Huey during the impeachment crisis, and many of the insiders agree with him. "I went broke getting him out of trouble when the Legislature was trying to impeach him," Earl said.

Later there came the big split. Earl begged for the job of governor in 1932, and Huey refused him. Earl stepped his goal down to that of lieutenant governor. Huey still refused. Earl announced he would be a candidate for lieutenant governor anyway. "I was going to cram myself down his throat and get him to agree he would not put a man out against me," Earl later said. But Huey called Earl's bluff by indeed putting up a candidate against him, and Earl was soundly defeated.

That's when Earl went before the Senate committee to testify against Huey. Earl toured the state calling his brother "a big-bellied coward" and "the yellowest creature that God ever let live." When the Roosevelt administration began pumping patronage to Huey's Louisiana enemies, Earl was considered qualified for the job as counsel to the Home Owners' Loan Corporation.

But in 1934 Earl went back into the fold. Specifically he went back to help Huey elect John Fournet as chief justice of the state Supreme Court. Earl stumped the state for Fournet. This did not end the Long family feud. Older brother Julius remained against Huey, and he stumped against Fournet.

One night Julius was making a speech, and Earl appeared to begin heckling him from the audience. Julius shouted back. The exchange became increasingly bitter and personal, until Earl shrieked, "I'll clean your plow!" and started toward the speaker's platform with fists clenched. Halted before he got there, he was hustled from the hall.

Huey put Earl back on the state payroll. Earl had been Inheritance Tax Commission attorney, but was fired when he began his fight with Huey. Now he was made counsel for the State Tax Commission, and when Huey died Earl was at the bedside.

It is inevitable that everyone in Louisiana—even Earl—

compare the two brothers who have dominated state politics for so many years.

Earl has said: "I ain't like Huey. He could go a-champing around and get away with it. I've gotta go slower. I might get my head knocked off. Maybe I ain't much as a genius, but I got more horse sense."

A veteran statehouse reporter put it this way: "He hasn't got Huey's brains and he hasn't got Huey's finesse. Where Huey was fiery, this fellow is just loud. Where Huey outsmarted his opposition, Earl just slams into the center of the line."

Naturally, Earl spent his entire political life competing against Huey. And once Earl got elected governor in his own right he seemed to make a special effort to show he was as good as Huey if not better. Seeking election in 1956, he said: "I've done more for the poor people of this state than any other governor. The only other governor who came close was my brother, Huey, and he was just starting out. I've got his experience and I've got my experience, and you'll see that I can make a better governor."

Nevertheless, Earl has an amazing political history. It is probably due to his doggedness, more than anything else, that there was such a thing as the Long dynasty, for—as has been seen—Huey's immediate heirs were too overwhelmed by their greed to perpetuate Longism in Louisiana.

In 1928 Earl was appointed inheritance-tax attorney by Huey. In 1932 he ran for lieutenant governor against Huey's ticket, and lost. In 1934 he was elected lieutenant governor under Leche. In 1939 he succeeded Leche as governor. In 1940, in the wake of the scandals, he ran for governor against reformer Sam Houston Jones, and lost. In 1944 he ran for lieutenant governor with ex-Congressman Lewis Morgan, and lost. In 1948 he ran for governor and won. In 1952, unable to succeed himself, he backed Judge Carlos Spaht for governor, and lost. In 1956 he ran for governor, again against reformer Jones, and this time he won.

In that record you can see the rewards implied by the old

saw, "If at first you don't succeed . . ." You can also see Earl
Long's infatuation with the job of governor.

Several times Earl has tried end runs instead of center
bucks into the statehouse. In 1940, after being defeated for
governor, he tried to get himself named Secretary of State
when the nominee died before taking office. In 1944, when he
ran on the ticket with Morgan, the first primary result placed
Morgan second to Jimmy Davis in the race for governor and
Earl first in the race for lieutenant governor. Under Louisiana
primary procedure a runoff election was called between the
two top candidates for each office. The rules also provided
that should one of these two top candidates for governor withdraw, the leading man for each office in the first primary
would be declared elected. Earl begged Morgan to withdraw
from the race. This would have left Morgan without a job,
but it would have made Earl lieutenant governor. Morgan
refused Earl's wheedles and promises, and the Morgan-Long
ticket was defeated in the second primary.

After Earl was elected in 1948, he attempted to call a constitutional convention to extend his term without a vote of
the people. After he was elected in 1956, he tried to beat the
law which says the governor cannot succeed himself. He
promised to resign before the end of his term so that he would
be succeeding his lieutenant governor, not himself, come
inauguration day. Both plans went awry.

Earl is a colorful campaigner, certainly his brother's match
in the invention of invective. Like Huey he concedes the city
vote to the opposition and concentrates on convincing the
great unwashed that he, too, hates to bathe. Campaigning
against reformer Jones, Earl made the damning revelation,
"High-hat, sweet-smellin', perfume-squirtin' corporation lawyer Sam Jones sleeps in pajamas." Ridiculing New Orleans'
dapper Mayor deLesseps Morrison, Earl said: "He wears
$400 suits. Put one of them $400 suits on Uncle Earl and it'd
look like socks on a rooster."

This, friends, is empathy in the backwoods. The gnarled

rednecks eat it up. They'd better. If not, Uncle Earl turns on them.

Campaigning in 1956 to unseat two uncooperative congressmen, Earl was heckled at Pine Prairie, and responded by calling his audience "ignorant jackasses." Booed at Mamou, he shouted: "Why don't you bray? That's what a jackass would do." As to one of the congressmen he was trying to unseat, Long said, in true Huey fashion, "We're going to take the sugar tit out of his mouth and he's going to cry, cry, cry." The congressman, T. A. Thompson, followed Long onto the platform to respond in kind: "Earl Long is like a mad dog."

Earl is not one for trite epithets. He thinks up his own. Campaigning against Robert Kennon, he said: "They tested Judge Kennon when he left the Army. They tested his feet and said they were no good for running. They tested his blood and it was 65 per cent champagne and 35 per cent talcum powder. They tested his ears and the doctor said: 'Judge, your ears are perfect. You can hear an election coming two years off!' "

One of the men to run against the Long ticket was a songwriter, Jimmy Davis. His big hit was "You Are My Sunshine." Davis was no political reformer. His campaign slogan, perhaps perfect for cynical Louisiana, was "Live and let live." But even he was shocked by the emotional rigors of pursuing office against Earl Long. Davis said, "I spent the first half of the campaign denying all the things he said I'd done and I spent the last half wondering why I had done such damn' fool things in the first place."

Earl, who refers to himself as "The Last of the Red Hot Papas," is no electronics campaigner. "TV makes me look like a monkey on a stick," he said. Huey was a great exploiter of the radio and would have been marvelous on TV, but Earl goes to see the people personally.

He is preceded by garish station wagons equipped with loud-speakers. A typical appearance was at French Settlement, a hamlet off the main highway between New Orleans and

Baton Rouge, a rural nowhere that no citified candidate would deign to visit.

A white pickup truck is parked under a majestic oak dripping with moss, and here, in an artist's Louisiana, Earl climbs upon the truck to make his speech. He takes off his coat to bare his wide suspenders. He loosens his tie. He tugs his pants well south of the border. He rattles the coins in his pocket and gazes curiously around for familiar faces as he's introduced.

And then, in his gravelly voice, he begins to shout. Occasionally the rasp breaks into a moment of falsetto, much in the fashion of an adolescent whose voice is changing. Sometimes Earl lapses into a staccato cough, the result of an old bronchial condition, and, amazingly, he continues to talk through the cough, not missing a syllable. He calls out to old friends in the audience—every audience has old friends—to back up his arguments, and invariably they reply, "You're right, Earl."

The crowd has sometimes waited for hours to hear Earl talk. It is a shabbily dressed crowd, more often transported to the speech by open truck than by closed passenger car. The people are seldom young. It is obvious that most of them hark back to Huey's day. But it would be wrong to assume that Earl has no following of his own. To these people, at least, he has firmly established himself as the friend of the poor farmer.

His speeches wander from campaign promises to Bible quotations to tart curses to long-winded jokes. He has the professional politician's phenomenal memory for precinct-by-precinct votes and face-by-face recognitions. His voice carries the fervor of the evangelist, and his arms fan the breeze with extravagant gestures.

At the end of the talk Earl eases himself gratefully into a chair on the truck, and it is then that he really begins winning votes. The people start coming up to chat with him personally. He'll linger for an hour, two hours, just talking with the little folk of Louisiana, the true believers in Long and Longism. They mention a bad stretch of road, and Earl knows that stretch, no matter how remote, and he also knows why the Highway Department hasn't repaired it yet. They ask for a job, and he says, "Come see me in Baton Rouge." This is the Earl Long who garners votes while the rest of the world wonders how Louisiana can elect such an uncouth governor.

Earl knows the voters and he knows their pappies, too. He can be confronted by an upstart in the legislature and immediately say: "You had a fine father—one of the best that ever lived. What was his name? Odum, wasn't it? And then you was brought up by a fine man named Rainach, but somewhere along the line you dropped something and you ain't never picked it up."

Earl scoffs at all talk of money. "I don't care about money," he said. "Huey didn't care about money. I get plenty of it but I don't need it. I'm happier at my farm at Winnfield, raising billy goats and eating beans, than I am anywhere else. It doesn't matter to me whether I have money or not. Of course, when I say that, my wife tells me I just say it because I have enough money."

Like Huey, Earl had picked up considerable change by having agencies of his own state government hire him from time to time as special attorney, a perfectly legal procedure. Once he drew as much as $10,000 as his fee for a two-day hearing. But, unlike Huey, his opponents do not concede that his legal cunning is worth that kind of money. Huey was commended for a brief he submitted to the United States Supreme Court. Earl had never tried a case as a lawyer before he got his first state appointment.

A political enemy once charged on the floor of Congress that Earl received $250,000 in graft and that he eventually paid a penalty for attempting to evade income-tax payment on it. The charge was never substantiated, and Earl frequently has called himself "the most investigated man in Louisiana." Under a new law passed by the reformers who followed in the wake of the scandals, the Louisiana governor must declare his net worth at the start and completion of each term. When Earl took office in 1956 he declared his worth as $150,000.

His farm at Winnfield contains 300 acres and is highly profit-able, despite the shoddy shack which is "the main house."

Those close to Earl say that he is amazed and grateful whenever he runs into honesty. He was overwhelmed with gratitude when he handed an aide $100 to rent a bus for his campaign claque and the man returned with $46 change. Earl expected the man to pocket the $46. Earl's highest accolade for a legislator is to tell the man's home district, "That fellow has never asked me for a dime."

The veteran observers at the statehouse say that Earl blows hot and cold between icy cynicism and a burning desire to make the state a good governor. Privately, Earl likes to consider himself a diamond in the rough.

He has said:

"There's a difference between character and reputation. Reputation is what people think you are and character is what you really are inside. You can be a son of a gun, but if people think you're all right you're in pretty good shape. But no matter how good you are, if people think you're rotten you might as well give up."

CHAPTER ELEVEN

"We'll improve on everything Huey did."

EARL LONG COULD NOT HAVE PICKED A WORSE TIME TO RUN FOR governor for the first time. The year was 1940. His brother's old pals were buried under an avalanche of indictments. The depression miseries which fueled the old Share-the-Wealth program were fast disappearing. And Earl himself was occupying the governor's office atop an administration which was not of his making and over which he had little control.

Earl tried hard to put over the point, "I'm only responsible for what goes on under my administration." As for the frauds of the past, he said, "My main object is to stop it."

Earl so desperately wanted to be governor that he did not consider sitting out the 1940 election. Launching his campaign on a single issue, "Remember Huey," he promised that, if elected, he'd turn back the clock to make Louisiana "just like under Huey." He induced Huey's widow to make speeches for him and he displayed Huey's sons on the platform. He brought back Gerald L. K. Smith, the old Share-the-Wealth preacher, to fire up the revivals and he put Huey's former secretary, Earle Christenberry, on the ticket as candidate for state treasurer.

Far from daring to trace the roots of the scandals back to Huey's dictatorship, the opposition candidates pleaded that they, too, loved Huey. Earl's two principal opponents were Jimmy Noe, who had indeed been a Huey man, and a corporation lawyer named Sam Jones, who had to be satisfied with saying, "My pappy voted for Huey."

Jones reminded the voters: "I'm not running against a dead man. I am running against a gang of rascals as live as any gang that ever lived."

The campaign was waged in the general vicinity of the gutter. Earl warned the back-country folk to "vote for one of your own kind . . . one who thinks like you and smells like you on Saturday night." Jones campaigners sang a ditty which went:

> "So long, Earl Long.
> We know that you got your part
> With Seymour, Dick and Monte Hart.
> So long, Earl Long."

Despite all his handicaps, Earl led the field in the first primary with 40.9 per cent of the total vote. He carried 41 of the state's 64 parishes. Sam Jones finished second with 28 per cent of the vote, carrying 11 parishes. That meant a Long-Jones runoff, and it meant that Jimmy Noe, who had placed third, held the balance of power. Noe was the man whose blood was pumped into Huey's veins in the first transfusion at Our Lady of the Lake Sanitarium. Noe also was the man whose affidavits launched the scandals. Which way would he turn? Noe dallied for a few days, then swung his support to Jones.

Earl was defeated in the runoff. And immediately the obituary writers unlimbered their typewriters. The Longs were dead. Louisiana was rid of Longism. The voters had wised up at last. These overeager morticians did not take time to examine the election returns properly. Despite the scandals, despite his pussyfooting avoidance of a cleanup, and despite the fact that his old defections still rankled the hardest core of Huey's following, Earl had polled 48.2 per cent of the vote. Under the most adverse of circumstances he had lost by only 19,000 votes.

Nevertheless, no man is more important than an unemployed dispenser of patronage. Earl summoned a special session of the legislature to attempt a few lame-duck didos, but the quorum failed to answer his call. He made his futile attempt to become the new secretary of state and in 1944 ran unsuccessfully for lieutenant governor.

Came 1948, and Earl once more sought the office of governor. He had little in the way of organized support. The old Long organization was smashed and, as Earl put it, "When I started out, practically every politician in the state gave me the cold shoulder."

But Earl had a program—Something for Everyone. He ran now as Earl Long rather than as Huey Long's brother. He promised to hike the old-age pension to $50. He promised free hot lunches to go with Huey's free schoolbooks. He promised to widen Huey's highways. He promised the teachers a minimum salary of $2,400 a year, a sharp reversal of his 1940 position, when he told the New Orleans Teachers Federation he was "not ready to turn the affairs of the state over to the teachers—not by a devil of a lot." He promised a veterans' bonus.

Again Earl's principal opponent was Sam Jones, and again Earl led the first primary, this time with 41.5 per cent of the vote, a shade more than he polled in 1944. It looked like history repeating. But the voters read one part of the history book while the political prognosticators read another. The voters read those chapters about Huey and his largesse for the poor. The prognosticators could see only as far back as Jones beating Long in the heat of scandal.

This time it was different. Earl polled one of the largest majorities in the state's history, winning 62 of the 64 parishes.

He shouted, "Happy days are here again! The Longs are back in the saddle. We'll improve on everything Huey did." And just to show that it was the Longs—with the plural s—he appointed Huey's son, Russell, fresh out of law school, to the job of governor's executive counsel.

Earl had said during the campaign: "The governor gets his house free, and his groceries, and everything free and I want you all to come up to the mansion and have a cup of coffee. You might as well because you're paying for it anyhow."

Now that he was elected he invited the entire state to his inauguration. He set the scene in LSU's football stadium.

The rednecks came. This was their Baton Rouge again. They had been outsiders during the administrations of corporation lawyer Jones and the songwriter Jimmy Davis. But Earl was one of them, and Earl meant it when he said the country folk were welcome to drop in any time.

The governor, who happened to be on a buttermilk kick at the moment, ordered for his guests 16,000 gallons of buttermilk plus 240,000 bottles of soda pop, 200,000 hot dogs plus cowboys, clowns, a baseball game, and a two-hour parade containing 140 high-school bands.

The *Times-Picayune*'s wide-eyed (and eared) correspondent set down this exchange between two old codgers from Tangipahoa Parish:

"God ahmighty, Slim. I never thought I'd live to see the day you'd drink buttermilk."

"Shucks, Jack, it's just that the governor sets such store in the stuff, but I aim to wash it down with something stronger."

There was a lot of the stronger stuff in evidence by the time the governor made his inaugural address to climax the day. The *Times-Picayune* summarized the speech by saying, "It would be hard for any official to promise more."

Earl inherited a solvent state. When he left office in 1940 Louisiana was $10,000,000 in debt. When he returned eight years later there was a general fund surplus of $30,000,000 plus $50,000,000 already available for highway expansion and $30,000,000 available for hospital and mental-institution expansion. (This was due only partly to the frugality of the reform administrations. It was also due to the fact that these administrations had spanned the war years when tax collections were high and the supply of construction materials was low.)

Despite this wealth, Earl had to increase taxes immediately. He had promised too much, and he needed money to keep his promises. Earl hiked the gasoline tax, doubled the severance tax on oil and natural gas and doubled the sales tax. He placed a tax on beer, too. (The New Orleans Brewers Association responded with full-page newspaper advertisements saying, "BEER IS THE WORKING MAN'S DRINK. Do your part at once to help kill the proposed 5 cent tax on beer." The ads did no good.)

Earl also promised: "I'm going to make the administration of hospitals and institutions my personal concern. The question as to who will run them is secondary to the welfare of the patients."

Perhaps. But it was not secondary to the patronage of Earl Long. He made a clean sweep of all appointive offices. Not only did the hospitals get new superintendents; the National Guard also got a new chief to replace Major General Raymond Fleming after forty years in command. Some boards, such as the powerful Orleans Parish Levee Board, were replaced in their entirety. Earl even stopped payment on the Levee Board staff's vacation paychecks.

He appointed his publicity woman, Mary Evelyn Dickerson, as executive director of the Department of Commerce and Industry a month after he promised he wouldn't. For head of the state police he selected Goldman Grant, who had been fired as a state trooper eight years earlier.

The first state legislature under Long smothered the civil service system and placed all state purchasing under the direct control of the governor. Once again a Long was operating the state government as a private domain, hiring whom he chose and buying what and where he chose. Cynicism became the state's code, moving Earl to tell his legislators that the veterans' bonus was advisable because "75,000 bonus checks means 75,000 local campaign managers."

Yes, the Longs were in the saddle again. Earl even turned the perpetual light back onto Huey's grave. It had been extinguished for the wartime blackout, and the reform administrations conveniently forgot to turn it back on after V-J Day.

Yet even as Earl indiscriminately refurbished the state payroll with his own people, he made an attempt to be a good governor. Intimates cite numerous cases where he stiff-armed the political crooks who rushed to Baton Rouge in the happy delusion that the election of a Long was a new license to steal. Earl maintained that political privilege was one thing and outright thievery another.

Furthermore, he made good on his campaign promises. He delivered the free lunches to the schools. He put across the veterans' bonus. He established the minimum-salary scale for teachers and equalized the pay of white and Negro teachers for the first time in the state's history. He established a sorely needed LSU extension in New Orleans. This gave him his excuse for clearing out the Levee Board. Because it refused to surrender title to the land Earl wanted for the branch university, he fired the whole board in the interests of higher education.

The one law that has always stymied the Longs—and the one they have never been able to eradicate or circumvent— is that which prohibits a Louisiana governor from succeeding himself. It was designed, of course, to prevent just such a man as Earl Long from perpetuating himself in office. Probably this law is the only force that could have pried Earl out of the Capitol in 1952, for even one of his bitterest enemies concedes, "If you believe in his philosophy of tax and spend, Earl Long was a good governor despite the abuses of his administration."

So it was no surprise that in 1956, when he was again eligible for the office, Earl became candidate for governor again. This time he was no underdog. This time he met no cold shoulder from the state's professional politicians. And this time he was certain he had the right formula for success.

The people elected him in 1948 because he promised free lunches in the schools. Fine, so this time he promised them free pencils and erasers in the schools. The people elected him in 1948 because he promised them a $50 old-age pension. Fine, so this time he promised them a $65 old-age pension. It was all so simple. Louisiana was truly the welfare state now. Huey? Share-the-Wealth was mostly promises. Earl's plans were not so grandiose, but he actually was delivering the goods.

Earl even knew how to sugar-coat his penchant for running every branch of the state government personally. He made it a campaign promise: "I will not hide behind any board or commissioners, but will accept the responsibilities of all the actions of the boards and the governor's office."

This time there was no runoff. Earl swept into office by winning the majority of votes over his combined opponents in the first primary, an unprecedented achievement in Louisiana gubernatorial elections.

But once elected he found himself in difficulty. The anti-Long legislatures which serve in Louisiana during those brief intervals the Longs are out of office have a fatalistic attitude: They know they'll be succeeded by still another Long administration, and so they devote their energies to hamstringing that new Long crowd they assume is on the horizon. The legislature which preceded Earl's 1956 inauguration did its work well. First of all, it prevented another big buttermilk, bourbon, and barbecue binge in the LSU stadium by limiting the incoming governor to $5,000 for inauguration expenses. Second, and far more important, it passed a constitutional amendment requiring a two-thirds vote of both houses for passage of any and all fiscal bills.

This made it much tougher for Earl to put across his new tax-and-spend program. He had always scraped together his simple majorities with difficulty, and now he was frequently hamstrung.

The legislature did not dare buck Earl on the key points of his program—the money for the schools and the increased old-age pension. But he couldn't get beyond that in expending the benefits of the welfare state. With a simple majority, however, he was able to curtail sharply the use of voting machines.

His administration produced the usual high jinks. The state prison convicts were found working on his Winnfield farm. A loyal Longite, Mrs. Mary Evelyn Parker, was voted a

$2,000 pay raise by the State Welfare Commission at a meeting which lacked a quorum. A Long leader in the legislature was caught hauling state sand to a privately owned project. The Welfare Commission approved the minutes of the quorumless meeting without even reading them. The legislative leader promised he wouldn't haul any more state sand to his projects.

Like Huey, Earl prowled the floor of the legislature while key bills were under consideration. He would drift in through a side door, moving slowly up the aisles, shaking hands here, chatting there, while the debate droned on. He sometimes would stoop to pick up a scrap of waste paper messing up *his* Capitol floor. He'd send a pageboy for a bottle of soda pop. And when his chats convinced him he had the support he needed, he would suddenly sing out in loud tones:

"Vote!"

Immediately a Long floor leader would respond to the cue and call for an end of the debate. The House speaker or the Senate president would be alert to grant it, and the red and the green lights would flicker the Yeas and Nays on the big electric board at the front of the chamber.

Earl would stare at the board, checking the results.

"Looks like you lost a vote there," said a reporter once when a light went unexpectedly Nay.

"Saves money," snickered Long, and moved along up the aisle.

Sometimes Earl caught an errant voter and bawled hell out of him right on the House or Senate floor. Sometimes he summoned the poor devil into the governor's office for a pithy dressing down that reverberated through the door and up the corridor. Earl was told often that these tactics created a sour impression, but he said, "I'm told that hiding these feelings don't contribute to longevity and I'm told it's better to belch 'em up."

Even Earl's attempts at finesse came out crudely. He would drop a hint to a legislator that a particularly choice piece of pork out of the barrel might be lost if the man didn't vote right on the governor's pet project of the moment. He made it plain that the voters back home would learn just why the governor was forced to veto that needed bridge or that new hospital.

Earl said: "Huey used to buy the Legislature like a sack of potatoes. Hell, I never bought one in my life. I just rent 'em. It's cheaper that way."

If Earl delivered more than Huey in the way of actual welfare benefits to the poor, Huey delivered more in the way of visible monuments. Earl was quite sensitive about this. He was inclined, therefore, to exaggerate his accomplishments.

A year after the start of his 1948 administration the state issued an eight-page progress report on Governor Long's works. It contained photographs of the Baton Rouge Bridge, the Morgan City Bridge, the big charity hospitals—all built well before Earl's time. It told of a $16,000,000 hospital expansion program but didn't mention that the money had been voted two years before Earl's inauguration. Confronted by reporters with the facts, Earl merely grinned, and said: "I just signed a report the way I do a thousand other things they put before me. But nobody's interested in the figures anyway. They're more interested in things like old-age pensions and free school lunches."

And with that he turned from the gentlemen of the press to receive a delegation from Ruston, a delegation to which he presented a bushel of peaches. He didn't mention that he had received the same peaches an hour earlier from a delegation from Lake Charles.

As governor, Earl always sought to duck the thorny issues that could only lose votes. This is not unusual in a politician, but it is unusual in a man who thrives on controversy. The paradox seems to be this: Earl is interested only in the controversies of his making. When Louisiana became embroiled in the right-to-work scrap, the best that Earl Long, the poor man's governor, could do was say, "I'll remain neutral." (He signed the bill when it passed the legislature.) When the State Senate passed a resolution asking him to help settle a year-old bus strike, he said he was "too busy." When the entire family of an LSU professor was killed when his car struck a cow on the highway after Long reneged on his promise to produce a sorely needed stock-fencing law, the best he could suggest was that the state build the fences (so that neither the rural cattlemen nor the city motorists would be angered).

Earl, it can be seen, was interested only in the administration of government—the control of the jobs. That was the secret of his power. And many in Louisiana thought that his hidden power was far more dangerous than the obvious dictatorial tactics of brother Huey. They felt that the average citizen knew what Huey was up to, whether he approved of it or not. But the average citizen had no idea what Earl was doing within the drone of the twenty-four new state agencies that he created in a period of four years. These agencies regulated everything from liquor sales and oil production to Highway Department purchases and to the hiring of state employees.

Earl insisted on determining personally who worked for the state government. He always wanted men with large families, for they were more dependent on the jobs and naturally had more relatives to vote for Long so that they could keep their jobs. In heavily Catholic Louisiana it is not difficult to find large families.

The Sam Jones administration put in a strong civil-service law as the answer to these Long policies. And during the 1948 election campaign the Louisiana Civil Service League asked each of the candidates if he would preserve the Jones civil-service law if elected. Earl was one of those who quickly answered Yes.

As soon as the votes were counted, however, Earl said that while he was "for civil service" he felt that a majority of the House and Senate might suspend it "because of a demand for jobs by supporters of the incoming administration."

The legislature had no sooner met than it was considering a bill to replace the existing Civil Service Commission with one which would serve only at the pleasure of the governor. In other words, civil service would be dead.

The debate was long and bitter. One representative cried, "Let's feed the horse that brought in the feed and fodder during the campaign."

Representative Ragan Madden, author of the bill, said, "Frankly, I am in favor of the spoils system."

Another Long supporter, Representative Henry Sevier, was asked, "Do you think this bill will destroy civil service?"

Sevier replied, "I hope it will."

Governor Long, obviously because of his campaign promise, never announced publicly that he favored the bill. But while it was under consideration in the House he moved about the floor, lobbying in its favor, and when it progressed into the Senate two weeks later he was there, too, urging its passage in stage whispers. He piously told reporters he might veto the bill, "but it's hard to go against two-thirds of the legislature." Naturally he signed it, and civil service died in Louisiana. Two years later, when his term neared its end, he tried to get civil service reinstated, obviously to preserve the jobs of those Longites who now permeated the government. But, alas, this was not the will of the legislature, and Earl's people were shoveled out of the jobs as fast as they were shoveled in.

CHAPTER TWELVE

"If the money runs out, there's more where that came from."

WHO WERE THE PEOPLE WHO VOTED FOR EARL LONG? ONE OF Louisiana's most seasoned political observers answered the question with two words: "His beneficiaries." At first thought that reply would seem to be an oversimplification, but actually it is an eloquent summation.

There were 656,000 votes cast in the 1948 second primary which gave Earl his first full term as governor. Within a year 239,000 persons were drawing some type of welfare check. These 239,000 represented more than one-third the total vote, more than one-half of Earl's vote, and more than all of opponent Sam Jones' vote. Yet they are only the hard core of the Long support. To them must be added their relatives, who owe Earl gratitude if only because he has removed a burden from their personal pocketbooks. And to these relatives must be added the state government employees (Louisiana ranks third in the number of state employees per thousand population) and *their* relatives. The total number of beneficiaries is formidable.

An analysis of Louisiana elections down through the years shows that Earl Long starts off with about 40 per cent of the vote, win or lose. The difference between victory and defeat hinges only on his success in swinging 10 per cent more.

These are the figures:

Year	Office Sought	Earl's First Primary Vote	Earl's Second Primary Vote
1940	Gov.	40.9%	48.2%
1944	Lt. Gov.	41.9	48.8
1948	Gov.	41.5	65.9
1956	Gov.	55.0	—

The first primary is the best test of a man's personal popularity, since the voters have a wide-open choice—five or six candidates—as against only two in a runoff or in a two-party general election. The theory that the Longs automatically get about 40 per cent of the vote is further substantiated by the fact that Russell Long, then an unknown quantity to any discriminating voter, polled 44 per cent in the first primary when he initially sought election to the United States Senate; he subsequently won the office in a runoff.

A vital portion of Earl's support was the Negro vote. This was, of course, a fantastic phenomenon in the Deep South. The Longs, both Huey and Earl, not only were willing to forgo the Southern demagogue's mainstay of white supremacy, but Earl actually bucked the tide when the long-dormant question of the Negro vote suddenly erupted throughout the South.

Huey had the poor white's prejudice against the Negro. He told "nigger jokes," and frequently likened opponents to the Negro (if, indeed, he did not falsely "expose" their Negro ancestry.) But Huey, although living in the era of Talmadge and Bilbo and Rankin, never attempted to exploit racial prejudice politically. He employed Negroes to a great degree on his public-works programs. He did so because they worked cheaper; nevertheless, he did so when these jobs meant a great deal to either whites or Negroes suffering from the depression. Undoubtedly Huey eschewed the easy road of the Bilbos because he knew this would endanger his national ambitions. He did not think of himself as a regional politician. Furthermore, even in the early 1930's any farsighted man could see erosions in white supremacy, and Huey chose a cause he felt to be more durable.

It was Earl who lived to capitalize on this unusual facet of Longism. The Negro vote became 10 per cent of the total by 1956 (as against 32.9 per cent of the population), and the poverty-ridden Negro lined up solidly behind Earl and his welfare benefits.

Earl was no liberal. He didn't advocate racial equality. Rather, as a Longite said: "He stands up there and tells them they were eating each other in Africa a hundred years ago and things like that and they just smile and applaud. They get the welfare and they know that nobody has done more for them than Earl Long, whatever he says."

The Negro is so accustomed to second-class treatment in Louisiana that he must be specifically told when he is to share the first-class largesse. Earl made certain the Negroes understood they'd get their share from him. Campaigning in 1948, he made it a point to say, "This veterans' bonus is going to be for everybody, including you colored folks who fought in the Army and the Navy. You'll get it even if you don't have the vote." Ten years later, when the Negroes' right to vote became an issue in the state, Earl said, "If those colored people helped build this country, if they could fight in its Army, then I'm for giving them the vote."

In previous eras it was difficult to predict how the slim Negro vote might go. Some Negro publications picked up tidy sums endorsing candidates. The money was paid by the opposition. The endorsements were bought so a candidate might wave the publication before the eyes of the bigoted poor whites and shout, "You see, Nigras want the other fellow to win, so you'd better vote for me."

But this particularly nasty bit of Louisiana political chicanery was rendered obsolete by Earl Long. Everyone knew the Negroes would vote for him. Endorsements, bought or otherwise, could not affect that. They supported him so openly in 1948 that a colored organization chartered a bus to carry its members to his inauguration party. Their vote was so solid in 1956 that they provided the margin which permitted Earl to win in the first primary rather than endure a runoff. Earl said after the election, "It is a victory for the people of all walks of life, and for the fine colored people."

Louisiana's intellectuals and liberals, such as they are—in some sections of north Louisiana a man is a liberal if he subscribes to the *New Yorker*—were very much opposed to Huey. They deplored his cavalier attitude toward civil rights of whites and Negroes alike, and they mourned the death of academic freedom and unfettered student expression at the state university. But these intellectuals and liberals tended to support Earl Long. The social consciousness seemingly reflected by the mammoth welfare program was accepted as ultimately good, no matter what the governor's motives. His attitude toward the Negro enhanced this support. His frequent jibes about cannibal ancestry and interracial hanky-panky behind the barn were obliterated by his support of the Negro vote and by his action in equalizing the pay of white and colored schoolteachers. Furthermore, the academicians of Louisiana naturally were delighted by the state's heavy expenditures on education.

Too often, however, these liberal supporters of Earl failed to look beyond the title of the bills passed by the legislature. The hard truth is that many an ignoble purpose is served by the noble contributions to education.

For example, each legislator is given a certain amount of money annually to be passed on to needy, deserving students in his district. This is a fine idea. In theory it plugs the hole in the impersonal state university scholarship setup by authorizing each legislator to help the youngsters he knows by personal contact really need help.

But what has been the practice? One senator granted scholarships to 127 students; his average grant was $36. One representative awarded 17 scholarships at $12.50 each. Still another representative got his scholarships down to $10 each so that he could spread them among even more constituents. Obviously a $10 or a $12.50 annual scholarship is not going to be much help to a boy or girl in college, even in Louisiana where the colleges are cheap. These niggling handouts were the rule rather than the exception. The Public Affairs Research Council found that the large proportion of scholarships was for $25 and $50 each. It found only one legislator who awarded his scholarships in substantial amounts after getting advice from the local school officials as to which students were good scholars and needed aid to go to college. It did find another legislator who also awarded substantial scholarships, but, by some strange coincidence, every recipient bore the same last name as the legislator himself.

There was a different sort of abuse in the establishing of trade schools throughout the state. Earl promised a trade school to every community that wanted one. The state would foot the entire bill. To make it easy on the legislators, Earl distributed predrafted bills, mimeographed, so that all a representative need do was fill in the blank giving the name of the town and then toss the bill into the hopper. He got his school. The result is that the trade schools were built not where they were needed, but simply where legislators chose to drop a chunk of pork out of the barrel. Trade schools appeared in completely rural areas. One such school was built at Greensburg (population 423) which couldn't even support its own high school.

Some of Earl's opponents facetiously claim to have detected that Earl Long had a harmful influence on the economy of the state. They noticed that every time he assumed office the number of Louisiana's aged, blind, sick, and indigent leaped. In 1957, for example, the number of persons receiving old-age assistance throughout the United States reached an all-time low for the decade. At the same time, the number receiving such aid in Louisiana reached an all-time high. Between 1951 and 1957 there was a steady decline in the number needing such aid across the nation; in Louisiana there was a steady increase. Furthermore, the average national payment was $59.19 a month as opposed to Louisiana's average of $63 a month.

And still Earl felt he could go higher. He offered to summon a special session of the legislature to hike the old-age pension to $100 a month in 1952 in order to aid the election chances of his hand-picked gubernatorial candidate Carlos Spaht, but Spaht talked him out of it. Earl did not, however, endorse all welfare benefits, but only those which he produced. The others, he charged, were a waste. He felt the same way about any construction. If Earl Long built the building it was a boon to mankind. If an opposition administration built the building, it was "to provide fat fees for their architect pals."

Despite the obvious political bent of Earl Long's welfare programs, it would be very wrong to overlook the obvious good they do or the obvious need they fulfill. In the case of the old-age pensions, for example, Louisiana has not enjoyed the full benefits of the federal Social Security program. Nationally, about three out of every four persons reaching the age of sixty-five become eligible for Social Security payments. But the ratio is much lower in Louisiana because of the large number of agricultural workers, many of them migrants not covered by Social Security until comparatively recently.

It is difficult to quarrel with Louisiana's free-lunch program in the schools, outsized though it may be. The Louisiana program has been the second-most costly in the nation, ranking only behind much more populous New York. One out of eight school children, both in public and in private schools, receives free lunches, and many more than that receive lunches financed in large part by state and matching federal funds. The Long trend is to make education absolutely free. The Public Affairs Research Council's report on school lunches concedes that not a single school child in Louisiana lacks a solid meal in school, and adds, "The problem does not appear to be one of determining which children are needy within the meaning of the lunch program regulations, but rather one of deciding whether the state and federal governments should continue to pay such a large share of the cost of lunches served to children who are not needy."

In addition to providing the obvious tuition, book, and lunch aids to education, the Longs have, at times, provided efficiencies both dramatic and unique. Huey, for example, noticed the vast empty space beneath the LSU football stadium. He filled this in with dormitory rooms. Thus, while most universities maintain stadiums which are largely a waste except for a few Saturdays a year, the LSU stadium serves the year round as a dorm for male students.

Earl made his promises of ever-increasing welfare benefits without any concern for what they might do to the state's budget. Campaigning in 1948, he told the voters: "If the money runs out, there's more where that came from. The school lunch program doesn't cost you a cent unless you happen to own an oil well."

A few months later he doubled the sales tax and added a few new levies at the same time. But he was not embarrassed. He went on a state-wide radio hookup to tell the people that "those taxes on gas and oil will go to the educational system. The tax on beer will go for the soldier-boy bonus and the free-lunch program for school children and there'll be some left to expand our hospital program. A lot of the need for hospital treatment comes from beer. It's only fair that some of the beer-tax surplus go to the hospitals."

Fair, perhaps, but not legal. The very bill Earl was endorsing allotted the full tax to fulfill the campaign promises for the bonus and the school lunches. There could be no diverting of funds to the hospitals.

Earl used Huey's technique in lumping all opposition to his ever-increasing taxes as minions of Wall Street. He said: "A lot of people cuss Huey and a lot of people cuss Roosevelt. Do you know why? Well, if you touch some people's pocketbooks you strike their heart. Just relieve them of a few dollars to help some poor devil and you will hear them yell."

Actually, of course, Earl touched everyone's pocketbook. His taxation was not discriminatory against the rich or even against the bogyman corporations. Louisiana's taxpayer did, however, get a big break when the United States Supreme Court awarded title to the offshore oil lands to the states. This will net Louisiana billions of dollars, and in Louisiana oil income traditionally is earmarked for education.

This money—or rather the way it's spent—accounts for the Long organization. It was the money which gave Earl that hard core of 40 per cent of the vote at the start of each election campaign and it was the money—the jobs, the road contracts, the state purchases—which attracted professional politicians to Earl's side. He had no permanent precinct captains or district leaders as were found in Tammany's Manhattan or Curley's Boston or Hague's Jersey City. He had a very few professionals who could even be considered permanent and indiscriminate Long men. Instead, he had an organization built upon the patronage and rewards of the moment. One man fell out and another stepped in. The state's payroll is the only tie that binds.

In one election Leander H. Perez was Earl's campaign manager, exhorting the people to elect Earl as savior of the state. Within a matter of months Earl was standing on the floor of the legislature during a regular session, shouting, "There is no bigger thief in Louisiana than Leander H. Perez." In between there had been a falling out, probably over the assignment of jobs in the new administration. The voting public was not shocked by this palace revolt. It has happened in every Long administration. Just as Huey came to wage a bitter fight against his lieutenant governor, Cyr, so Earl came to decry his lieutenant governor as "big bad Bill Dodd."

Earl recognized these defections as part of the game. He took them lightly. He said: "We fall out but we can always get together when we see the need. We've always got tunnels of communication to one another."

There are some who say Earl kept his hand free of the state's purse strings but always purposely placed temptation in the paths of his chief underlings. "He wanted them to step out of line," said one veteran Capitol newspaperman. "He wanted to have an ax over their heads. He wanted to know where the bodies were buried, and so he permitted these characters to bury a few with his blessing."

One opponent told an Associated Press reporter: "The Longs believe in the plantation system of government. They're the big boss in the white house on the hill. The legislators and the people at the district level are the field foremen. And the voters are the main crop to be harvested."

Earl was quite serious when he made his comment about renting legislators instead of buying them. Before an election he would tour the state to talk to the legislative delegations and determine whether each man had a price for his support in the forthcoming election. Most would strike a bargain, and it would hold for that election only. There was no attempt to make the Earl Long organization permanent. There were some men, of course, who habitually fell in line for campaign after campaign, and these, in a sense, could be called Long district leaders. But, except for the New Orleans Choctaw Club, a city political machine in the classic sense, there was never any attempt to make these relationships any more formal than they were permanent.

Earl could count on the permanent support of Robert Maestri, the unlettered baron of the New Orleans machine. Earl also got some timely support from oil man William C. Feazel.

Back in 1948, when Earl first announced his candidacy for governor after his defeat in the wake of the scandals, he was desperate for financial backing. Earl is not an expensive campaigner. One of his opponents has said, "He can do more with $1,000 than most candidates can do with $10,000 because he knows where to go and who to talk to and how to spend it." Yet the professionals had so little faith in Earl's recuperative powers that he was forced to pass the hat at his hill-country rallies to get the gasoline money to proceed to the next stop.

Feazel was one who noticed that Earl did get that gasoline money. And he reasoned that folks who would kick in a buck or two for Earl would kick in a vote or two. He decided to support the campaign.

Feazel was not exactly a stranger to the Long crowd. He had been involved in a natural-gas deal with Governor Leche, and in this deal, the Federal Power Commission reported, he netted $237,628 without any capital investment. Leche, the FPC said, was "paid his share in cash." Now Feazel backed Earl, and his judgment was vindicated at the polls.

When Senator John Overton died, Earl appointed Feazel to fill out Overton's unexpired term. And, what's more, Feazel's lawyer was appointed to the Conservation Commission which had jurisdiction over oil-man Feazel's oil operations.

After the 1948 election Earl did not need any single angel to back him. His candidacy of 1956 was supported by as many of the professionals as could jostle their way onto the bandwagon. The old crowd which had elbowed him out of the way during the Leche administration suddenly reappeared to look upon Earl as an exalted leader. In his hotel suite to celebrate the election victory were Maestri, Abe Shushan, Leche, and Seymour Weiss.

Once Huey sewed up Louisiana, he began his campaign for the Presidency of the United States. Though Earl never attained Huey's continuity of power in the state, he made it plain that he did not aspire to strength beyond Louisiana's borders. Part of this was a simple matter of facing reality. He had neither Huey's colorful personality nor Huey's unique opportunity of proposing Share-the-Wealth in a nation befuddled by depression. But, beyond that, he did not have Huey's ambition, either. One of his closest friends said: "Earl wanted to run Louisiana, and that's all he wanted to do. He never wanted to see anyone else run Louisiana and he never wanted to see Earl Long run anything else."

Earl snubbed any attempts to solidify the South politically, either under Arkansas' Governor Orval Faubus for purposes of fighting school integration or under the more progressive Southern governors for purposes of giving the South a larger voice in Democratic party councils. Earl supported Harry Truman for President in 1948 and Adlai Stevenson in 1952 and 1956, not so much out of conviction as because it was the automatic thing to do. True, his Negro vote made him incompatible with the Dixiecrats who opposed Truman, and his welfare-state program made him incompatible with the moneyed Louisiana Democrats who supported General Eisenhower against Stevenson in 1952 and 1956. But Earl did not fight for Truman and for Stevenson. He simply did not oppose them. These were not Louisiana fights and, consequently, they did not interest Earl Long.

CHAPTER THIRTEEN

"Dammit, when a man's being kidnaped, he has a right to know who's running the show."

WHEN THE SUPREME COURT OUTLAWED PUBLIC-SCHOOL SEGRE-gation in 1954, the South—contrary to the general impression —did not explode with an immediate outcry of defiance. Rather, the first reaction was resentment, but a resentment that seemed to foreshadow grudging acceptance of an unpopular law. It was not until six months to a year later that the South's politicians realized they could make defiance of court ruling a glorious cause.

That's when the White Citizens Councils began sprouting. Soon every politician, from United States senator to county tax collector, was seeking office on the promise to preserve segregation in the public schools. Louisiana was the last of the Deep South states to be infected by this madness. Although Southern by custom as well as by geography, Louisiana had seldom been plagued by phony racial issues in its political campaigns. This was due partly to the attitude of the Longs. It was due also to the attitude of the powerful Catholic Church and to the cosmopolitan influence of New Orleans.

But as the fear of integration was whipped up to a frenzy by various demagogues throughout the South, a steely-eyed band of Earl Long's political enemies saw that here, at last, was an issue to challenge Longism. It was an issue that had to split Earl's support into two sections. Earl's poor whites, steeped in generations of bigotry, would be rabidly for segregation. Earl's intellectuals, liberals, and Negroes would be for integration. Raise the issue, and Earl had to lose half his voting bloc no matter which way he swung.

The lead was seized in 1955 by two men, Leander Perez, the boss of St. Bernard and Plaquemine parishes south of New Orleans, and William E. Rainach, a wildly ambitious but obscure state senator from the hard-bitten north country. With no pretense at grass-roots inspiration, they organized a network of White Citizens Councils from the top down, and with this they set out to ride the racial issue to power.

Even they were stunned by the magnitude of their success. The issue was electric. It even shocked the Catholic Church. Traditionally unquestioned in south Louisiana where it claimed some 90 per cent of the white population, the church suddenly found its members in open defiance. Archbishop Joseph Francis Rummel announced integration of the parochial schools in New Orleans, and then had to back down because the objection was so intense. A Negro priest assigned to Jesuit Bend was forcibly blocked from entering the mission to say mass, and the church had to replace him with a white priest. A cross was burned on the lawn of the archbishop's residence. Catholic laymen took newspaper advertisements to challenge the attitude of their church. A Catholic lay group went over the archbishop's head and asked (but did not get) sanction from the pope to defy integration of the church.

Earl Long was caught in the middle, just as Rainach and Perez intended he should be. And Louisiana saw a strange reversal of history. Here was a Long trying desperately to talk reason to a people captivated by the cries of demagogues.

He said: "There are extremists on both sides who are injuring the cause. I think there are a lot of fakers trying to make themselves politically by using that issue to befuddle the people. I don't think we need the NAACP down here. I think the colored people will get a square deal without them.

"I don't see any need to pass a lot of segregation bills—even though I would favor them—when the Supreme Court probably would knock them out anyway.

"Even though I received a splendid Negro vote I didn't make any promises to the white citizens or the colored people which could be considered unreasonable on either side."

Under Rainach's whip, the legislature rushed through segregation bills which ran from the ludicrous to the impossible. Interracial meetings were outlawed, even on private premises. Interracial sports events were outlawed. Interracial theatrical performances were outlawed. Rainach even introduced a resolution calling for the impeachment of the United States Supreme Court. Earl told him, "You can't kick the Supreme Court in the slats on the one hand and expect a square deal on the other." Still the bills poured forth, and, after feebly protesting their unconstitutionality, Earl signed them as he fished about for some escape from his dilemma.

He went to the floor of the legislature to question the motives of the segregationists. He told Rainach: "A lot of people are following you not because they agree with you but because they are scared not to be. It's easy to say 'nigger' and scare everybody in the state. I'm for segregation 100 per cent but I don't believe you should run for office on it."

The Rainach-Perez cabal didn't stop. They announced a bill for the 1959 legislature to toughen the voter registration laws. Ostensibly this was a gimmick to disenfranchise the Negroes. Every Negro lost was a Long vote lost. But, beyond that, Earl saw in this bill a license for anti-Long registrars to disenfranchise all Long voters, regardless of color. He became desperate.

He decided, among other things, that only he could save Louisiana from the madness of the segregationists. And he decided, furthermore, he could do so only by getting re-elected as governor. He would resign before the end of his term and thus would be technically eligible to serve again, for he would not be succeeding himself. His wife, Blanche, objected strenuously. For one thing, she did not think Earl would get away with his gimmick to circumvent the nonsuccession law. For another, she feared for his health; he had suffered a heart attack a few years before and he had passed his sixty-second birthday.

They fought over his decision. "I'm gonna run for governor, and you can vote for Jimmie Davis and I'll beat the hell out of both of you," Earl shouted.

As the pressure mounted in early 1959, Earl began changing his ways. He had given up smoking and drinking—he was never a big drinker—after the heart attack. Now he was smoking and drinking heavily. Earl, as befitting a man of the people, had always forbidden his state police chauffeur to exceed the speed limits or to use the siren on the governor's official car; now he insisted on speeds of one hundred miles per hour, and the siren was always screaming. He was rash in almost every action. Always a frugal man, he would now suddenly drop into a supermarket and buy $500 worth of groceries in a matter of minutes. Earl fretted constantly about all the segregationists who were "out to get me." He became abusive to his friends, and frequently accused them of defection to the enemy or desertion under fire.

His public-relations consultant, Mrs. Cora Schley, was in the process of adopting a baby when Earl telephoned her one 5:00 A.M. and said: "I'm your friend but I'm going to see that you don't keep this baby. I'm the head of the Welfare Department and I'll stop it. You have other work to do." Suddenly the baby's unwed mother demanded return of the child, and was chauffeured to court in a state police car to press her claim.

Another morning, at five-thirty, Earl summoned Jesse Bankston, the state's director of hospitals, to the executive mansion. As Bankston told the Civil Service Commission, he arrived to find the governor sobbing, his head wrapped in a cold towel. He told Bankston he had been given tranquilizers by a doctor, but that actually, "I know they're poison."

His arguments with his wife grew hotter. She was urging him to take a rest, a long rest. He accused her of consorting with the enemy. At least once she appeared in public wearing dark glasses which obviously hid blackened eyes. She later charged in her separation petition that Earl had attempted to kill her.

Earl began appearing in the French Quarter night clubs, and he popped up at the Kentucky Derby dandling a couple of pretty girls on his knee. His horse betting had been more or less surreptitious before, but now he was openly wagering $500 to $2,000 on a single race. He flew a National Guard plane to Atlanta to pick up some entertainers for a party he threw at the executive mansion, and at the party he danced and sang and guzzled and hugged the wriggling girl dancers while Mrs. Long hunched frozen with embarrassment in a corner of the room.

The political pressure from the segregationists was squeezing all of the reason out of Earl, and suddenly he had a new worry. The Internal Revenue Service, which had found nothing awry with his income-tax returns during the scandals, was investigating him again. At first Earl scoffed and said, "They'll never find a thing." But then disturbing rumors reached his ears. A bodyguard Earl recently fired was reported "singing." A former political ally was claiming evidence that Earl was the secret owner of several businesses. A New Orleans oil man charged that he left $5,000 on the governor's desk the day he asked Earl to veto a pay hike for the river pilots.

Long went to Washington to see if he could get the investigation halted or, at least, postponed until after his campaign for re-election. He dropped in to see his nephew, Russell, at Russell's Washington apartment. "He was very much under a strain and needed a rest," Russell said later.

On May 13th the legislature convened for its annual message from the governor. The session was scheduled to start at 8:00 P.M. But the minutes ticked by and Earl did not appear. At 8:45 Lieutenant Governor Luther Frazar rose and announced he would read the governor's address. He had barely started when there was a rustle at one side and Long loped in. The governor pulled out a bright red handkerchief and loudly blew his nose. Then he waved the handkerchief for the benefit of news photographers.

The governor walked up to the rostrum, and Frazar handed him the bulky manuscript. Long fumbled with it and almost dropped it. He mumbled, "Did you finish page four?" Frazar nodded. Long rustled the pages, then put down the manuscript and began to speak off the cuff.

He talked of any and everything.

He announced the Internal Revenue investigation of his income tax. "I haven't defrauded the federal government and I haven't defrauded anybody else," he said.

He announced his intentions to seek re-election. "I'll be back, and my administration will be as pure as the drifted snow," he said.

He attacked his political opponents. "There are anti-Long meetings all across the state," he said, "but the most recent at Alexandria attracted only forty persons and except for a few of my friends and stooges they wouldn't have had twenty."

As to the business at hand, the 1959 legislature, he said: "I'm going to call a spade a spade this time. Look at me and look at me good. I don't possess one crooked or illegal dollar to the detriment of the taxpayer of Louisiana. Do you think I ought to be a bloodhound and follow people to their door?"

The legislature giggled with embarrassment. What was this all about?

"The monuments to good, honest, fair government are evident all over this state," Earl said. "They stand to the credit of the Longs and all their friends and helpers in public affairs."

At this he inexplicably twisted his hips and paced seductively across the platform. Then he returned to attack tax increases, outline his spending program, and shout to fidgeting newspaper reporters, "If you're getting tired, get up and go."

In all, his strange talk lasted forty minutes. Suddenly he stopped and walked listlessly into his office.

On May 25th he suddenly summoned reporters to his office

at midnight for a press conference. It lasted three hours. He ranted about the foe and spoke tenderly of Huey in his youth. He noticed that one reporter was wearing scuffed shoes and immediately summoned a servant from the executive mansion and ordered him to polish the shoes. He talked of his boyhood. And he predicted ultimate victory over the segregationists. Little of what he said could be printed. The language was too profane.

On May 26th the legislature's committee met to consider the voter registration bill. This was the showdown. So many legislators wanted to attend that the committee met in the House chamber. The galleries were packed. The entire official proceeding was televised live throughout the state. Governor Long showed up to fight his cause. He heckled the speakers constantly. He wandered about the hall sipping bourbon and grape juice from a pop bottle. He seized the microphone frequently to interject his latest thoughts on the subject at hand, or any other subject. He grew more profane by the moment.

Once he leaped up to say: "About 1908 or 1906 I had an uncle killed. He got drunk one night and went down to the colored quarters in Winnfield. He knocked a nigger man out of bed and got in with the woman. The nigger man came back and shot him. Oh, yes, that's the trouble here. They're just trying to protect their women. You know up there around Alexandria there's some people who keep two families. The trouble goes on all over this state and that's where the trouble starts."

Later he said, "Look at the nigger leaders. About 90 per cent of the intelligent niggers come from the white race and that's what causes the trouble."

A member of the White Citizens Council grabbed the microphone to apologize for the governor's profanity. Long, he said, had "constipation of the brain" and "diarrhea of the mouth." Long interrupted. He was asked to be quiet.

"I'll interrupt that bastard any time I want to," shouted the governor, with millions watching on TV. "He's got no right to slander a sick man."

Then Long was given the microphone again. He wanted to apologize, he said. He had just been informed that there were school children and nuns in the gallery. "I sent for my Bible and I'm gonna swear off cussin'," he told the school children. "Let's you and I and the good nuns keep from cussing as long as possible."

The hearing on the voter registration bill became more heated, and Long lounged against the speaker's rostrum, puffing cigarettes and swilling from his pop bottle. He shouted every time he was provoked, and there was plenty to provoke the man. White Citizens Council leader Willie Rainach at one time turned to the governor and shouted, "We're gonna stomp you when you get out of line."

Earl replied, "They've been doing this kind of thing in Georgia long before you thought of it."

Sometimes Earl defended the Negro and sometimes he attacked him. During the hearing Earl said, "I'd let a Negro out of jail if he'd vote for me." And later, telling a story, Earl talked of "a colored lady—I mean a colored woman—a slip of the tongue."

Back at the mansion Mrs. Long saw all of this on TV, just as did so many others in the state. It was a shocking performance. The governor, whose perfect memory for names and dates was fabled throughout the state, now was reduced to shouting to a senator, "Hey, you Simmesport man, what's your name?"

The next day Earl sent word to the legislature that he realized how terrible the whole shoddy episode looked on TV and that he'd like to appear before a joint session of the state legislature to apologize. The session was called. But as soon as he got to the rostrum, Long resumed the same shouting, cursing assault of the previous night. He told one legislator, "You've got a little dago in you." He called another "the biggest hypocrite who ever lived." He said still another was "in league with the wineheads."

This lasted an hour and a half. Then aides led him to an adjoining office, and there he remained for several hours until he was slipped through a little-used door and taken back to the mansion.

The next day Long appeared in the Senate for the third time. He got into an argument with Rainach, but was persuaded to return to his office. He sent for the loud-speaker station wagon he uses on campaign tours, and ordered it parked under the window of the governor's office. "Play Guy Lombardo loud," he told the driver. All afternoon the Lombardo music screamed behind the Capitol.

That evening at home, according to testimony taken at a hearing of the Louisiana Civil Service Commission, Mrs. Long summoned the governor's family. Bankston testified that at 11:30 P.M. he was called to the executive mansion and asked to provide some male nurses who would be willing to leave their homes for a few days and who could be trusted to keep their mouths shut. Dr. Arthur Long, a psychiatrist who is also a cousin of the governor, testified that he was called by Russell, the governor's nephew. "We're having some trouble at the mansion," Russell said. Dr. Long guessed what the trouble was, but said he couldn't come until morning.

The next day, Friday, May 29th, as Bankston testified at the hearing, he reported to the mansion with four attendants he had procured from the East Louisiana State Hospital. Dr. Long arrived. So did Russell, Mrs. Long's two sisters, and one of Earl's sisters. Four additional doctors were summoned. They had a council and decided that Earl was mentally ill. He needed treatment immediately. But where? This was the governor of Louisiana. John Nealy Hospital in Galveston was selected, Bankston said, because it was nearby, because it was good, and because it was in Texas, where Long would not have the powers of governor.

Mrs. Long told reporters at noon that the governor was ill and needed a long rest. That's all she said.

The male nurses, two at a time, were assigned to the governor's bedroom. Keep him there, they were told. The governor was given sedatives, but they didn't work.

During the afternoon the governor caught on to what was

up. He tried to get away. Once, according to Russell's testimony at the hearing, he burst past his guarded bedroom door and reached the mansion elevator. There he was stopped by Russell and Arthur Long and two other men, and they wrestled him back to the bedroom. He began screaming. He began crying. He began hurling things out the window, trying to attract attention on the street below.

The state police who normally guard the mansion had been instructed to remain away from the family quarters on the second floor. Dr. Long told the family that Earl was a victim of manic depressive psychosis—a condition of overactivity and, at times, of violence. Dr. Long testified that Earl was dangerous, and that, furthermore, Earl's condition was such that he might die at any moment if he were not restrained and given medication and rest.

At 5:00 P.M. Earl was raising so much ruckus that Mrs. Long, trying to make arrangements with the Galveston hospital by telephone, told State Police Sergeant William Abadie to go upstairs to help restrain the governor. Abadie had been the governor's chauffeur but was relieved at his own request when the hundred-mile-an-hour auto rides became too much for him. He had been called back to duty because of the new emergency.

Abadie went upstairs and, he said, Long shouted at him: "Get out of here! I don't want you around." Abadie returned to his post downstairs.

Russell testified that at one point Earl's family actually frisked him, and that he, Russell, took away the pocketknife that the governor normally carried. But Earl broke pieces of furniture to acquire new weapons and new objects to hurl out of the window. The telephone was removed from his room.

National Guard Commander Raymond Hufft was summoned. He was asked to arrange to fly the governor to Texas. Hufft decided to use the Guard's plane because it contained bunks to which the governor might be strapped.

It was a harrowing night in the mansion. Hufft told the

Civil Service Commission that the governor did not sleep despite the sedatives. The next morning, just before nine, a station wagon was brought to the back door. Earl was strapped to a stretcher by the male nurses and carted, screaming and writhing, into the vehicle.

Hufft said that Earl called, "Ray, don't let them hurt me."

"I put my arm over him on the litter. I walked down the steps of the mansion with him. I said: 'Governor, I promise you no one is going to hurt you. I am going with you wherever you go.' "

At the airport Earl spotted Victor Bussie, the state AFL-CIO chairman who had been at the mansion through the night. "Bussie, are these some of your labor goons?" Earl asked. "Are you in charge, Vic? Are you in charge, Ray? Dammit, when a man's being kidnaped he has a right to know who's running the show."

Finally his fury settled on Hufft. "Dammit, Hufft, you ain't gonna be a general no more. As of this moment I'm demoting you to private and I'm promoting this sergeant here to general. Hey, sergeant, make this SOB salute you right now. You're his boss."

Earl was strapped onto a bunk on the plane and flown to Galveston. Mrs. Long was too nervous to make the flight. She followed by automobile. Then, with Earl incarcerated, the Long family announced the truth to the public: The governor was confined to a mental hospital and would have to remain under treatment for some time.

Actually, Earl Long was not the first governor treated at John Sealy. He was the third. But the others, spirited in and out under the veil of secrecy, provided nothing like the circus which attended Earl Long's seventeen-day incarceration. Earl refused to cooperate with the doctors. He was interviewed by reporters who sneaked under cover of night to whistle beneath his room window. He even was interviewed over the radio until the phone was yanked from his room. Two of his most trusted pals were caught sneaking whisky to him. One of his sisters arrived and insisted that she be permitted to cook his meals; she did—catfish and mustard greens and corn bread and huckleberry pie. Earl kept firing orders back to Louisiana by any courier who'd carry the message.

He fought his incarceration, and loudly berated his family in the preliminary hearing. Then he turned foxy. He told his wife he'd stay in the hospital if she'd let him go back to Louisiana. She decided to risk it. The shame and the weariness and the worry were weighting her beyond endurance. Earl was told he could go to Louisiana if he'd promise to accept medical and psychiatric treatment, and if he'd sign a paper releasing his family from kidnaping charges.

He signed, and was flown to the Oschner Clinic in New Orleans. He didn't stay twenty-four hours. He simply walked out of his room, got into a state police car, and ordered the driver to take him to Baton Rouge. He was governor again.

Mrs. Long was prepared for this. She telephoned to Baton Rouge and asked the parish coroner to commit her husband by force. As Earl's state police car crossed into Baton Rouge, the parish officials were waiting. Sheriff's deputies forced the Long car to the curb and ordered it to the courthouse.

Because Governor Long refused to leave the car for a hearing, the formalities were conducted in the basement garage of the courthouse. The governor screamed to bystanders for aid. Then he noticed a newspaper reporter wearing Bermuda shorts. "McLean, go shave your legs," he shouted. The governor was ordered committed and driven immediately to the state hospital at Mandeville, a hospital which, ironically, his administration had established as part of his campaign for better mental facilities.

Mrs. Long signed the commitment papers. Now, to the general public, the question seemed resolved. But behind the scenes the lawyers knew that because Earl was governor he could soon engineer his own release. Longism was partly responsible. The governor hired and fired all of the hospital superintendents. Their star patient would fire them all the moment someone slipped him the proper paper to sign.

Long demanded his right of a sanity hearing in court. On

the morning of the hearing, with the courtroom packed, Long arrived with documents to announce that he had replaced the hospital superintendent and that he had been released by the new superintendent, a seventy-two-year-old country doctor. He had the papers to support this and, furthermore, the papers were countersigned by Lieutenant Governor Frazar. There was nothing anyone could do. Long was a free man.

How could this be? When they wrote the law they didn't anticipate a governor going crazy. The law did provide that the lieutenant governor would supersede the governor if the governor were incapacitated, but it made no attempt to define "incapacitated" nor did it stipulate who would decide when the governor was incapacitated. True, the governor could be impeached by the legislature. But, just as true, the only practical means of convening the legislature in special session was on order of the governor and, even then, only to handle business specifically authorized by the governor.

Those in Long's official family who felt he should be committed were faced with the problem of legal ethics. Any lawyer assigned to him would be bound to follow his wishes, and his wishes were to get free. They tried to circumvent this problem by appointing a committee of prominent lawyers to represent the state bar, rather than the governor as a client, but no prominent lawyer would serve. So it became a case of Earl asking one after another of his lawyer pals to get him free. One after the other refused, but inevitably he found one who agreed to represent him—and after that it was only a matter of time.

J. Arthur Sims was the attorney who agreed to represent Earl. He drew up the papers which permitted Earl to replace the hospital superintendent. The one man remaining who might have challenged this was Lieutenant Governor Frazar. But Frazar, who had been president of McNeese Junior College prior to his election, had only one ambition now—to become president of LSU. Earl was his only hope of getting the job. He went along with Earl and cosigned the ouster of the hospital superintendent. Frazar told his friends he did not think Earl was mentally unbalanced—no more than usual, anyway.

The medical and psychiatric reports issued on Earl before and after his release said in substance that he had suffered a series of minor strokes which had caused a certain amount of organic brain damage; his intellect was unimpaired but he had no inhibitions; he was paranoic, that is, he suffered from delusions of persecution, and he was potentially dangerous, to himself and to others. One doctor was of the opinion that Earl really wanted to kill himself. The others said that his continued excesses at work and play could produce a stroke which would kill him instantly.

Earl's inner circle was split now. On one side were those who felt the governor should be committed; on the other side were those who felt he had to be freed. Of those who wanted him free, there were some who sincerely thought that they could induce him to hole up at his beloved "peapatch" farm and get as much rest as in a hospital. There were others who didn't care; they either were too terrified to cross vindictive old Earl or else they were concerned with the boodle they could grab by humoring him and presenting themselves as his only loyal friends.

At any rate, as soon as Earl stepped free of the hospital, Louisiana was legally under the direction of a governor who had been described as mentally unfit by psychiatrists at three different institutions. And from far and wide reporters rushed in to chronicle the administration of "the crazy governor."

CHAPTER FOURTEEN

"If I'm crazy now, I've always been crazy."

EARL BOUNDED OUT OF THE MANDEVILLE HOSPITAL FULL OF plans and full of promises. First he'd take a long vacation, he said, and then he would summon a special session of the legislature to deal with his enemies. He was wifeless now and without restraint. Blanche Long had gone—she fled the state to hide out in Colorado Springs and sent Theo Cangelosi, a lawyer and family friend, into court to seek a legal separation.

Earl holed up in Winnfield at the farm for a few days, long enough to fire most of the medical staff he had promised to obey, and then set out on his bizarre tour through the Southwest. He made headlines every day.

At Fort Worth he attempted to thwart photographers who met him at the airport by putting a pillowcase over his head, then a pillow atop the pillowcase and his hat atop the pillow. His state police bodyguard slugged a reporter, and Earl shouted, "You reporters are going to drive me nuts!" Later he quieted down long enough to give an interview. He said his vacation was being financed by campaign-fund contributions he had kept hidden since 1928. He said he had made a fortune of $300,000 from one wildcat oil well. He summoned Lieutenant Governor Frazar and three other lieutenants, and they came rushing from Louisiana for a gubernatorial conference.

At Big Spring, Texas, he announced, "If I'm crazy now, I've always been crazy." He had a new doctor, Dr. M. O. Motter, of New Orleans, who pronounced him "much improved." He said he suspected his wife of "trying to make up."

At El Paso he said: "I'll never make up with her. We've fought for twenty-five years. It's a wonder we haven't killed each other. When the money gets low the love gets low."

At Pecos, Texas, he said he expected the first bill before his special session of the legislature would be to impeach him. "I'm ready for the bastards," he said.

And back home who was minding the store? "Things are going about as well as could be expected under the circumstances," said one administrative official in Baton Rouge.

At Ruidoso, New Mexico, he got into a hassle with the deputy sheriff assigned to accompany him to the race track when the deputy refused to let him change his seat. Earl stalked out of the track, pausing to wag his finger at the deputy and say: "If ever I saw a convict, he's one. Why do you turn these people on a sick man?"

At Juarez, Mexico, he visited some of the hot spots and got into a screaming hassle with photographers who followed him.

At Santa Fe, New Mexico, he said that Mexico, not Alaska, should have been admitted to the Union. He philosophized about psychiatrists, saying, "I think they all might be crazy." He went on a wild car ride trying to elude photographers, and one of his suitcases broke loose from its mooring atop the limousine. Earl sat in the car and laughed as his state policemen retrieved polka-dot undershorts which lay scattered about the roadway.

At Albuquerque he read a local newspaper story which said that the governor—who had boasted to reporters he was toting a gun—would have to check his firearms at the hotel during his visit. Asked for comment, Long told reporters to "take that newspaper and shove it."

And meanwhile, back home a Long political foe complained that he had received a crate of cantaloupes, collect.

At Taos, New Mexico, he stood on the street and swapped risqué stories with local merchants. The exchange got so raw that a fluttery state cop began urging the women in the crowd to move on. One lady objected strenuously. "I want to hear

Governor Long cuss," she wailed. Earl later went to his hotel and fell into such a deep sleep that his aides called a doctor and a nurse. They thought he had died.

At Denver he dropped between $4,000 and $6,000 at the races and wailed that one of his entourage had bought a ticket on the wrong horse in the seventh. He was delighted to hear that he had launched a new craze. All over the Southwest wags were checking into hotels with pillowcases over their heads; invariably the rumor spread that Governor Long of Louisiana was in town.

And back at home the opposition leaders announced they had decided to forgo impeachment proceedings against the governor because he was wrecking his organization in his own way.

At Independence, Missouri, he met former President Truman, and said, "All I did was tell him a lot of bad jokes." As he left the Truman Library he tipped the guard $100 and scrawled into an autograph book: "Earl K. Long. Three times Gov. of La. and maybe (?) four times."

And back home the New Orleans Young Men's Business Club passed a resolution condemning the governor's tour as "undignified."

At Hot Springs, Arkansas, he sparked a thirty-eight-year-old Memphis divorcee, parking with her under an Arkansas moon in his $10,000 Cadillac. He invited her to come visit him in Baton Rouge, but later she told reporters, "He invites everybody, doesn't he?"

And, back home in Louisiana at last, the governor called a meeting of his legislative supporters to blueprint the special session he was calling. Fifteen attended.

Long walked into the meeting room wearing a wilted suit and a sagging panama hat. He sat silent for a few moments, and then said, "Let's get down to business."

He turned to Representative Buford Smith. "Let's start out with you, Smith. You got something to sing? I see you been popping off in the papers."

Smith screwed up his nerve, and said, "I don't think you ought to call a special session at this time, Governor."

"Who knows the most, you or I?" Long snapped.

Smith paid flowery tribute to the chief executive's capabilities. The governor spun around and began checking the absentees. He'd deal with them later, he said. Now he wanted to outline what he would have that special session do.

Other men got up to say that they, too, objected to the session. It wasn't, er, timely. Long said, "I'll say this. The governor has rights and, like Caesar's wife, you ought not inquire into them."

He went ahead with his proposals for the special session. One was a bill that would forbid airlines to fire hostesses because they marry.

"You aren't serious about that, are you?" asked Senator C. H. Downs.

"Sure I am. It ain't fair."

Another of his proposals was to require seven neighbors to attest to a person's insanity before he could be locked up.

"Today, in a modern state like Louisiana, it's just a case of who gets to the courthouse first, the man or the woman," Long said.

"One day I was walking down the hall at Mandeville and I heard this nice-looking blonde lady talking kind of loud and screaming. I just sat down and looked at her, and she said her husband had run off to California with a blonde and in order to take that trip he had locked her up."

Long said he had ordered her freed. He also revealed that he had become fond of another inmate in Galveston, a fourteen-year-old boy, and that he attempted to adopt the child but the lad's parents had objected.

The meeting broke up, and the legislators scattered to their home bases. Earl called other such meetings elsewhere in the state. Everywhere he went his old supporters in the House and Senate pleaded with him to abandon his plan to call the special session. He was adamant. At the same time he was wearing his closest lieutenants to a frazzle. He slept little—

three or four hours at most in a stretch—yet he seemed to be thriving. Far from collapsing in sudden death as the doctors had warned, his coloring was improving and he seemed livelier than ever.

Earl had never been a wencher, but now he talked incessantly about his love for the ladies. Privately he admitted to a reporter his consistent lack of success with the fair sex. Publicly he winked and leered as if he were the world's greatest roué. He had first taken on this new attitude just about the time he was showing the strain of the segregationists' threat in the legislature in early May. His infatuation for a twenty-three-year-old redheaded strip teaser named Blaze Starr soon brightened the newspapers.

Earl had gone into a French Quarter bistro named the Sho-Bar with some cronies just before the start of the legislature, and there he saw Miss Starr perform. "He was mad for her. He came back nearly every night for two weeks," said Frank Caracci, the owner of the night club.

Miss Starr visited Long once at his farm in Winnfield and once in his suite in the Roosevelt Hotel. Each time the event was heralded in big black headlines. Later, after she took her act to Miami, Miss Starr flew a thousand miles, apparently only for a brief rendezvous with the governor at the home of a friend. Miss Starr said later: "We had a few soft drinks and milk shakes and that's all there was to it. If people got the wrong idea, it's pathetic. He's just a good guy and I like to be with him. He's entitled to a little happiness."

Earl telephoned the newspapers to cuss out the editors for "harassing that poor woman" with their stories, and with good cause. The New Orleans newspapers have always been especially discreet about personal peccadilloes of the state's more prominent figures. Now they seemed to be climbing all over Earl with an attitude of "anything goes."

Everywhere Earl went he was followed by an entourage of henchmen who did his every bidding, no matter how unreasonable. The hotel-suite parties at the end of the day were long and loud. Earl gave one party at the executive mansion, and a surprising number of legislators attended. Some were plainly curious. Others simply were afraid to absent themselves. As one put it, "If he fires my people from their state jobs, they're fired—whether he's crazy or not. I have to go along with him."

The mansion party was raucous, and Earl ran every moment of it. "Everybody dance," he'd shout, and obediently, if sheepishly, the guests rose to their feet to dance. "Everybody down," he'd shout, and everyone would shuffle back to seats to watch Earl perform along with the floor show he had imported from the French Quarter.

Meanwhile, who was minding the store? Long was away from the governor's office seventy-four days. Lieutenant Governor Frazar steadfastly refused to usurp the prerogatives. How did Louisiana function? Reporters sent to find out learned something startling about government. The governor has the power to do many things. But if he does nothing, the government still operates close to normal. The only problem created by Earl's seventy-four-day absence from his office was that of 150 convicts who had to remain in prison because there was no one to sign their paroles.

Of course, the situation would deteriorate as it was extended. And around the nation experts in government operation watched Louisiana not nearly so amused as was the general public. The North Carolina *Medical Journal* published a paper on what was called the "tragicomedy" of Governor Long. It cited four lessons to be learned:

1. "The importance of the state's being prepared to deal with such a problem should it arise." The *Journal* said a survey discovered that only two states, Alabama and Oregon, have definite provisions for determining a governor's sanity should it be questioned.

2. "No layman, not even a governor, should have the right to discharge the head of the state mental hospital." The *Journal* said that "in too many states politics plays a great part in the care of the mentally sick."

3. "The danger over a patient's trying to diagnose his own case."

4. "The very threat to medical prestige arising from the conflicting testimony given by psychiatrists. It is hard to understand how doctors appointed by Long to replace the ousted head of the state hospital could have justified their action in declaring him sane. Surely they must have realized that they were selling their medical birthright for a very sorry mess of political pottage."

Long had ousted a psychiatrist, Dr. Charles Belcher, as superintendent of the hospital at Mandeville and replaced him with Dr. Jesse J. McClendon, a seventy-two-year-old country physician. Dr. McClendon replied to the *Medical Journal*'s editorial by saying that "two head psychiatrists from Tulane and Louisiana State University examined him and declared him sane." Dr. McClendon said, "I've been practicing medicine more than fifty years and I've known Governor Long a long time. When you know somebody and have been in contact with him for years you know whether they're crazy or not. The governor had the right to appoint and discharge the heads of all the state hospitals."

The ouster of Dr. Belcher was only the beginning for Earl. He returned to Louisiana from his Southwestern tour in a vindictive rage. He fired the head of the state's hospital system; he fired the state police chief and his bodyguard (for permitting his removal from the mansion for the enforced trip to Galveston); and then he set his sights on attorney Theo Cangelosi. He had two grudges against Cangelosi: one, that he refused to help the governor escape Mandeville and, two, that Cangelosi represented Mrs. Long when she filed her separation suit. Earl was determined to oust Cangelosi from his position as chairman of the LSU Board of Supervisors, but this was one of the rare state jobs over which the governor had no control.

Long made the Cangelosi affair part of his call for a special session of the legislature. This came out as a bill to "remove certain officeholders from office." The governor had eighteen

other measures up for consideration, ranging from his salvation of married airlines hostesses to a raft of pay hikes for
those state officials who might be involved in his campaign for
re-election.

The great majority of the members of the legislature did
not know what to do. They deplored going into session under
a governor they considered mentally unsound. This was an
election year, and they were fearful of the reaction to kowtow-
ing to Long and they were equally fearful of the reaction to
kicking him when he was down. They gathered at Baton
Rouge the morning of the session to find a way off the hook.
They quickly eliminated the possibility of impeachment, although Long had dared them to try it and had even made it
legally possible. Secretly the Long and anti-Long forces came
to an agreement, and then all sat back to await the opening
of the session on August 10th at 5:00 P.M.

The governor was told the House and Senate would organize at that hour, and then would recess until 8:00 P.M. when
it would hear his message. Long left the Capitol and went
to the executive mansion to take a nap before his speech. He
awoke at five and turned on the radio to hear the legislative
proceedings while the barber shaved him in his bedroom.

He was just in time to hear the legislature adjourning out
from under him!

In the House Long's own floor leader, Representative Ben
Holt, made the motion to adjourn. "I am in no way angry
with Governor Long," he said, "but I cannot permit friendship and loyalty to circumvent or prevail over the right of the
people. I would feel the same way if any close friend or
brother became ill and could not carry on the responsibility
of great office." Holt said the special session was called only
for "vindictive, personal and political reasons," and he told
his fellow Long supporters, "You owe it to the governor to
go along with a measure to end the session to save embarrassment and harassment."

Governor Long leaped from his chair at those words and,
half shaved, quickly dressed and rushed back to the Capitol.

As he rode he heard the House pass the adjournment, 71 to 25. And he heard the radio broadcast switch to the Senate, where Senator J. D. De Blieux called out, "Since the House has seen fit to adjourn, I make a motion that the Senate adjourn sine die."

The Senate had just voted to quit, 26 to 9, when Governor Long panted into the chamber. He was too late. But he walked up to the microphone and began an informal address. Everyone in the packed hall winced. The legislators expected a tirade even more intense than those which had erupted before the governor had been committed in Galveston.

Earl stood somber and on the verge of tears before the Senate and stared into the faces of those who had humiliated him. He was dressed as if for a funeral, black suit, black tie, white shirt. His voice quavered a bit as he started to speak and then, all the more bitter because his own floor leader had made the motion to adjourn, he warmed up:

"Gentlemen, if this is the way you look at it, I don't know much I can do. I'm going to carry my fight to the people."

And then he shouted:

"If I was crazy, then I'm still crazy. So you're getting the opportunity to see a crazy governor. I don't know what made them send me off, but I got a bill this morning from the hospital in Galveston. Do you think I ought to pay it?"

There were some cries of Yes, and others of No.

Earl chuckled. "Don't you worry about that bill because Uncle Earl's not worrying."

Then he went into an attack on those who moved to adjourn. Representative Holt "likes notoriety," Earl said. "I think he wants to run for governor, but he won't carry Rapides Parish."

Earl rambled for ten minutes. The Senate was quiet. Most members stared forward. One woman gulped to fight back the tears. Two young boys, squeezed onto the same bench as their senator-father, sat transfixed, their chins resting on their fists as they gaped in awe.

Soon it was over. The governor ended with, "Go home,

think it over, let your consciences be your guide, good luck and God bless you." There was light applause, and Earl Long sat down heavily and stared blankly into space.

Then the well-wishers stepped forward. One wizened old supporter, obviously a Longite since the first days of Huey, came up to shake his hand and say, "The people are still with you, Earl." The governor replied, "Yeah, but they don't know it," and swept his hand toward the legislature which had deserted him. Lieutenant Governor Frazar told him not to be upset. "I'm upset-proof," Earl said.

Earl announced that the next day he would go to New Orleans to speak on behalf of his re-election. He scheduled a rally at Canal Street and Claiborne Avenue, one of the most accessible intersections in the city, and he arrived to find no Long-type crowd. Instead, there was a motley band of the curious. Many were college and high-school students, obviously on a lark. Smack in front of them all was Tony Morrison, the teenage son of Earl's hated political rival, Mayor deLesseps S. Morrison.

Earl tried to speak, and the ill-mannered kids heckled him badly. Once the heckling became so loud that Earl walked away from the microphone while a fellow candidate lectured the audience on good manners. Earl slumped in his seat during this interval. A reporter asked him, "Does this bother you?" He expected to get a bombastic "Hell, no," but instead Earl mumbled, "Yes, very much."

He continued to stump the state. Sometimes, as at Amite, there were cheers and tears for the game campaigner who brayed on even when his voice broke or his cough seemed to become uncontrollable.

The hecklers popped up everywhere, and Earl tried to bite them off with the old Long insult. A typical instance occurred at Lake Charles.

As Earl talked, a heckler from up front shouted, "You got a big mouth."

Earl replied: "If it ever closed I'd be in a devil of a fix. You be quiet. If you fellows didn't talk sometimes I wouldn't be able to tell you smell and need a bath."

Later in the talk Earl said, "I am guilty of no wrongdoing," and the hecklers responded with raucous laughter.

Earl shouted: "Now you be respectful to me. If the water is too hot sneak out and go about your business."

He finished his speech, as he finished dozens of others, on the brink of exhaustion. Then he sat and chatted with the old-timers who filed up for a handshake with the governor and a plea for alms from the government. Sometimes Earl would sing with these late-stayers. His favorite was "I'm Looking Over a Four-Leaf Clover."

Sometimes in his speeches Earl made light of his commitment to the mental wards and sometimes he painted it as a dark political plot. "I just thought you'd like to see what a crazy governor looks like," Earl would tell the crowds. "Well, here I am. If I'm nuts now, then I've always been nuts."

The income-tax investigation continued to plague him, and he announced that the government agreed to halt its investigation until after the political campaign. The Internal Revenue Service people denied this, but there was every indication that Long was telling the truth. For one thing, Senator Ellender said he had arranged the delay in Washington.

There was a new attempt by Mrs. Long to get the governor to withdraw from the election campaign and take the rest his doctors advised. One day Earl and Mrs. Long met at the New Orleans home of her brother, Paul Revere. The governor was there for an hour and ten minutes. Several times he was heard to shout, "No, no, no!"

And No it was. He continued to campaign. But the hecklers and the small crowds and the mass desertions eventually got through to him.

As the deadline for qualifying for the election ballot neared, Earl still had not resigned as governor. He kept pushing the date back, and once even suggested to reporters that actually he didn't have to resign until ten minutes before the inauguration. If he did that, he still wouldn't be succeeding himself, would he?

Came the day of the deadline, and Earl produced his anti-climax. He wasn't running for governor after all, he said. He was running for lieutenant governor on a ticket headed by Jimmy Noe.

And so now, at last, Jimmy Noe—who had been shoved aside by Huey's successors twenty-four years ago—was the Long candidate for governor. Earl maintained that he had said all along he "didn't necessarily want to run for governor," and now that Noe was willing to run, well, it wasn't necessary for Earl to run.

He filled out his papers to run for lieutenant governor and signed them in the presence of photographers. "Tell 'em I have the money [the qualifying fee], 210 bucks, cash in hand, better than anybody's check. Honestly and truly it feels better to be lieutenant governor under the right man than governor."

Why did Earl withdraw after staking his home, his career, his life on his desperate bid for re-election? For one thing, he saw he couldn't get elected governor. For another, he dared not resign because he felt the powers of office were his only means of stemming a mounting tide of defections in his political camp. So Earl ran for lieutenant governor, and he was badly beaten; he finished third (although he polled 40,000 more votes than Noe, his running mate) and he was eliminated in the first primary. The segregationists played a major role in his defeat. Their candidate for governor, Rainach, ran third, but he did poll 138,000 votes. This back-woods vote had once belonged to Earl, but Rainach had wooed the poor whites away. The final blow, probably, came when the New Orleans Choctaw Club withdrew its support from Earl. In the end, he even failed to get elected to the state Democratic Committee from his home parish.

The Long organization might continue, but it would no longer be run by Earl K.

CHAPTER FIFTEEN

"Do they want me to go back and apologize for free school books, for building roads, for charity hospitals, for old-age pensions, for free school lunches?"

THE LATE-MODEL LONG IS RUSSELL, WHO SEEMS TO SPEND HALF his time deploring comparisons with Huey and the other half manufacturing them.

Russell's physical appearance is a constant reminder of his father. He has the same bulbous nose, the same cleft chin, the same unruly hair, the same little eyes, and the same pot-likker drawl. Much of the Long dynasty is simply the wish of the redneck voters that there be a dynasty, and to these people Russell is Huey reincarnated. When Russell spoke at his Uncle Earl's 1948 inauguration, he drew more applause than the new governor.

The late Kingfish's eldest child was born the senior King-prince and spent his entire life training himself for the assumption of power. As a matter of fact, he literally almost became a Huey. He was born on November 3, 1918, in Shreveport on a day when his father was out of the city campaigning. Mrs. Long selected the name of Huey Pierce Long III for her child. When Huey returned home he objected, and the name became Russell Billiu Long. No one remembered to change the birth certificate, and as a result Russell became entangled in considerable red tape when he joined the Navy.

Russell spent the first twelve years of his life in Shreveport, where being Huey Long's son involved him in numerous schoolboy fistfights. The city of Shreveport, and particularly the upper-class neighborhood in which he lived, were always hotbeds of anti-Long feeling.

The family moved to the executive mansion when Huey was elected governor, and then New Orleans two years later when Huey was elected to the United States Senate. Russell was left behind in Baton Rouge briefly to live in the home of LSU President James Monroe Smith while he completed the year in the LSU experimental high school. It was in the Smith home, at the age of thirteen, that Russell granted his first newspaper interview.

"I miss my father a lot since he went to Washington," Russell said. "Of course, I miss my mother and my sister and my brother who are in New Orleans but I miss Dad the most because I do not get to see him often. . . . I would rather hear him speak than do most anything else I know."

And as the interview ended, Russell very formally escorted the reporter to the door, shook his hand, and said, "When I get big and run for office I want you to remember the promise you made to vote for me."

At sixteen Russell finished high school at Fortier in New Orleans. He wanted to go to Princeton, as befitting his Audubon Boulevard upbringing. But Huey's career was based on his loyalty to the poor folks, and hadn't he given the poor folks a better college at LSU for free than the rich nabobs got up East? Russell had to go to LSU. He was entered for September, 1935. Three weeks before the start of classes Huey was assassinated.

At the funeral the widowed Mrs. Long told an old friend: "Russell is going to follow in his father's footsteps. He will go to LSU, the school in which Huey took such pride, and he will study law. If the public needs him, as it needed my husband, he will go into politics. Perhaps the things that Huey fought for can be carried on by his son."

Within a year he was indeed carrying on. He spent his Christmas holidays campaigning for Richard Leche. He'd be trotted out at every stop and introduced by his Uncle Earl. Then he would recite the identical speech for each audience:

"I have come here because I know all of you were my father's friends and I want to thank you for the appreciation and support you have given him. . . . I'd like to meet all of you and shake hands with you, but I really came just to thank you for your friendship to my father."

Russell ran his own campaign for the first time in 1938. He sought election as president of the LSU student body, and he soon brought a new dimension to campus politics—the Long dimension. Pretty co-eds paraded the campus with "Long" painted on their bare backs. Airplanes dropped vote-for-Long leaflets. Russell imported name dance bands. He gave away ice-cream cones at his rallies.

One of his opponents was the head cheerleader, Blondy Bennett, who was working his way through college by operating a campus laundry. Russell promised a cheaper campus co-operative laundry if elected. He was Huey all over again as he put an advertisement in the college humor magazine saying Bennett only sought election to "keep from losing the laundry racket, the juiciest pickings that have come down the pike in many a day."

One afternoon Bennett grabbed Russell in the Huey P. Long Field House and, with five hundred students gaping, charged that Russell offered him $1,200 cash and a job as assistant secretary of the State Senate if he would withdraw from the election.

Russell turned red and shouted, "It's a damn' lie!"

Russell overwhelmed Bennett, who finished third in the three-man race. Years later Russell said, "Though it was only college politics, it seemed to me that my whole political future depended upon that election."

Russell's campus political career emulated his father's political career. Just as Huey worked out of his mansions in better sections of Shreveport and New Orleans as a fighter for the underprivileged, so Russell operated out of the Delta Kappa Epsilon fraternity house as a fighter for the neglected nonfraternity men. And just as Huey had been a brilliant law student, so Russell finished law school third in his class.

He married his campus sweetheart, Katherine Mae Hattic, on June 3, 1939, and then went into the Navy. He served as a landing boat officer in North Africa, Sicily, Anzio, and southern France and returned to peacetime Baton Rouge a lieutenant. He practiced law for two years, and then his Uncle Earl ran for governor in 1948.

Earl and Russell had never been close. There was the old feud before Huey's death, and there was Earl's crudity which horrified a boy reared on Audubon Boulevard. But Russell began his campaign for Earl by assuring the suspicious rednecks that "the family is satisfied my father and uncle patched up their differences, and if we are satisfied you should be."

Earl was grateful for the help. Upon his election he said the job for governor's executive counsel "has been offered to Russell Long, but he handed it back. If he wants it, it will be given to him." Russell replied, "I don't want Earl to feel obligated to me, but if I can be of any substantial aid to him I might take it."

The niceties over, Russell took it. He was one of the principal drafters of the big tax bills which Earl needed to fulfill his campaign promises. Again Russell walked in Huey's shadow as he testified before a committee on increased oil taxes. The big oil companies were threatening to leave Louisiana if their taxes were hiked, but Russell said:

"When the oil and gas are gone they are going to pick up and leave, and that's the last we'll see of them. Some say they can't afford to pay the tax, but when oil was selling for eighty cents a barrel they were paying eight cents tax and were doing all right."

"The people are paying a sales tax, which is a poor man's tax, and a beer tax with the money going back to help them. This is a rich man's tax that won't hurt the rich and will help everybody."

Russell worked for Earl for two months. Then United States Senator John Overton died, and Earl, after appointing

William Feazel to serve out the current session, immediately announced that he was supporting his nephew in the election to name a successor.

Russell began his campaign in true Long style. He said: "We are feeding every Jap, every Chinaman, every Hindu and every Arab we can find to feed. I intend to see that we get our share of that money to feed the people at home."

The crowds turned out for Russell. But just about the time that his campaign reached high gear, the $50,000,000 in new Earl Long taxes began to hit the populace. There was considerable grumbling. Russell became frightened. He thought that perhaps this was not the year for a Long to run. Earl insisted that he remain in the race. The words got harsh, and at one point Earl was heard to say, "You little SOB, you'll stay in that race if you only get two votes—mine and yours."

Russell began to bear down on his inheritance of the Long name. He was deft in reminding the folks who he was. He said in one speech: "Don't think that you owe Russell Long anything for whatever he has been able to do for you. It's just the other way around. You folks have been good to my family, and I owe you far more than you could ever owe me."

But, if perchance the people still loved Huey, then, "I'll try to achieve all the things for which he stood—such things as old-age pensions, federal aid to education, and state welfare programs."

Russell also showed that he could turn a phrase in the manner of his father. Commenting on his opponent, Judge Robert Kennon, he said, "From where I sit it looks as though the judge wants to be everybody's sweetheart and nobody's gal."

The election was close, harrowingly so. Russell won by only 10,475 votes. He didn't carry his home parish of Baton Rouge, and he trailed Kennon by 25,000 votes in New Orleans. Once again it was obvious that the country folks went for the Longs and the city folks didn't, moving Russell to say, "I want to thank especially the boys who laid down their cotton sacks, plows and hoes to go to the polls and elect Russell Long."

Normally the Democratic primary is the only thing that counts in one-party Louisiana, but the opposition to this extension generation of the Long dynasty was such that a Republican, Clem S. Clarke, announced he would run against Russell in the general election. He did, and although Russell won, Clarke piled up the highest Republican total in Louisiana since the Reconstruction.

In 1952 Russell and his uncle, Earl, split bitterly. And here the difference between the two men was pointed up sharply. Both were Longs and both knew and used the techniques of whipping up the back-country folk against the city people—the rednecks against the whitenecks, so to speak. Earl and Huey came by the rednecks naturally. They were Winn Parish boys, reared on the farm and indoctrinated by their father to hate the rich snobs. Russell was of the same blood line but was reared differently. He was the city boy from Shreveport and New Orleans. He was whiteneck by environment even if a redneck by philosophy.

His old friends were the fraternity-house set. Congressman T. Hale Boggs belonged to the set, too. He was a Tulane graduate, supported by Mayor deLesseps Morrison and the "better people" in New Orleans, and it was natural that he and Russell would become close friends in Washington. In 1952 Boggs decided to run for governor. Russell yearned to support him, but Uncle Earl insisted on a hand-picked pro, somebody he thought he could control. Earl threw his support to a Baton Rouge city judge, Carlos Spaht, and even put himself on the ticket for lieutenant governor.

Russell would have none of it. He decided to stump for Boggs. And so once again it was Long against Long on the speaking platforms of Louisiana, and once again Earl showed that his bitterness knows no bounds.

He charged that as a teen-ager Russell was "Louisiana's leading deadhead." He said that during the Leche administration Russell "was on the payroll for $200 a month and he didn't do a lick of work."

Russell replied that "Earl is getting as bitter toward me as he was toward my father." (Apparently the family was no longer "satisfied" that all was well between Earl and Huey.) Russell continued: "I have always earned my salary in every job I have ever held. Certainly if Earl Long thought otherwise, he should not have recommended me to the people of Louisiana for the United States Senate."

Earl castigated Russell for going over to the city slickers, the old enemies of the Longs. Russell replied that "blessed are the peacemakers," and urged the people to forget the hoary political feuds which had ripped Louisiana apart for decades.

Earl said that maybe this was all his fault. After all, he had foisted Russell on the people. "Russell Long was picked too green on the vine." Russell replied, "If I was picked too green on the vine, then Uncle Earl is too ripe on the vine and should be picked at once."

The trouble with Uncle Earl, Russell said, was that he was suffering from "mansionitis, an ailment that comes from sitting in that big mansion with all those servants and all those limousines and chauffeurs."

The result was a tie. Both Longs lost. Their men were defeated by Kennon, the judge Russell had licked in the senatorial primary.

Russell wasn't too happy with the reception he got from the whitenecks. He felt he was one of them, and yet that they wouldn't accept him only because his name was Long. When he ran for the full Senate term in 1950 and again in 1956, the "better people" refused to back him. They would support Boggs and not Long, and yet Boggs and Long had almost identical records in Washington. Obviously this was pure prejudice against the memory of Huey.

Russell snorted, "Do they want me to go back and apologize for free schoolbooks, for building roads, for charity hospitals, for old-age pensions, for free school lunches?"

Convinced of the folly of having Long battle Long on the

speaking platforms, Russell sat out Earl's successful 1956 gubernatorial campaign. He wouldn't make speeches on behalf of Earl, but he certainly would not support someone in opposition to Earl. And so gradually the two Longs came to a guarded truce which lasted until Earl's breakdown.

Russell moved in to handle the family crisis on the eve of Earl's dispatch to the hospital in Galveston. Earl has accused Russell of engineering a plot to get rid of Earl so that Russell could run for governor.

Actually, Russell was in New Orleans to make a commencement-day address at Loyola University when Earl's wife summoned him to the executive mansion in Baton Rouge. Russell made the decision to send Earl to Galveston, and Russell felt that, as a member of the family, it was up to him to report to the legislature on the condition of the governor.

Once again the ghost of Huey rose up to haunt his son. In any other state Russell's appearance under the circumstances would be unusual but understandable, and no one would search for ulterior motives. But this was Louisiana. In too many minds there still burned the memory of United States Senator Huey Long coming down from Washington to harangue the legislature from the podium. Now here was another Senator Long deciding, without invitation, that he would address the legislature. A minority—very small but very loud—objected.

When the legislature assembled in joint session, six members of the House pointedly walked out. Russell, on the podium ready to speak, was infuriated and *he* started to walk out.

A senator shouted: "Go back. I think you have made the biggest mistake of your life."

Russell hesitated, then returned to the rostrum. The legislature cheered. He took the microphone and said that someone suggested that he apologize for his appearance.

"I am sorry. I cannot make an apology," he said.

He asked if anyone still objected to his speaking. Three

men jumped up. Russell glared, then started up the aisle again.

There were cries of "Come back, Russell," and he did come back. Then he began to speak. He said, "Governor Long has had a breakdown in his health. The duties and great burdens of this great office have been more than he could stand.

"He is now away from Louisiana under the treatment of good doctors. I am sure that you know how distressing this matter is to the governor's family. We find the situation extremely regrettable. We will do whatever we can to assist him in any way possible. With reference to the political situation, Governor Frazar is now your governor. He is a peaceful and gentle man, but he will need your devoted help if he is to be a successful governor.

"This state is in a serious political and governmental crisis. There is nothing about it that responsible men with good will cannot handle with ease."

There were cries the next day that Russell was grabbing Earl's mantle as if this were a kingdom. Russell replied: "My uncle and I have differed politically in the past. He has his following and I have mine. As far as I'm concerned Lieutenant Governor Frazar is the head of the Long forces now. I'm available for help but not here to put pressure on things."

After Earl was freed from the hospitals, he was bitter about Russell's part in having him committed. "That wasn't his duty to go before the legislature—it was the lieutenant governor's duty if it was anybody's," Earl said.

Earl complained that Russell pulled out his telephones at the executive mansion and in the hospital at Galveston. "Ripped 'em right off the wall," Earl said. "Left the wire hanging."

Russell subsequently testified before the Louisiana Civil Service Commission concerning his actions. A state policeman whom Earl fired for failing to block his removal to Galveston appealed for reinstatement, and Russell appeared on behalf of the man to absolve him of any responsibility.

"My understandings of the law," Russell testified, "is that

a person can be physically sick unto death, and if he refuses treatment that he is right. If he is mentally sick, that duty falls on his wife and next of kin.

"My feeling was that it was my duty to see that the man [Earl] received the treatment and rest needed to protect his life and health. I didn't see that I had any right to decline that duty. I tried to explain it to him that way. We tried to get him to stay in the mansion and take the rest needed. The moment he tried to get out and we stopped him he became violent."

Earl said that after the turmoil Russell, who had returned to Washington, tried to kiss and make up. "Senator Ellender came around as a peacemaker," Earl said. "I still think Russell should have stayed in Washington rather than listen to my wife. But he's my nephew and I've got no children. He helped me get elected governor in 1948. I helped him become senator in 1950."

Earl's chief objection to Russell politically is that hankering for the whitenecks. Earl appraised Russell this way: "He's a little like Huey. He's smart. But he doesn't know the people —the country people. He was born with a silver spoon in his mouth. He's pretty well posted, pretty studious about his job. He's a digger, but he's not politically dependable—not as politically dependable as Senator Ellender, for example.

"Russell was very ungrateful, after all I've done for him. It beats me why he should want to leave Washington to be governor."

The constant comparisons to his father tend to become odious to Russell, even though he is quick to utilize them when they suit his purposes. He seldom grants an interview that the subject doesn't come up.

Columnist Robert Ruark came away from one of these sessions with the impression that "he is obsessed with the idea of fumigating his father's memory."

To Cabell Phillips, of the New York *Times,* Russell said: "I think my father was one of the greatest men of his time. He was certainly the greatest man I ever knew. He truly gave his life fighting for the poor and underprivileged, not only of this state, but of the nation.

"Naturally he was cursed and vilified by every entrenched interest there is. They said he was a dictator and a crook. They tried to impeach him when he was governor and they did everything they could to blacken his character.

"But he figured if your enemies try to low rate you the only thing to do is to low rate them right back—only do it better. He did it better, too, and that's why they can't forgive him even after he is dead."

To Edward Stagg, of the New Orleans *Item,* Russell said: "He was the only hope for millions of poor people when other leaders were looking out only for themselves. My father was really an idealist. He was the only man on his side who felt the benefits had to be provided. That's why he had to have power."

To Charles W. Graham, Russell said: "He had many human faults but everything he did was intended to help the common people and the poor. . . . He believed that every family was entitled to a home and a living, and he didn't believe in great accumulations of wealth. I would not be in politics if his enemies, including the press, had given him credit for the good things he did. I am going to try to carry out some of his ideals, and if I can't do it, I shall help someone else who can."

When he was first elected to the Senate, Russell made it plain he felt he was following in his father's footsteps. He said:

"My main concern, just like my father's, will be for social legislation. I think we ought to have wider Social Security benefits, more public health and hospital services, more federal aid to education, free school lunches and that sort of thing. We've got all of these things in Louisiana now, but many people outside of Louisiana don't give Huey Long credit for it.

"I think it's the sort of thing we've got to have for the country as a whole. It's not only simple justice to our people.

We've got to do it in the national self-interest if we don't want the Communists to take over in the next depression.

"I guess the main difference between me and my father is that the only way he knew to get things he wanted was to fight and raise hell for them. He wanted all these good things to happen right now—fast.

"I know you can't get things that fast, and I'm satisfied to take my time."

Actually, Russell did not know his father very well. Huey was not a family man. He lived alone in Washington, and frequently he stayed in his suite in the Roosevelt Hotel in New Orleans rather than in the house uptown. But as the eldest son, Russell was granted a few trips with his father and he was old enough to hear his father speak and understand what Huey was saying. They were idol and worshiper rather than father and son.

However, in one way Russell has surpassed his father already. He has wider public acceptance than Huey enjoyed even in his heyday. After his close 1948 election for Overton's incomplete Senate term, Russell ran for the full term in 1950. He said, "I'm not running on Earl Long's record and I'm not running on Huey Long's record. I'm running on Russell Long's record."

Russell polled 69 per cent of the votes. The highest Huey ever polled was 57 per cent.

CHAPTER SIXTEEN

*"It seems that a man who is a liberal in Louisiana
is just a moderate here in Washington."*

IN THE SENATE RUSSELL LONG ALWAYS TALKS LIKE A LIBERAL
and frequently acts like a conservative. But primarily he is,
by his own definition, a "Louisiana firster." He devotes a
large portion of his time to plucking the federal vine for
fruit to ship to the folks back home. Other senators choose as
their executive assistants either publicity men or political
sharpshooters, but Russell filled this job with a bright young
chap from the Corps of Engineers, a man who would be
especially adept at snaring the rivers and harbors projects
which are so vital to waterlogged Louisiana.

This does not mean that Russell avoids the more mo-
mentous issues of our time. But it does mean that he performs
the day's pork barreling first, and only then does he dart off
into the entertainment of legislation.

Russell went into the Senate with a lot to live up to, and
a lot to live down. He was Huey's son, and Washington immediately wanted to know if he were "another Huey." The
answer, of course, is No. He's got all of Huey's mannerisms
and a few of Huey's tactics, but that's as far as it goes.

Label-happy Washington is not satisfied, however, to accept
Russell as the workaday salesman that he is but feels it must
peg him as a liberal or a conservative. Drew Pearson put the
question up to Russell personally, and the reply came out
like this:

"Why, it seems that a man who is a liberal in Louisiana is

just a moderate here in Washington. I was regarded as a wild liberal down in Louisiana but here I am barely over the line."

The analysis is pretty good.

He could be called a liberal because he voted for a long-range housing bill, for federal aid to education, for a liberal labor law, for a liberal displaced-persons bill, for expansion of Social Security, for reciprocal trade, and for expansion of the free-school-lunch program.

Or he could be called conservative because he voted against organizing a Department of Welfare, against confirmation of New Dealer Leland Olds to the Federal Power Commission, for the Kerr natural-gas bill, against equal rights for women, for trimming European aid, for permitting "local option" in rent control, and against public power as opposed to private power.

Huey's entire program in the Senate was Share-the-Wealth. Russell rode Huey's memory to the Senate, and so it was only natural to ask him to compare his economic philosophy with Share-the-Wealth.

Russell believes, he said, in the notion of a United States where "nobody is too rich or too poor." He believes that low interest loans and long-term credit are the most practical means of attaining this ideal.

"I think," he said, "that if we can get a fair share of the national income into the hands of the working classes the Share-the-Wealth idea will take care of itself."

The key factor in Huey's Share-the-Wealth plan was a capital tax, or, as he put it, the seizure by the government of the fortunes that Huey thought were too big. Russell doesn't go nearly that far, although he has talked of capital taxes in the past. Russell does not fear the word "socialism" when he's talking about his philosophy.

"It's just a matter of using our government as our servant and agent," he says. He gets impatient with his opponents who use sweeping catch phrases to cloak their fight against a specific benefit. He said in the Senate, "Instead of talking about 'cradle-to-grave security,' come out and say whether you are for or against old-age pensions and the money it takes to pay for them."

Russell was an opponent of McCarthyism, although not especially vocal until after censure put McCarthy on the skids. Then Russell did have a few open clashes with the Wisconsin pepperpot. Russell once mailed his constituents a blistering attack on McCarthy and then learned to everyone's chagrin that the Senate mail room erroneously sent these out in franked envelopes of Senator Wiley of Wisconsin!

Russell's claim to liberalism runs into particular difficulty on three counts—civil rights, government spending, and oil and power legislation.

On the matter of civil rights he certainly is no Jim Eastland of Mississippi, but he stands solidly with the Southern Democrats. It is a position his father and his uncle avoided. Huey was not faced with the head-and-head crisis produced by the Supreme Court integration decision, of course, but Earl invited political disaster by his steadfast protection of the Negro's vote. Russell gives the soft sell to questioners about his position on civil rights. He thinks education for the Negroes—good education but segregated education—is the panacea. He is against laws "to regulate prejudice," he says.

A vital part of the civil-rights fight in the Senate involves the filibuster rule. Russell, son of a frequent filibusterer, came to the Senate saying, "I'm talkative but I've never filibustered," but in his first session he made a four-hour speech. (He prepared himself for this by going on a low-liquid diet so that he would not be betrayed by an attraction for the men's room.) Russell's maiden speech had been in defense of the filibuster rule. He said it served as protection for minorities from "some oppressive group grinding them to dust." The filibuster, he said, "is one of our most precious heritages." Besides, Russell said later, what is a filibuster anyway? "When a senator makes a speech you agree with, it's enlightening debate; but if you disagree with it it's filibuster."

Yet despite this position, Russell is not glued to the Dixiecrat party line. He sided with the Republicans in supporting statehood for Hawaii and he specifically deplored talk of a Southern filibuster in this instance. "It wouldn't do the Southern cause any good because it would be against states' rights, not for states' rights," he said. His fellow Southern Democrats were particularly outraged by his position on Hawaii, but he did not waver in the face of their blandishments.

Furthermore, he showed particular courage in the 1952 Democratic National Convention when he staged a revolt within a revolt. Governor Robert Kennon (who subsequently supported President Eisenhower in the election) called for a walkout over the issue of the loyalty oath. Kennon proposed that Louisiana put Eisenhower on the ballot as a Democrat.

Russell refused to go along. He said he'd remain in the convention "if I'm the only one in the delegation who does." He made a speech from the floor, saying:

"What has the Louisiana delegation been asked to do by this pledge [the loyalty oath]? They've been asked to give the people of my state a chance to vote on the Democratic nominees. That's all they've been asked to do.

"I don't care what it costs me politically. It's time we stopped passing those state laws that say politicians have the right to prevent the people from voting for the candidates of their choice."

Russell's words were loudly cheered. The Washington *Post* cited him for his "courageous stand," calling his speech "one of the dramatic and heartening events" of the convention. Russell supported Adlai Stevenson in the election, and his judgment was vindicated at least by Louisiana's vote: Stevenson carried the state.

The unending paradox of Russell Long as a senator comes into sharpest focus on the issue of government spending. The one basic tenet of Longism, as practiced and preached by both Huey and Earl, was tax and spend. Russell seems a little reluctant to do either. He is a staunch ally of Senator Byrd in such matters as curtailing foreign aid, military spending, and the national debt.

Russell has been especially rabid on the issue of foreign aid. For years he has attacked the "waste" in the program. In 1950 he succeeded in getting the Senate to slash $500,000,000 from the administration's bill. That was the largest single cut ever made on the Senate floor.

But more often Russell has simply shouted to the winds. In 1955, when he was attempting to strip $318,000,000 from the foreign-aid bill, Senator Walter George, of Georgia, suddenly rose from his seat and boomed into the face of his younger colleague, "Do you want any allies? Do you want any friends abroad?" Russell's attempts at economy failed, and two years later he failed again when he tried to trim $390,-000,000 from the aid bill, charging "enormous waste and bureaucratic bungling."

His closest colleagues in the Senate think he carried this fight off the deep end when he opposed the appointment of C. Douglas Dillon as Undersecretary of State following the death of Secretary of State Dulles. Russell was the only man in the Senate to raise objection to Dillon; furthermore, he did so with what many considered unreasoning fury.

In the Foreign Relations Committee Russell accused Dillon of "horrible mismanagement" of the foreign-aid program. He told Dillon he doubted whether he was "capable of recognizing obvious mistakes when you see them."

The committee recommended Dillon's confirmation by a 16-to-1 vote (Russell, of course, was the 1), but still the senator from Louisiana wouldn't give up. He carried his fight to the floor, unleashing a speech worthy of the old Huey. He castigated Dillon as a "Wall Street banker" who was responsible for just about every sin since the original one. When Senator Prescott Bush of Connecticut rose to call the talk "quite offensive," Russell forced Bush to take his seat under a Senate rule which forbids derogatory remarks about a fellow senator. That done, Russell continued his assault on Dillon.

Russell accomplished nothing. Dillon was approved by a voice vote. There was considerable tongue wagging as Washington tried to figure out just why Russell, standing alone, should be so bitter about Dillon. There apparently was nothing personal between the two men. There were suggestions that Russell had come too close to the grape or that he was under an unusual strain because of his uncle (this was while Earl was in the Galveston hospital), but Russell explained that his overseas inspection tours had convinced him of Dillon's mismanagement and that any other motives others might assign to him were pure hokum.

In support of his position Russell cited a luncheon the Foreign Relations Committee gave for a legislator from Singapore. The man was asked to give a frank appraisal of America. He did: "Our people think you are corrupt," he said. The startled senators asked him to explain. He said: "You people come along and drive down the street in a big car with a corrupt local politician. We say there goes another corrupt American. Why don't you do something for the people, not for the corrupt politicians? Why don't you tell these politicians that when you give them foreign aid you're going to watch them and make sure how they use the money?"

Russell said, "We've got to stop feeding the corrupt politicians abroad and do more about helping the common people who want to defeat Communism."

Russell carries authority on the foreign-aid program because of his seat on the Senate Foreign Relations Committee. He carries the same authority on military matters because of his seat on the Senate Armed Services Committee, and here again he operates as a fund cutter worthy of Harry Byrd.

Russell has joked about his own military career. He tells the story of his "private invasion" of southern France when his landing boat hit the wrong beach. But he also poses as something of a military expert. He led the opposition against confirmation of General Mark Clark as Far East commander in 1952 on purely military grounds. Clark's crossing of the Rapido River during the Italian campaign of World War II had been criticized in Congress before, but Russell sought to block this appointment on the basis of all his authority as a former lieutenant in the Navy. He said:

"I was in the area with the Navy at the time of the Rapido crossing and I know that many of the officers with whom I associated did not think too highly of Clark's ability as a field commander."

There was considerable grumbling in the Pentagon over young Long passing professional judgment on Clark.

But this was just a passing incident for Russell. His main concern, militarily, has been the money spent for foreign bases. His charge is simple—too much too soon.

In 1952 he and Senator Saltonstall of Massachusetts announced that the Armed Services Committee was holding up "considerable" money for overseas bases. Russell said, "There are several items I consider to be totally unnecessary and for that matter entirely wasteful."

He said, "We can get more defense at less cost." And when the Washington *Post* criticized the committee's action, Russell again showed shades of old Huey as he wrote a letter to the editor in which he accused the *Post* of being "the mouthpiece and spokesman for the military wastrels."

Russell said his objections to the foreign bases were born of a tour he and Senator Wayne Morse made from Newfoundland to the Middle East. They gave the Armed Forces Committee a "startling" report on waste. The report, heavily censored before its release, contained such charges as "100 or even 200 groups of men in units of 2,000 to 5,000 are sitting idly in the muck and mire of Europe, Asia, Africa and the Arctic Circle waiting for a war which we hope to avoid."

The report also said:

1. That "untold millions" were spent on bases without any arrangements made to defend them from "easy capture."

2. That taxpayers were led "unsuspectingly" to build huge cities to house "perhaps 750,000 service men for the next generation."

3. That European forces were "top-heavy and overstaffed."

4. That the Navy and Air Force increased costs by refusing to use one another's facilities.

These were old charges, undoubtedly true to some extent and the result of oversimplification to another extent. Russell rode them hard on his economy kick.

Russell cited his record in support of reciprocal trade, to show that despite his assault on money spent overseas on aid and military bases he is no isolationist. As a matter of fact, Russell gave himself credit for saving President Eisenhower's entire trade program in 1955. He told it this way in a newsletter to his constituents:

"The Senate finance committee had reached a tie vote on the foreign trade bill. The Republicans were voting almost unanimously in favor of an amendment to cripple the President's foreign trade program, while the Democrats were voting almost unanimously to uphold the hand of the President. I was in New Orleans but was able to vote by telephone and break the tie in favor of the President's program."

If Huey could return to castigate his son about one thing, it would be the matter of the power companies. Huey fought the big utilities constantly. They were a dragon to be slain and slain again in every new election campaign. Russell, on the other hand, is one of big power's best friends in the Senate.

The issue is public power versus private power, and here Russell operates in direct conflict with the public-power sentiments that dominate the South. He crossed the party line to vote in favor of the Dixon-Yates project, and he proved to be the Number One block to public development of the Hell's Canyon Dam project in the first years of the Eisenhower administration.

The Democrats put forth a bill to authorize the federal government to develop Hell's Canyon. The Republicans opposed it; they wanted the project to go to the Idaho Power Company. Russell was the key man in two respects. He was chairman of the Senate Interior Committee which held the bill, and he was the swing vote: the committee was composed of eight Democrats and seven Republicans. Had they voted straight party line, the bill would have been reported favorably. But Russell was swinging to the Republican side when he was kicked upstairs.

Alben Barkley's seat became vacant on the Foreign Affairs Committee, and Russell was given the promotion from the Interior Committee. He was entitled to the promotion anyway on the basis of the Senate seniority system, but the Democratic leadership made no attempt to hide the fact that it was scooting Russell out of Interior as fast as it could to salvage the Hell's Canyon bill.

Russell also votes for legislation favorable to the big oil companies. This is understandable on both selfish and unselfish grounds. Russell is an oil man himself. The most valuable property he inherited from his father was stock in the Win-or-Lose Oil Company, one of the moneymakers engineered by Seymour Weiss. Russell confided to Drew Pearson that his stock in Win-or-Lose is now worth more than $25,000 a share. He draws a handsome income from it, enough so that he need not worry about his Senate salary or any other means of earning a living. But Russell's interest in oil is more general than his Win-or-Lose stock. Louisiana is an oil state, and it would be naïve to expect Louisiana's congressmen or senators to vote any way except with oil.

Thus it was no surprise when Russell backed the Kerr bill which would exempt the gas companies from Federal Power Commission regulation. As a matter of fact, when the Kerr bill failed Russell introduced his own "little Kerr bill" to apply only to the smaller companies, but with a similar lack of success. Russell has been a steady opponent of regulation by the FPC and also the Federal Trade Commission, and he voted against President Truman's plan to give these regulatory agencies increased authority. However, Russell was quick to support the FTC when it attacked an alleged "international oil cartel" which was importing foreign oil at the expense of the domestic product.

Russell has not introduced a major piece of legislation since he has been in the Senate. However, he has attempted some commendable minor bills. He tried to find a way to award federal employees for merit, and he finally came up with a bill to give them up to 25 per cent of any money they saved the government through increased efficiency. The bill passed but the plan was slow to catch on. After sixteen months only one award had been made, that of $1,500 to fifty-four Treasury Department employees. Russell blames the failure on the Budget Bureau's bewildering ten pages of introduction on how to administer the program.

Generally, Russell has been a plugger in the Senate, and certainly not one to rival his father's color or bombast. Veteran capital correspondent Jack Bell summed him up as a man "willing to work in harness." Bell adds, "He knows how to keep his mouth shut but can speak and argue with force when the time comes."

Perhaps Russell's greatest shortcoming is his lack of spontaneous humor. He is a good storyteller in the good old Southern political tradition, but he has neither his father's nor his uncle's ability to throw out the quips.

One reporter recalls the opening day of Russell's campaign for the Senate. His Uncle Earl gave him a party at the executive mansion. The reporter went up to Russell and jokingly said, "Say, I hear your opponent had thirteen hundred people to hear him speak today."

Russell spun around, livid. "Only six hundred," he snapped. "We had somebody there to count them."

The reporter was flabbergasted. What had been meant as a friendly and transparent jest had been seized on by Russell as a point of argument.

Even when his fellow senators deplored Huey as a detriment to the nation, they had to be amused by his antics on the floor. Russell puts on no such performance. He is, however, prankish.

One night the Senate was deserted except for three men—Senator Morse, who was making a speech about home rule for the District of Columbia; Senator Lausche, who was acting as temporary president; and Russell, who was the

Southern sentry guarding against sneak civil-rights legislation. Russell suddenly rose to say, "I notice that not one
Republican is now on the floor of the Senate. If the Senator
from Oregon would yield for that purpose, I would move to
abolish the Republican party."

Morse replied that he had a long-established policy of pro-
tecting the rights of minorities—even Republican minorities.

Russell said it was a shame that the Republicans were
forced to rely on a Democratic senator to save their party
for them.

In Washington, Russell is like his father in one respect—he
lives in an apartment alone. His wife and two daughters did
stay in Washington for a few years but subsequently moved
back to Baton Rouge. His closest friends are two strongly
liberal senators, Hubert Humphrey and Paul Douglas, who
think very much of him personally as well as politically. They
seem to be quite tolerant and understanding of his transgressions from liberalism.

Russell maintains an even relationship with his fellow
members of the Louisiana congressional delegation. Allen
Ellender was installed in the Senate by Huey but remained
to become a sturdy and well-reasoned member of the Southern
bloc, a man accepted by all factions of Louisiana politics.
Ellender shows a fatherly tolerance toward Russell. He con-
siders Russell's liberal talk a little wild at times but certainly
not dangerous.

Earl complained frequently that "you could never find
Russell when you needed him in Washington," but this
seemed to be more Earl's personal problem than anyone else's.
Russell does not have a bad absentee record, and he is not
a man to avoid work. His staff sometimes is overwhelmed by
the enthusiasm with which he will dive into the routine of the
office.

Russell could have a pat and secure future. Because of the
Senate's devotion to seniority, all he need do is sit tight
until time gives him power. But Russell wants to be, as his
Dad was, governor of Louisiana. In 1955 he was fishing for

support, particularly soliciting Mayor Morrison and the "nice people" in New Orleans, when his Uncle Earl jumped into the race. Russell had to bow out then. He again began talking about running when Earl was shipped off to Galveston. He even went so far as to ask the voters how they felt. The response was not enthusiastic, however, and shortly thereafter Russell announced he would not run for governor in 1959.

This does not mean his ambition has cooled. It means only that he must wait until the memory of Uncle Earl is dimmed. Four years from now will be right, Russell figures. The Longs always do best after Louisiana has been bored by a calmer administration. Then Russell can launch the third generation of Longism. Every man a king? Maybe. But every Long a king? Certainly.

CHAPTER SEVENTEEN

"You can make it illegal but you can't make it unpopular."

LAW AFTER LAW IN LOUISIANA STIPULATES "EXCEPT NEW OR-leans" or "only New Orleans" or "applicable only to cities exceeding 500,000 population." For generations the legislatures have passed one set of laws for the big city and another set for the remainder of the state. Sometimes this double standard has been the result of bitter war between City Hall and Baton Rouge; sometimes it has been the result of a benign peace. It would be difficult to determine under which circumstance the city's residents were fleeced the most—under war or under peace.

But if New Orleans has always had its special set of laws, it also has always had its special set of morals. The city is traditionally wide open. Vice is considered an industry, and a cherished one because of the tourist dollars it reaps. The taxi driver's supreme insult is to call an outlander a "ten and ten man." This means the fellow arrived in New Orleans with the Ten Commandments in one hand and a ten-dollar bill in the other, and that he left New Orleans without breaking either.

New Orleans was a sin city from its founding. The French brought over prostitutes by the boatload. In the days before the Civil War, the bawdyhouses advertised in the newspapers. New Orleans' proudest contribution to American culture, jazz, was spawned in these houses. The octaroon balls were an open market place where one could select anything from a mistress to a companion for the night.

It was inevitable that a city which accepted vice as a tradition would produce a powerful political organization to feed off vice. This was the Choctaw Club, also known as the Old Regulars, also known as The Ring. The organization fought the Longs for half their political lives and was married to them for half. The people took it on the chin under both circumstances.

The Choctaws were formed in 1898 upon adoption of the post-Reconstruction election laws which made the Democratic primary the decisive election in the state. Within a few years the Choctaws were celebrated as the "Tammany Hall of the South," and, indeed, the New Orleans branch of the family did occasionally import Tammany goons for specialized election work.

The first boss of the organization was Martin Behrman, a massive ex-beer salesman who was mayor from 1904 to 1926. He was in the classic city-boss tradition: fat, bediamonded, unlettered, and a wizard at organizing the vote block by block, precinct by precinct, ward by ward. His bon mots were cherished throughout the city. When asked by a committee of church ladies to stamp out prostitution, he said, "You can make it illegal but you can't make it unpopular." When asked to design the proposed new Municipal Auditorium in the style of a Greek theater, he rejected the idea because "there aren't enough Greeks living here to make it worth while."

As was disclosed by a special Attorney General's hearing held by Huey, the Choctaw Club drew regular tribute from the gamblers and the madams. In return for this franchise, its men in the legislature ran the errands and protected the interests of the city's utilities and businesses. To make its voice effective in the legislature, the Choctaw Club maintained a careful alliance with the upstate planter class. This was the combination that Huey Long set out to defeat when he first entered politics. The battle lasted his lifetime. Furthermore, when Earl Long finally made peace with the Choctaws, he found they had been driven off the reservation and replaced by a rival faction. Thus he had to fight Huey's old war against the city of New Orleans all over again.

When Huey first ran for governor in 1924, without any organized support in New Orleans, his city vote was niggling. This did not surprise him. For his second attempt at election he induced one of the Choctaw leaders, John Sullivan, to break away from the club and support him. Huey did no better in New Orleans with Sullivan than without him. He realized then that it would have to be all or nothing—he must capture New Orleans or he must fight it forever.

T. Semmes Walmsley had become both mayor of the city and chief of the Choctaws when Behrman died, and it was Walmsley whom Huey fought down through the years. Huey used two weapons. The first was the vice raid, conducted by the state militia, which smashed the furnishings and terrified the customers of this keystone of the Choctaw Club income. The second was the legislature, which passed one discriminatory bill after another to bankrupt the city government and reduce it to a façade.

The first of Huey's "vice cleanups" came on February 13, 1929, a year after he had become governor. He sent the National Guard into the city to raid a number of select gambling houses, and he made plans to lead the men personally. However, first he stopped off at a party given by his pal, Alfred Danzinger. During the festivities somebody blabbed, and word of the impending raids reached the gambling houses before the troops. The militia found no gambling activity at all. The customers were searched for chips. Those who objected were held overnight and forcibly searched. One woman told the newspapers she was undressed in the process. The raids were a propaganda flop.

But if this failed, the other half of Huey's pincer did not. His legislature began stabbing New Orleans in the pocketbook. The city government was bankrupt; its employees were on half-pay. And when the city fathers suddenly came upon a way to raise quick cash, Huey's legislators thwarted them. The city offered a 2 per cent discount on all taxes paid in advance. But the legislature then passed a bill halting all tax collections for six months. The city employees went unpaid.

When Huey ran for the Senate in 1930, he faced heavy opposition in New Orleans. His feud with City Hall was so bitter that he brought in his own state policemen to direct traffic at a Long-for-Senator rally. The city cops objected to this invasion of their jurisdiction. And thus, while Huey spoke, the better show was going on outside where the state and city policemen battled one another with blackjacks and nightsticks in a free-for-all still cherished by Donnybrook fanciers.

Huey's margin of victory in his election to the Senate was so great—and the legislature's stranglehold on the city so tight—that the Old Regulars attempted to surrender. Mayor Walmsley went up to Huey's hotel suite to hand over his sword, and peace reigned from 1930 until 1933.

But then Walmsley, still leader of the Old Regulars, announced he would run for mayor again. Huey didn't want that. Even in peace he didn't trust Walmsley. He wanted his own man in City Hall.

First Huey met Walmsley's challenge by reassembling the legislature. It stripped $800,000 in appropriations from the city. It gave the governor control over the police, fire, and judicial appointments in the city.

It also passed the following laws:

1. The attorney general was authorized to supersede the district attorney in any lawsuit.

2. The attorney general was authorized to appoint or discharge any of the district attorney's assistants.

3. The courts were forbidden to interfere with the governor's use of the militia.

4. The municipality was forbidden to levy any new tax without permission of the legislature.

5. Courts were forbidden to seize records of the registrar of voters.

6. A state tax was levied on advertisements in newspapers of more than twenty thousand circulation.

7. No policeman was authorized to carry firearms without the consent of the governor.

8. The state usurped the city's property assessment powers.

Huey put up John Klorer to run against Walmsley for mayor. Walmsley quickly seized the city's voting records, saying he anticipated fraud. The distribution of Huey's campaign literature was blocked for want of a city license. Huey responded by getting on the radio to malign "Turkey Head Walmsley" with every libel known to man.

Walmsley won by 15,747 votes—New Orleans was not yet ready to surrender to the country bumpkin Long—and old "Turkey Head" immediately left for Washington to fulfill his Number One campaign promise. He would punch Huey Long in the nose, he said. For several days he camped in the lobby of Huey's hotel, waiting to make good his promise. Huey remained in the suite, even for his meals. Walmsley finally grew discouraged and returned to New Orleans.

He found that his victory was only part of the fight. A congressional election was next, and the Old Regulars needed control of the city delegation to maintain their liaison with the New Deal administration which was beginning to feed them money and jobs to fight Huey. So once again Huey announced a "vice cleanup" in New Orleans. He went on the radio to warn "lottery kings, racketeers, ward bosses, dives, and bawdyhouses" to get out of town. Huey said he'd move in if the mayor didn't enforce the cleanup. Walmsley ignored him. Suddenly, in the middle of the night, the National Guard clanked into New Orleans.

Walmsley shouted, "I warn you, Huey Long, that if a life is spent in defense of this city you shall pay the penalty as other carpetbaggers have done before you."

The National Guard, bent on its mission of ridding the city of insidious vice, selected a strange target. It marched past the gambling dens and bawdyhouses and set up camp in the voting registrars' building. Proclamations were plastered throughout the city declaring "partial martial law."

The city government countered by hiring five hundred extra policemen and buying $5,000 worth of bombs and machine guns. It rushed in a South American soldier of fortune to head this force. Seventy-five cops stood guard at City Hall pointing their rifles at the voting registrars' building across the street, and the National Guardsmen pointed their machine guns back.

Civic organizations roared in protest at the invasion of the troops. Huey laughed and said it was awful, but "I can't do anything with Governor Allen. He defied me, told me to go right to hell." Besides, said Huey, the troops were just watching the voting records until they moved on to the gambling dens, and surely the good people of New Orleans wanted those dens cleaned up.

Mayor Walmsley appealed to Washington to help New Orleans rid itself of the invaders. Huey scoffed. "Roosevelt is no damn' fool," he said. "He's running his business and I'm running mine. He knows his place."

Then Huey called a hearing to expose the New Orleans vice graft. He would conduct it himself as a special attorney general. He strode into the hearing room surrounded by his National Guardsmen, and ordered all reporters and spectators out. The hearings would be broadcast on the radio. That would be enough. (Reporters ask questions but radio microphones don't.)

Over the airwaves came a motley parade of whores and madams. They testified of payoffs running from $1 per girl per day for the cop on the beat to $1,335 weekly for the Old Regular bigshots at the Choctaw Club. The testimony was sordid. Also, it was true.

Election Day dawned with the troops still in the city, but discreetly clear of the polls. Huey spent the day hopping from his bed to the radio microphone and back again, going on the air for five minutes every hour to urge the election of his candidates. And his candidates all won.

The vice hearing folded then, but Huey's legislature received one of those special New-Orleans-only laws: this one would transfer all New Orleans Parish gambling cases into the Long-dominated state courts.

"Why not extend it to cover gambling in St. Bernard Parish and other parishes?" asked an indignant New Orleans representative.

"Do you know of any gambling in St. Bernard Parish?" asked Huey.

The legislature howled with laughter. St. Bernard was notorious as the biggest gambling parish of them all.

"Well," said the representative, "I see pictures of St. Bernard Parish gambling on the front pages of the newspapers."

"You better quit believing what you read in the newspapers," Huey said.

At Huey's death he had New Orleans under his thumb. Walmsley was still mayor and the nominal head of the Old Regulars. But most of the organization had deserted to Huey. When the Leche crowd took over the statehouse, both sides yearned for peace. The statehouse sent City Hall its terms: make Bob Maestri mayor.

It was an incredible suggestion. Robert W. Maestri, the son of an Italian-American poultry peddler, had quit school after the third grade. Bob's father set him up in a furniture store and, legend has it, Bob's customers were the madams who operated the bawdyhouses: by special arrangement with Bob's police pals, the madams had to rebuy the same furniture over and over after periodic "raids." Bob was a wealthy man by the time he reached thirty.

He had been an early Huey Long supporter and remained, as Huey said, "the greatest of all friends in foul weather."

Huey credited Maestri with financing his fight against impeachment. Things looked bad, Huey said, when Maestri arrived at the hotel suite.

"Do you need money?" he asked.

"All the silver in India and all the tea in China," Huey replied.

"How fast do you need it?" asked Maestri.

"Just as fast as a printing office can turn out circulars and the government can sell stamps," said Huey.

"I'll take care of that," said Maestri.

And Maestri did take care of it. Huey subsequently made his friend chairman of the Conservation Commission. Maestri went into oil speculation and added to the millions he already had stashed in the bank. Later Maestri was the cool head who took charge of the squabblers when Huey was killed, and now he wanted to come from behind the scenes and be the mayor of New Orleans.

Obviously he could not carry his dese-dem-dose oratory into an election campaign. The boys in Baton Rouge would have to devise a way to make Bob mayor without an election. They did. They induced the weary and defeated and lonely Walmsley to resign. But before he did, Maestri was appointed city commissioner of finance, the office in line for succession in the event of any mayor's resignation. Now Bob was mayor. To keep him there the boys had to cope with a forthcoming election. They induced all of the qualified candidates to withdraw, leaving Maestri the only man in the race. Furthermore, the legislature passed still another New-Orleans-only law: it extended the term of the mayor from four years to six.

Thus Bob Maestri was safely in the mayor's office for seven years without risking an appearance before the electorate.

New Orleans was never gayer. The bawdyhouses were wide open, peppered throughout the French Quarter. They catered to young and old alike, and many a father escaped the ordeal of a birds-and-bees explanation by slipping his adolescent son two dollars and a French Quarter address. The racing handbooks likewise flourished (except when the Fair Grounds Race Track was open, in which case all bookmakers took a sabbatical in order not to furnish "unfair" competition). One

of the most popular handbooks in town operated across the
street from City Hall, in full view of the mayor's office.

One day the Board of Health closed a saloon a block from
City Hall when it discovered there was no running water in
the men's room. The next afternoon the cop on the beat
noticed a steady flow of customers in and out of the saloon.

"I thought this place was ordered closed," the cop told the
saloon keeper.

"I'm not serving—these people are just going in and out
of the handbook," explained the saloonkeeper. This explanation satisfied the cop.

Maestri nevertheless set out to make the city a good mayor.
The government he inherited was in terrible financial shape.
It had been starved by the state until it was only a shell. The
streets were in decay; the employees were disgruntled and
usually unpaid; there had been no new construction for
years. Maestri began by lending the city $100,000 of his own
money, interest free. He helped engineer the Second Louisiana Purchase which made peace between Baton Rouge and
Washington and freed millions in WPA money.

The purpose of the WPA was to provide jobs. Feather-
bedding was a virtue of the system, but Maestri would have
none of that. He wanted only to build, build, build. He
utilized work-saving machines and he made every man produce. He had no WPA jobs for the white-collar class—only
for the men who could do things with their hands. He stam-
peded the suppliers into giving the city 25 per cent off on
this item, 10 per cent off on that one, 50 per cent off on a
third. Contractors "loaned" the city such handy little gadgets
as steam shovels.

The city's conservative businessmen, who opposed Huey to
the end, did not find fault with Maestri. He was putting the
city on a sound basis. And, lest there be any doubt as to his
loyalties, he eliminated them when the city's taxi drivers
went on strike. All he had to do was put a policeman in
beside the scab driver in every cab to break the strike. CIO
organizers were run out of town by the cops.

The mayor was quite civic-minded. He bought into the New Orleans Pelican baseball club, and then made certain that it won the Southern Association Award for the largest opening-day attendance: city employees and public school-children were issued tickets and then packed off to the ball game by bus. Maestri's baseball team presented a new twist to an old excuse: A city employee had to tell a sad tale about his grandmother's funeral in order to get *out* of going to the baseball park.

Maestri's photograph was taken often at dedications and other civic functions, but he never made a speech. He was too self-conscious about the deses, dems, and doses which fell out of his mouth. When President Roosevelt visited New Orleans in 1937 and was paraded through the streets, Governor Leche sat on one side of FDR and the embarrassed Maestri on the other throughout a day of festivity. Leche did what he could to keep the conversational ball away from the mayor, but during the formal luncheon at Antoine's Restaurant the governor had to excuse himself, leaving a great void between Maestri and Roosevelt. The mayor felt he had to say at least one thing to the President before the day ended. He leaned over and asked, "How you like dem ersters, huh?" They say in Louisiana that Roosevelt was still laughing when he died eight years later.

When the scandals broke in 1939, the investigators tried hard to pin something on Maestri. They centered their interest in his term as chairman of the Conservation Commission. He had indeed issued illegal hot-oil orders, but Prosecutor Rogge said Seymour Weiss and Governor Leche had used deception "to cause and induce" Maestri to issue these orders. Weiss, Leche, and a Texas oil operator named Freeman Buford were indicted. But a Texas federal judge refused to turn over Buford for arraignment. He said from the bench, "Governor Leche of Louisiana and his political boss, Seymour Weiss, could not have pulled down this money and put it in their pockets but for J. A. Shaw and Maestri. Shaw and Maestri are just as guilty as are the other men indicted in this case."

Rogge later issued a statement saying that Maestri made $1,157,000 from the oil business while he was Conservation Commission chairman but that the federal government had no criminal case against the mayor.

Eventually Maestri did have to face an election, and he did so just as Johnny came marching home. Or, to be exact, when deLesseps came marching home. DeLesseps S. Morrison was a blue-blooded but not wealthy Louisiana boy who was selected by the "better element" to run for mayor against Maestri in 1945. Morrison campaigned in his army major's uniform. Maestri campaigned principally with a very few carefully coached radio speeches. Morrison, promising reform, won.

Thus, when Earl Long was elected governor in 1948, he found himself in the same position as Huey: in command of the statehouse but in sharp opposition to the New Orleans city government. Morrison has cleaned up New Orleans, chasing the racing handbooks underground and driving the prostitutes from their French Quarter cribs. (These girls were replaced by the modern models: the call girls who operate out of ritzy apartment buildings. New Orleans still has not given up on sin.)

And faced with Huey's problem, Earl used Huey's solution. He set his legislature to gnawing at the city's pocketbook. Huey's 1948 legislature cut the city sales tax in half (at the same time it was doubling the state sales tax). It killed Morrison's pet construction projects. It stripped the city of control of its public utilities. When Morrison complained that the city could not operate with its stripped income, Earl told him to "practice economy." Earl said: "If he's not big enough to run the city he ought to quit. He's just a boy trying to do a man's job."

Morrison was able to use some of Huey's techniques himself. There was no gambling in New Orleans, but the handbooks were wide open in the Long parishes of St. Bernard and Jefferson, those parishes on the New Orleans border. Morrison taunted Earl about using the governor's powers to halt this sinning. Suddenly St. Bernard's handbooks did close. What happened? Sheriff C. F. Rowley said he wired the governor asking him what he wanted done. "I got a sanctimonious telegram from him telling me to stop racehorse betting, so I did," Rowley said.

The sheriff wasn't happy about it. "We were getting along O.K. here," he said. "We were minding our own business. Those guys ought to get together and say their talk about home rule is just so much baloney and stop trying to fool us country people."

Within a month the St. Bernard handbooks were flourishing again.

Morrison became Earl's public enemy Number One. Once Morrison ran for governor against Earl, but he didn't get very far. He was the city slicker, and the country vote had always overwhelmed city candidates for governor in Louisiana. Thereafter Earl found himself unable to make a speech without castigating and ridiculing Morrison. This did not hold only for campaign speeches. It held for every occasion from a sweet-potato festival to a press conference to a social chat.

In 1957 three men were charged with wiretapping Morrison's home telephone during the 1956 gubernatorial election campaign. The government said that Earl and Mrs. Long were seen listening to recordings of these wiretaps in their hotel suite. In the trial of the three men Morrison testified that a couple of days after the election—when Earl was returned to the statehouse—a friend told him that the wiretaps were all over town. Morrison said he looked about his house and saw a wire running from the roof to another house in the middle of the block.

A number of persons testified that they heard the tapped telephone conversations played back in Long's hotel suite. Mrs. Long was a witness, and she testified that she had heard the recordings and that later she had been given a transcript of them.

The three accused men, two former telephone company employees and a private detective named Sidney Massicot, were convicted of the wiretaps and sent to jail. Oddly, at no time was Massicot asked in court who hired him to do the job. The wiretaps admitted into evidence were innocuous conversations between Morrison and his wife, and Morrison and an assistant.

Just as Walmsley reached a truce with Huey Long in 1930, so a truce was reported in 1950 between Morrison and Earl. The city's motive for surrender both times was the same: anything to get back the revenue which had been shredded by the legislature. According to insiders at the time, the agreement was that the Morrison forces would support Russell Long for senator in return for restoration of the old city sales tax. The truce never came to pass. Morrison denied it was ever considered. Earl said that the agreement was made but that Morrison was induced to renege. Russell said that Morrison was forced by "wealthier, powerful people prejudiced against my father" to forgo his support of any Long for any office whatever.

Yet slowly Russell moved into the Morrison circle. When they both supported Hale Boggs for governor in opposition to Earl's hand-picked candidate, Russell said: "What's so hard to understand about advocating that we live in peace and harmony with each other? The really important thing is that we have put aside factional differences for the common good of all of us in Louisiana. The fact is that Russell Long and Chep Morrison and Hale Boggs have always stood for progressive, alert, honest, efficient government."

If there was a spin left in old Huey, he was surely back at it in his grave again.

". . . one brother, one sister, one uncle, eighteen cousins and two brothers-in-law."

IT IS THE MISFORTUNE OF THE LOUISIANA TAXPAYER THAT THE Longs are so prolific. The big family has meant a big payroll. Back when Huey was governor the Louisiana Constitutional League published a list of Longs known to be on the state payroll: ". . . one brother, one sister, one uncle, eighteen cousins and two brothers-in-law drawing a total of $75,849 a year."

But this does not mean that the Longs always stick together. Aside from temporary feuds, there was a permanent feud involving oldest brother Julius. He was against everybody named Long. He was against Huey, he was against Earl and, at eighty-two, he was turning against Russell.

Not only did Julius join Earl in testifying against Huey during the Senate investigation of 1933, but he campaigned against both Huey and Earl and their candidates as long as his age and health permitted. Julius summed up his feelings for Huey in a single sentence, "He would even say he had Negro blood if it meant votes."

Huey didn't answer Julius. Huey said, "In no campaign have I ever denied a charge my brothers made and in no campaign, public or private, have I ever made a charge against one of them. I cannot attack my own blood."

Earl explained Julius as a sorehead, jealous of the success of his younger brothers. "He was older," Earl said, "and he thought we should have waited for him to blaze the trail. But we'd still be waiting for him to blaze.

"Back before Huey was elected railroad commissioner, Julius ran for judge in Winnfield. As fast as me and Huey went around making friends for him, he'd go around making enemies. He'd go out of his way to do it. He hunted 'em up to cuss 'em out.

"And he stayed the sorehead all his life. When my other brother died he came to the funeral. I had a hotel suite and I invited Julius and his family down for breakfast or coffee. His wife and children wanted to come but he refused. That's the way he is."

Julius never got a job from Huey or Earl—maybe that was the trouble—but he eked out a fairly prosperous existence without them, practicing law in Winnfield and in Shreveport. He never stopped damning his politically successful kinfolk. He used to write long letters to the newspapers, diatribes against whichever Long happened to be in power at the moment.

George Long, the third of the four Long brothers, was Julius' exact opposite. George was a jolly good fellow who didn't mind anyone else's success but naturally wanted a little piece for himself. George left Louisiana young. He became a dentist and for twenty-five years practiced in Tulsa, Oklahoma. He served a term in the Oklahoma legislature, and an eventful term it was. That particular legislature impeached not one but two governors!

George said he—not Earl, as other members of the family maintained—staked Huey to a year of college at the University of Oklahoma. "I staked him to $1,500," George said. "Therefore I claim the distinction of being the first Long ever to lend a Long money."

George returned to Louisiana to go into politics, and immediately began getting into trouble with Earl. After Earl was elected governor in 1948, he made George superintendent of the Pineville State Colony. George promptly got into a hassle with the colony business manager. The man charged that George insisted upon buying large amounts of canned goods from a crony, even though the food was delivered in small household-size cans. The business manager refused to accept delivery, and George fired him. Earl heard about it and fired George.

George ran for Congress three times before he made it. The first two times Earl opposed him, and he lost. The third time, in 1952, Earl backed him. George shouted, "There is no question that my election represents a comeback for the Longs in Louisiana," and he was right. But when he got to Washington he developed some big ideas. "Folks always said that me, Huey and our dad bore the strongest likeness," he said. That seemed to qualify George for governor.

Actually, Earl wanted him out of Congress. It was reported in 1956 that Earl urged George to retire so that Earl's wife, Blanche, could run for his congressional seat. Mrs. Long denied this—"It's unheard of," she said. George said, "Earl thought I should retire. He did not give me any reason. But I have no intention of retiring."

He wanted to run for governor in 1956. So did Earl. So did Russell. They had a council of war and admitted publicly that they were rival candidates. George began making speeches warning the voters that Earl's health was bad, and so, "If you love Earl don't vote for him."

But after Russell withdrew from contention, so did George, and George campaigned for Earl. At the inauguration, George chuckled, "We always seem to get together at this time of year, particularly every four years."

George tried to emulate an old Long foe. Politico Dudley J. LeBlanc made a fortune after he invented the patent medicine Hadacol, which was the medicinal equivalent of a dry Martini. George decided he could do as well. He invented Vitalong, which was a patent medicine with sherry as a base. George used to leave bottles of Vitalong on the desks of the Louisiana legislators as a good-will gesture. Got him a lot of good will, too.

George was most distinguished in Washington for his organization of the prayer room just off the Capitol rotunda. He never let a constituent leave the building without inspecting this accomplishment.

George was elected to three terms in Congress before he died on March 22, 1958.

Huey's other son was Palmer Reed Long, three years Russell's junior. Palmer has never dabbled in politics, although his mother has said that Huey thought Palmer would be the Long to carry on the family's business.

Palmer has always been the quiet one in the family. He even avoided Russell's brand of politics at LSU. He married a fifteen-year-old beauty queen while he was still in college, but that lasted only a matter of weeks. (She said he married her merely to spite another girl.) Palmer has since remarried and lives in Shreveport, where he is in the oil business.

Of his political ambitions, he has said: "I have none whatsoever, unless something happens to my brother. Russell stays up in Washington and helps run the country. He'll never get rich on his salary, and since the man doesn't live who can grease his palm, keeping up the family exchequer is my business."

Uncle Earl said of Palmer, "He's always helped me, but if it came to a showdown I guess he'd be for his brother, Russell."

The beauty queen who divorced Palmer, Cleo Moore, went on to Hollywood to become a movie starlet and a minor actress. If Palmer has no political ambitions, she does. On a couple of occasions she has said she may become Louisiana's first woman governor.

"Some people in Louisiana want me to run," she said. "I can't mention their names but they want to bill me as The White Goddess. I may run. I have sense enough to know what they want to do. They want me to put across their ideas. They know that people would listen to me and even if I didn't get one vote they at least would have an audience in

Louisiana who would listen to them. And I would be sincere enough to want to help these thousands of people who still live in some other century and are kept in ignorance.

"As a gimmick and a novelty—and I have sense enough to know this—I could put across the good things they stand for. And besides they'd run me as Cleo Moore Long. There's a feeling in Louisiana that anyone with the name Long can be elected to anything."

The newest Long is Speedy O. Long, a third cousin. At thirty he recently was elected to the Louisiana state Senate.

Speedy said, "I was brought up to think that Huey Long was God Almighty, Earl was Jesus Christ and George was St. Peter. I think Earl sponsored some good legislation. I favored increased old-age pensions and increases in pay for low-salaried state employees. No man in the history of the state has done as much for the schoolteachers."

Because of his youth and because of his distant relationship, Speedy remains a question mark. Some of the Louisiana political experts consider him as a real comer. They also think it is inevitable he will tangle with Russell in the not too distant future.

Huey's wife was Rose McConnell, a Yankee. But although born in Indiana, she had moved to Shreveport at the age of seven. Huey met her when he was peddling the cooking compound Cottolene. She baked Huey a cake and she saved him from jail.

What happened was this:

Huey met Rose when she won a cake-baking contest he ran for Cottolene. They began dating, and one morning Huey was unjustly accused of shooting a man. He was arrested for the lack of a strong alibi.

Actually, he had been attending a concert with Rose at the time of the shooting. A string saver by nature, she began digging into her personal effects until she found the ticket stubs.

Huey was freed as soon as she produced them, and shortly thereafter they were married.

She kept a one-room apartment on a budget of next to nothing when he attended law school in New Orleans, helping him whip through the three-year course in a single year. "She had a typewriter," Huey said, "and immediately after reading a book I would set her down at the machine where I could dictate to her, and I would extract that book from hell to breakfast while it was fresh in my mind, and I would practically memorize the extract I dictated." When Huey campaigned for railroad commissioner, Mrs. Long did all of the clerical work. After Huey was elected governor, she retired to the background—so the public thought.

Actually, she traveled Huey's campaign routes incognito. She used the pseudonym Mrs. Hardee. "That way I could go out among the crowd and not be conspicuous," she said. "I could understand better how people reacted to his speeches. Afterward he would ask me, 'What did you make of my speech?' and I would just tell him."

Mrs. Long literally sneaked in many a kind deed while her husband was in power. Once she received a plaintive letter from a state penitentiary inmate who protested his innocence. She made a secret visit to the prison to investigate personally, and then prevailed upon Huey to give the man a pardon. Years later he appeared at her back door for a handout, and she gave it to him and sent him on his way.

While Huey surrounded himself with bodyguards, Mrs. Long often picked up hitchhikers so she could question them about political sentiments.

After Huey moved from the executive mansion in Baton Rouge to the Mayflower Hotel in Washington, his family saw less and less of him. But when he decided to make a push toward the Presidency he made certain that Rose was available for newspaper interviews when she visited New York and Washington.

After Huey died, his political survivors had the state buy the Long mansion at an inflated price for use as a "Huey P.

Long Museum" and they appointed Mrs. Long to serve one year of Huey's unexpired term in the Senate.

For a few brief moments it looked as though Mrs. Long would seriously attempt to carry on Huey's Share-the-Wealth campaign in the Senate. She announced: "I am having all of our files and records sent up. I am 100 per cent for labor and the farmers and will vote for everything to help them. In my mind, I have a hazy idea about the things I want to do but I am not yet ready to announce them."

Furthermore, Gerald L. K. Smith said that he recognized her as "titular head of the Share-the-Wealth Society." Smith said, "I, as national organizer, shall continue the work of recruiting the masses for the great cause and I am instructing organizers all over America to that effect."

But Gerald soon got a different set of instructions from the real heirs of Huey Long, and was sent packing. Earl was shuffled out of authority, and Mrs. Long served out her year in the Senate meekly. Her main contribution was to make it possible, at a later date, for Russell to become the first man in history to follow both his father *and* his mother into the Senate.

Rose soon forgot Share-the-Wealth. Far from emulating Huey as a harping enemy of the Roosevelt administration, she voted New Deal policies without exception.

She made one speech in the Senate. Hardly a filibuster, it was four hundred words long, an appeal for enlargement of New Orleans' federally owned Chalmette Park. She was so nervous her tongue got twisted. She wanted to say "delightful party on the patio," but it came out, "delightful patty in the partio."

After her year of glory she returned to retirement, first in Baton Rouge and later in Shreveport.

Her Baton Rouge palace was on an artificial lake just off the LSU campus. It included a sunken garden and a fishpond. The fishpond brought a breath of the scandals to Mrs. Long when a federal indictment, later dropped, charged that Governor Leche saw to it that $644.50 worth of WPA labor and materials were used to build the pond. Mrs. Long was not implicated either in this or in any other facet of the scandals.

Rose emerged from obscurity to help Earl when he asked the family to support his candidacy in 1940 and 1948. Her principal contribution was the assurance that as Huey's widow she had no objection to Earl's election as governor. It was part of the campaign to convince the old Huey loyalists that the feud between the two brothers should be forgiven and forgotten.

Mrs. Long had always been a beautiful if plumpish woman. She attracted considerable attention from the senatorial bachelors during her year in Washington, but when a close friend of the family asked her a few years ago why she never remarried she exclaimed, "What—and give up the name Long!"

In addition to the two sons, the Longs had one daughter, Rose Lolita, the first of the three children.

She was at LSU when her father hit the peak of his power, and naturally she was elected the Queen of everything in sight. She was on the campus when James Monroe Smith expelled the student editors for daring to criticize the Kingfish. Subsequently she made a trip to New York, and immediately the reporters who interviewed her wanted the Princessfish's version of the campus uproar.

"The rest of the students didn't apppreciate the editors' stand," she said. "We felt sorry for them. After all, they were students of journalism and it was a shame they could no more care for their profession than to do things like that. They were terrible. They called the university authorities a lot of bad names. As far as Daddy was concerned, he told us personally he was going to ask the president to put the boys back in school—"

"Oh, I don't think he would," Mrs. Long interrupted.

"I don't know how much I really should say," Rose said. "But every college publication has a board of supervision. College students can't be left to turn out everything they want to, because there are radicals in college just like in anything else."

Just as Russell wanted to go to Princeton, Rose wanted to go to Wellesley. She came closer than her brother. At first Huey insisted that if LSU was good enough for the other kids of Louisiana it was good enough for Rose. But Mrs. Long lectured him on the hard time Rose was having, what with all her accomplishments belittled as tribute automatically paid the dictator's daughter.

Huey didn't say Yes and he didn't say No, but in one of his radio speeches he announced that he was sending his daughter to Wellesley to halt the talk about favoritism on the LSU campus. Rose never made it. Her father was killed before she could transfer.

Instead, Rose went to Washington with her mother. She was the official hostess of the office, and frequently prompted her mother at press conferences.

When Rose was married to Dr. Oswynn McFarland, the wedding had all Louisiana agog. The chef at the Roosevelt Hotel baked a five-foot wedding cake which was carted to Baton Rouge by a truck creeping the eighty miles at five miles per hour. The "New Orleans boys" of the Leche administration gave her a $12,000 set of silverware. Her fiancé was appointed medical adviser to the state's Huey P. Long Memorial Hospital, and with the job went a free house and free groceries. And the state employees were so happy that they kicked in part of their salaries to buy her a gold service. At least, everyone thought they were happy, but nobody really asked them. The contributions were deducted automatically.

Blanche Long was the beauty among the Long women. Blanche Long also was the shrewdest political operator among the Long women. Blanche Long met the most vexing crisis among the Long women.

A country girl from Covington, Blanche went to business school in New Orleans and there, working at the Monteleone Hotel, she met Earl, just completing his law course. They went all the way to Estes Park, Colorado, to get married because that's where Blanche had relatives who could put on the ceremony right.

Rose Long was a way station where Huey could stop to rest and salve his wounds. Blanche Long traveled the main line all the way with Earl. Earl heeded her advice often, and there were occasions where she handled some of the delicate negotiations often necessary to fuse various factions for an election campaign.

Even after their estrangement, Earl conceded that Blanche's political advice was usually good. "She gave me only one really bum steer," he said. "When I was running in 1948 she helped them talk me into saying I wouldn't raise taxes when we knew all along we had to raise them to fulfill the program I was promising."

Blanche was elected Democratic National Committeewoman from Louisiana at a time when Earl was governor, Russell was senator, and George was in Congress. Her influence, and a series of appointments Earl gave to women, started Louisiana editorialists sniffing about "petticoat government" during Earl's 1948–1952 administration. Blanche thought this hilarious, but Earl bristled with indignation.

The Earl Longs were exact opposites. Earl was profane, crude, purposely vulgar. Blanche was sedate, prim, socially ambitious. Earl said, "She wanted to be known as the best-dressed woman in Baton Rouge, the most intelligent, the best of everything. That woman's got all kinds of ambitions."

With her love of the elegant, Blanche flatly refused even to spend weekends in the squalor of Earl's beloved peapatch farm. She liked the social life of New Orleans, and next best the small-townish society of Baton Rouge. As the state's First Lady she was the perfect hostess. She could entertain the fanciest of official guests, and she could also manage the drop-ins of Earl's redneck worshipers without a wince on her smiling face.

Her dream was a great home of her own, the kind the other big shots built during the era when Earl was out in the political cold. After Earl was elected governor in 1948, she finally saw her opportunity and began working on him. Earl was hesitant. He didn't want to spend the money, and he was worried about what the folks in the hill country would say when they learned that Old Earl had finally succumbed to snooty ways.

Blanche finally got her home, and moved into it without Earl. It was completed just about the time they separated. Blanche engineered the entire house deal herself. First she bought the land, 53,000 square feet, for $8,045. It has been unofficially appraised by real-estate people at $40,000. The man who sold her a good part of it, Ernest Wilson, president of the North Baton Rouge Development Corporation, was appointed by Earl to the Baton Rouge Port Commission. Then she built the house. Real-estate men appraised it at $150,000. Mrs. Long says it cost $60,000, but she conceded that she got a few items "at cost" and a few more for free. The house was built by George Caldwell, the former LSU construction superintendent who served four years in prison for his part in the Louisiana Scandals. Caldwell built the house at the same time he was building a $1,500,000 Highway Department headquarters for the state.

Mrs. Long was, of course, first to note that Earl was showing signs of a breakdown. She realized that his sudden self-appointment as Louisiana's greatest Romeo was completely out of character. She noted that at times Earl would work in a burst of furious activity and at times would shuffle about listlessly. She nudged him to the doctors in wifely fashion, and labored mightily to force him to take the rest they recommended.

When Earl became violent, he picked her as his first victim. She was terrified, but she did not flee. She kept going back to the doctors for help. When she finally called Russell to the executive mansion during the week Earl was shipped to Galveston, she was at her wit's end. Russell said, "She said she had been asking the doctor, please, to find some way to help and she was not getting any help."

Earl blamed her for the humiliation of his incarceration. He accused her of everything from petty jealousy to traitorous politics. His denunciations and threats were so intense that she did not dare remain in Louisiana when he was first freed from mental care. She fled to a secret hideaway—with the relatives in Colorado—and told the lawyer back home to file for a legal separation. Then she returned to Baton Rouge, and moved into that elegant mansion which didn't seem so elegant any more.

Blanche—Earl calls her only "Miz Blanche" in public and in private—took the money with her when she left. Some estimate the total as high as $750,000. She was a shrewd businesswoman, and her friends say she is a silent partner in numerous enterprises. Earl said: "She got the money, all right. You won't have to worry about Miz Blanche. She's got plenty to take care of herself and she has plenty left over to take care of Uncle Earl if she wants to."

Blanche has made it plain right along that she left Earl because she feared him and because she could no longer stand the anguish of watching him drive himself twenty hours a day while doctors were insisting upon a long and absolute rest. She would go back to him the moment he agreed to heed their advice. She was not embittered, only humiliated, by his various antics because she considered them symptoms of his mental illness.

Earl blew hot and cold on a reconciliation. He telephoned her often just after his return to Louisiana from his wild tour of the Southwest. He would start each conversation with conciliatory murmurings, inquire solicitously into her well-being, and then he would mention the horror of his commitment. That set him off again. Over the telephone his fury would come out in a stream of profanity and recriminations. There would be no more talk of reconciliation—until the next night when the same telephone conversation would be repeated.

One or two of Blanche's sisters appeared at each political crisis Earl faced, apparently to report back to Blanche on his reaction. Earl saw them and was friendly and gentle with them. He agreed to meet with Blanche secretly at least once, but was not prepared to pay her price of a reconciliation— absolute retirement from politics immediately.

Partly because they were childless, Blanche and Earl spent most of their lives as the closest of all the Longs. They wound up the farthest apart.

CHAPTER NINETEEN

*"If it is necessary to teach them decency at the end
of a hemp rope, I, for one, am willing to swing
the rope."*

HUEY SENT IN HIS TROOPS TO CAPTURE A CITY WHEN HIS BLAN-
dishments of the voters failed. Did anybody care? Did anybody
fight? Earl ran the government as a private business, uncere-
moniously firing any official who balked at his whims. Did
anybody care? Did anybody fight?

There were indeed men who cried for constitutional government in Louisiana. And there were a few horrible moments in the last three decades when these men were poised
on the brink of bloody rebellion.

One member of the state legislature, Mason Spencer, rose
to the floor in 1935 to warn against the ultimate dangers of
Longism. He said:

"When this ugly thing is boiled down in its own juices, it
disenfranchises the white people of Louisiana. I am not gifted
with second sight. Nor did I see a spot of blood on the moon
last night. But I can see blood on the polished floor of this
Capitol. For if you ride this thing through, you will travel
with the white horse of death. White men have ever made
poor slaves."

The prophecy came true all too soon. There was indeed
blood on the polished floor of that Capitol within a few
months—Huey Long's blood. No living man knows what
thoughts coursed through the mind of Dr. Carl Austin Weiss

the night he became an assassin, but every indication is that he was obsessed by freedom and the horror of losing it. Men like Dr. Weiss had been goaded for years with warnings that only the rope or the bullet could free Louisiana from Huey.

No less a public figure than the mayor of Alexandria, George W. Hardy, Jr., had told a meeting of anti-Long people, "If it is necessary to teach them decency at the end of a hemp rope, I, for one, am willing to swing the rope."

Shortly after he uttered those words in 1934, Louisiana came very close to open revolt.

Huey's second attempt to put the discriminatory "occupational tax" on Standard Oil touched it off. Standard threatened to close its Louisiana plant and, to show it meant business, it released nine hundred men from the Baton Rouge refinery. Huey settled the oil fight with his secret deal which permitted the tax but rebated most of it. Standard hired the nine hundred men back—but at a loss of their pension rights.

There is no doubt that Standard did this deliberately to set the men against Huey. The stunt worked. Far from becoming angered at their employer for the cheap trick, the men turned their fury on Huey. They banded together with a batch of disgruntled former state government employees and formed the Square Deal Association. They organized along military lines and armed their members to fight for Louisiana's freedom.

Two Square Dealers were arrested, charged with plotting to assassinate Huey. That was the fuse. The next day three hundred Square Dealers, armed with shotguns and rifles, seized the Baton Rouge courthouse and demanded that the two men be freed. They held the building for three hours, until their brethren were released.

Huey, then the United States Senator junketing in New Orleans, called for martial law, and Governor Allen obediently mobilized the state militia. The Square Dealers mobilized, too. They summoned their forces to the Baton Rouge airfield. The vanguard of Square Dealers arrived and began deploying

sentries. But before they really got started they found themselves surrounded by National Guardsmen.

A gunfight seemed certain. "I'll get the officers first, and
you start picking off the soldiers," shouted Square Dealer
Tobey LeBlanc, who earlier had announced his appointment
as executioner to "shoot down like a dog" any Square Dealer
who deserted.

"Don't shoot, Tobey," called a voice. "There ain't anybody
here but us."

Tobey looked around. Sure enough, he and one lieutenant
stood alone. The other Square Dealers were fleeing, and leading the retreat was Ernest J. Bourgeous, president of the association, who clambered up and over a six-foot fence. Bourgeous fell as he landed on the other side of the fence. He
shook his gun to see if it was clogged by mud, and it went off,
wounding one Square Dealer and accounting for the only
casualty of the battle.

But the Square Deal Association did not die despite its
Keystone Cop debacle. The members drilled in secret. And,
it should be added, the martial law remained in force. Governor Allen frequently marched his bristling troops through
the streets of Baton Rouge as a warning to the citizenry against
further revolt. In Congress Representative J. Y. Sanders, Jr.,
bewailed the "dictatorship . . . coercion . . . and intimidation"
in his home state, but to no avail.

Huey finally snuffed out the revolt through the use of two
very familiar Long techniques. First, he conducted a hearing
in which an ex-deputy sheriff testified that he had been engaged by a Square Dealer to assassinate the Kingfish. Second,
he announced to the people of Baton Rouge that as special
attorney for the Public Service Commission he had just secured a 22 to 37 per cent cut in their electric rates.

The revolt died off right there and then. The Square Dealers were dispirited even by the obviously fake testimony of
the assassination plot, and the remainder of the citizenry was
bought off for the hard cash sliced from the monthly electric
bill.

Journalists cherish the idea that all other freedoms are safe as long as the people retain a free press. The Longs disproved this. They were never able to stifle the press, and yet the press was never able to stifle them. Huey was one of the first of the big-time politicians fully to exploit the radio. That was his primary answer to the press, although he did have other techniques. He used the phrase "them lying newspapers" so often that it became part of standard political jargon in Louisiana; even Huey's opposition used it in jest as often as he used it in earnest. He planted very deeply in the minds of thousands of Louisianians the idea that they should not believe the political stories they read in the newspapers—and after that Huey had no fear of the press. Actually, he became very close to some newspapermen, but they were not Louisiana newspapermen. They were Washington correspondents of papers such as the New York *Times* and the St. Louis *Post-Dispatch*.

Huey's radio shows were exactly that—shows, rather than mere political speeches. He peppered them with music (often he claimed to have written the songs, and he was a passable piano player); he told jokes; he had guest stars. He even had a theme song, his "Every Man a King." Furthermore, his show on the state-wide network came in radio's golden age, when a depression-fettered people sat glued to the set every night for hours on end. He adopted the "Kingfish" label at a time when Amos 'n' Andy were at the peak of their popularity. It was because of his skill and effectiveness on the radio that he included a free set for every home in his Share-the-Wealth plan.

In addition to the radio, Huey had his printed circulars. He first used these in his railroad-commissioner days, before he could afford to buy radio time and before he was powerful enough to demand free time from the radio stations. The problem with circulars is not writing them or printing them, but distributing them. It is an expensive proposition. But Huey licked that. He maintained a card file of devoted Long followers in every neighborhood, and they became his district circulation managers. Once in power, he used the state's facilities—trucks, police cars, even ambulances—to fan the bundles out to these district men. He refined the system to a point where he could write a circular at noon, have it printed in the afternoon, and know that it would be on every doorstep in Louisiana by the following morning. He could answer the newspapers as fast as they could fire their charges at him.

His circulars were garish, burdened with heavy black type, and full of colorful invective. People actually looked forward to getting them. They would contain such diatribes as this, against a gubernatorial candidate who headed a burial and insurance business:

"He operates a nigger burial lodge and shroud and coffin club. He charges for a coffin and he charges $7.50 for a shroud. I am informed that a nigger is laid out, and after the mourners have left, he takes the body into a back room, takes off the shroud, nails them up in a pine box and buries them at a total cost of $3.67½ cents."

What could he answer to that? And how? No newspaper wanted to get involved in such a discussion.

Huey ran his own newspaper, too. It was first called the *Louisiana Progress* (and was printed in Mississippi) and later changed to the *American Progress*. It was primarily a house organ for the Share-the-Wealth Clubs, although it was used during election campaigns to print the libels that no legitimate newspaper would touch. It was never a daily newspaper—usually a weekly, and sometimes suspended if Huey felt no particular need for it.

The newspapers of the state were amazingly consistent in their opposition to Huey. Colonel John Ewing, who operated the New Orleans *States*, as well as papers in Monroe and Shreveport, did support Huey for his second try at becoming governor, but the association was short lived (and so, for that matter, was Ewing's control of the New Orleans *States:* he sold it shortly afterward). The New Orleans *Item,* hard pressed for survival during the depression, swung to Huey after he was in full power.

But the two strongest papers in the state, the New Orleans *Times-Picayune* and the Baton Rouge *State Times,* were consistent in their opposition to the Longs, Huey and Earl, down through the years. The *Times-Picayune* (a morning newspaper which bought the afternoon *States* from Ewing and restored it to financial health) is the giant of the state's press, with large circulation in the rural areas as well as in the city. This was the paper the Longs feared most, and it was, of course, the paper they hated most.

One night Huey became so infuriated at the *Times-Picayune* that he ordered his adjutant general to take the militia to the newspaper office and "break every goddam machine they got." Luckily cooler heads prevailed in the Kingfishery, and the order was delayed until Huey could be induced to withdraw it.

He personally ordered the newspaper's assessments doubled. He canceled its privilege of storing newsprint free in the waterfront warehouses, and his legislature passed a discriminatory half-cent-per-copy tax that had exactly the opposite effect Huey intended: The papers took this to the United States Supreme Court and permanently established the principle that discriminatory taxes on newspapers violate freedom of the press.

Huey was tough on the newspaper reporters themselves. He chortled as his bodyguards slugged photographers with blackjacks. Associated Press photographer Leon Trice was left unconscious by one of these attacks. On another occasion Huey's bodyguards held the arms of a reporter while Huey slugged him.

Earl inherited Huey's hatred of the newspapers, just as he inherited the newspapers' hatred of the Longs. He became rabid on the subject. He did not have Huey's techniques of fighting back. He was not as colorful a radio performer, he was not the vivid circular writer that Huey was, and he had no *Louisiana Progress* because Dick Leche had killed it. Furthermore, Earl emerged in the new era of television, and this worked to his disadvantage. A veteran statehouse correspondent said, for example: "For years we wrote about Earl's unsavory antics in the legislature, but the disgusting spectacle never came across to the reader. Somehow, it seemed to come out amusing or simply colorful in cold print. But when the people actually saw him for themselves on television they grasped for the first time just how outrageous it was for their governor to be acting this way."

Earl reached the point where he could not conduct a press conference or make a speech or even chat with a casual visitor without a diatribe on the *Times-Picayune*. He would tell such stories as this: "There was this old hog in the ditch and two drunk *Times-Picayune* reporters fell down with him. A nice lady came along and saw this and said, 'Well, you certainly know people by the company they keep.' The hog got up and left. He was right, too. He was an honest hog."

Earl thinks the newspapers are very unfair to him. He said, "If you believe them, I've got a pistol in each pocket and a blackjack in each hand and you'd believe I grab senators by the neck and legislators by the tail."

Earl had no bodyguard to slug photographers, but at a meeting of the legislature he did suddenly hurl a newspaper into the face of reporter Emile Comar of the New Orleans *States* and shout: "You're a goddam professional liar, a murderer, that's what you are! If you want to fight I'll get somebody to fight you." Comar had written the stories which revealed that state-prison convicts were working on the governor's Winnfield farm.

The newspapers, especially the *Times-Picayune,* can carry criticism to extremes, sometimes to the point of bad taste. Too, they often have been more concerned with the "creeping socialism" of the Longs than with the corruption. When Earl called for free school lunches and more free hospital beds during his 1948 inaugural address, the *Times-Picayune* sniffed, "It is possible that this can be overdone in a time of full employment." The papers often paid tribute to Mayor

Maestri, especially during his taxi-union-busting phase, knowing full well the faults of his administration. But their praise was a fleeting thing. Over thirty years of Longism, the newspapers have been remarkably consistent in their criticism and exposés, especially in the face of such apathy by the voting readership.

Perhaps this apathy has been justified by the dull records of the non-Long governors who have been elected during the three Long decades. Sam Jones, the man who succeeded the Leche regime, had to devote all of his energies to undoing what the Leche crowd had done; he had little time or resources left to create anything new. Jimmy Davis, the songwriting governor, was known as a do-nothing governor. ("Don't deride him for that," one political observer said. "There are times when Louisiana desperately needs a do-nothing governor just to rest up from the others. Davis gave us a period of good feeling, between the abuses of the Longs and the get-even of the reformers.") Robert Kennon spent a great deal of his time trying to convert Louisiana to Eisenhower Republicanism, an effort that probably, as much as anything else, helped to reinstall Earl Long in the statehouse. The rednecks who have become dependent upon the Long largesse are not likely converts to Republicanism—Eisenhower, Kennon, or whatever brand.

Because of his musical campaigning and his promises to "live and let live," Davis is probably the most underrated governor of the Long era. It is true that he is a writer of hillbilly songs, but it is also true that he has a master's degree in psychology and taught the subject at LSU. It is true that he was inclined to do nothing, but it is also true that he left a $30,000,000 surplus in the state general fund. It is true that he disappeared from public view to avoid taking sides in a bitter two-week milk strike, but it is also true that he made the first real improvements in the notorious Angola State Prison.

The only professional outside New Orleans who has continued in power over the full thirty years of Longism is

Leander Perez, the Big Daddy of Plaquemine Parish. He was an original supporter of Huey and was Earl's 1948 campaign manager. But he subsequently split with Longism and was a key force behind Earl's breakup.

Originally Perez ruled St. Bernard and Plaquemine parishes, those just below New Orleans. He lost his grip on St. Bernard to considerable extent when Earl's legislature divided the two-parish district attorney jurisdictions in half. He was further undermined by the arrival of New Orleans people suddenly turned exurbanites. These new voters were not dependent upon Perez' handouts for their bread and butter; they were not dependent upon Perez-controlled businesses for their jobs; and they were not schooled to fear Perez' deputy sheriffs.

But in Plaquemine he still reigns supreme. He concedes no other authority. In 1943 when the parish sheriff died, Governor Jones appointed Walter J. Blaize as acting sheriff as provided by law. But Perez doesn't recognize any but his own law. He appointed his own acting sheriff, Ben R. Slater. The only way the governor could install his man was to declare martial law and send the National Guard to march Slater out of the sheriff's office and Blaize into it. Perez had mustered his own "Home Guard" troops but they didn't show up to fight.

Perez was the moving spirit behind the Dixiecrats who challenged President Truman with a third party in 1948. The public issue was Negro rights, but this was not Perez' real concern. He was involved in offshore oil, and his strategy was to use the Dixiecrat movement to force Truman into ceding the offshore oil lands to the states where Perez could exercise his control. He failed. He then forgot about the Negro peril until he began his challenge of Earl Long, and it was then that he organized the White Citizens Councils in Louisiana.

Perez does not have many friends. In 1941 he loaned some friends his speedboat, and they came close to death when the ignition key touched off a bomb, obviously a botched attempt to assassinate the owner.

For thirty years the election returns of Perez' Plaquemine Parish have been a joke in Louisiana. The best the anti-Perez candidates can ever muster—in national, state, or parish elections alike—is ten to fifteen votes. Sometimes they get only one or two. The unanimity of opinion is remarkable.

Russell Long got into a hassle with Perez on the floor of the 1952 Democratic convention—over the loyalty-oath issue, of course—and Russell made the usual charge of stolen votes in Plaquemine Parish. But this time the charge was different. This time Russell was charging the votes were stolen *for him* once and against him once.

Russell's bitter words were overheard by eight or ten delegates at the convention, and were reported by Alex Vuillemot in the New Orleans *States*. What happened, Vuillemot wrote, was this:

When Russell refused to bolt the convention over the oath, Perez made some political threats. Russell heard about them and blew up. He shouted:

"I accepted all Perez did, the stolen votes and the ruse to confuse the voters by the marking of the ballot. I am sorry I did. It was wrong and I regret it.

"In 1948, he gave me the votes and in 1952 he did not. So the way I look at it now is this—once for me and once against me and now it's even. I don't believe I needed the stolen votes because I would have beaten Kennon anyway."

Perez wasn't present at the outbreak. Told about it later, Perez snapped, "His rash and untrue statement is the result of too much liquor."

Still later, shaken by the furor he caused, Russell tried to back off. On the convention floor he said: "I have never to my knowledge received a single stolen vote and could not prove that I have or have not ever received such votes at all.

"To be perfectly truthful, however, I have always heard it said that you either get all the votes in Plaquemine Parish or you get none at all.

"The first time I ran for office Mr. Leander Perez was for me and I carried that parish by ten to one. The second time

I ran Mr. Perez was against me and I lost the parish by ten to one although I carried every other parish in Louisiana.

"Public officials seeking state office in Louisiana generally feel that it doesn't make any difference whether you campaign in Plaquemine or not. Perez decides everything."

Does it fall only to the professionals like Perez and the New Orleans Ring to fight the Longs? Over the long run, Yes. The "better people," that is, the upper-middle and upper classes, have consistently opposed the Longs in their parlor conversations, and occasionally they band together in good government organizations to fight corruption and dictatorship. But they have shown no stamina in the fight. In Huey's era the good-government forces formed what they called the Constitutional League. Huey immediately dubbed it the Constipational League, and described it as a band of the old mob he had scattered from the trough. These outs yearning to get back in certainly were a part of the Constitutional League. But the sincere good-government elements were in it, too, and the league was dogged in its exposures of Longism's excesses. Its lack of success was monumental.

Upon the outbreak of the scandals the good-government forces reached their peak in popularity and efficiency. The young lawyers of New Orleans, weary of fighting the palm-greasing old guard in the corrupt courts, were particularly active in attempting to clean up the state's politics. These forces did a lot to show the man in the street how he had been duped and fleeced by the Leche crowd, but mostly they were the caboose of someone else's train. Rogge's federal investigators were the men who actually cleaned out Louisiana politics for the moment, and any help they got was incidental.

The Boston Club set, which represents New Orleans' big money, had mixed feelings about the Leche administration. It was corrupt, and the Boston Clubbers opposed that. But it was kind to business, and the Boston Clubbers liked that. They were grateful to Leche for dispensing with the rabble rousing that marked Huey's every speech. They did not show the antipathy to Leche that they showed first to Huey, and later to Earl, until Dick Leche was on his way to jail.

Longism is complicated enough to escape the colorings of black and white. Many people who objected to corruption and dictatorship heartily sided with both Huey and Earl in their social reforms. On the other hand, many people who scorned the social reforms were quite happy to make profitable deals with the Long state governments. These conflicts account to a large measure for the fact that Louisiana never has mustered a solid opposition to the demagoguery which has fettered it for three decades.

There are too many people satisfied with just one slice of that pie in the sky.

CHAPTER TWENTY

"He kept faith with his people and they with him."

THIRTY YEARS IS AN AWFULLY LONG TIME. THE BABIES BORN ON the day Huey Long became governor have seen one and a half wars, wringing depression and overflowing prosperity, the birth of the atomic age and the space age and the television age and jet age and even the juvenile-delinquency age.

And because thirty years is such a long time, some political Houdini might gouge out the bronze memorials which the Longs have embedded in their bridges and highways and roads, and might even root the Longs themselves out of public office, yet still not eradicate the stamp which the Longs have placed on Louisiana's politics.

Huey Long created a class revolution. There can be no doubt about that, whatever degree of sincerity you grant him. He made the mass of voters a power to be catered to and reckoned with, a healthy change from the old order in which the voters catered to the officeholders. He was not 100 per cent demagogue. The issues he raised were real, and his promises of solutions were at least partly fulfilled. If he made a single contribution to Louisiana politics, it is this: The candidates for office must now tell the voters exactly what they propose to give them. No longer can a man get elected on a flowery tribute to the glories of the Confederacy.

His brother Earl is not unimportant in this change. Huey might have been a political meteor, momentarily glimpsed, had not Earl picked up the policies and demonstrated their durability. This is Russell's importance, too, for he shows that he can modernize Longism with just a little retooling and carry it forward another decade or two.

Louisiana has every possible excuse to challenge Arkansas and Mississippi and Alabama for the backwards championship of America. Yet because of the Longs, Louisiana has been a pioneer in many social improvements, challenging such traditionally progressive states as New York and California in every category where a state helps its have-nots pull up to a level approximating decent existence.

It may be said that Long did these things during a period of general social change and that few states fail to provide the benefits maintained in Louisiana. This would be only partly true. Long began his social changes before the New Deal—he had completed his term as governor and was in the Senate before Franklin Roosevelt's election. In addition, Louisiana moved faster than most states in adopting state welfare programs even after the New Deal set the pattern in the 1930's.

What has been the effect on government? On the people? On business? On education?

The blessings are, of course, mixed. The government of Louisiana is top-heavy and laden with crass patronage. At last count, there were 207 state agencies (a jump of 34 over a five-year period), and 87 per cent of these were administered by multimembered boards or commissions. Furthermore, the Public Affairs Research Council reveals, more than two-thirds of the 1,317 executive positions in the government are filled by gubernatorial appointment. These people do not answer directly to the electorate and they have no protection from civil service.

They do administer the mammoth Louisiana welfare and construction programs with efficiency, if not with economy. There is little bureaucratic callousness toward the public. Earl Long has taught them that the customer is always right. Mussolini made the trains run on time. Earl Long made the pension-check deliveries on time.

Huey's use of the militia and the packed parish boards has

made home rule a touchy political issue in Louisiana. The grass-roots politicians pledge their lives upon it, in theory. But as is usual in the case of big government, home rule is always eagerly surrendered when the state agrees to finance a town or parish function.

Important politically is the fact that the Longs gave Louisiana the two-party system—not Democrats and Republicans, but Longs and anti-Longs. This is an asset. The legislatures are not reduced to chaos by a scattershot of splinter groups. The voters can select a straight ticket and know approximately what they are getting. Campaign funds, although often unsavory in the collection, become a virtue in the spending: The money filters down through the entire ticket and gives a little man a chance to run for a little office without going on some selfish interest's retainer.

Of course, Louisiana's unique two-party system is not all to the good. The Long party has the advantage in that it is organized, with a single purpose, while the anti-Longs are continually rent by varying shades of opinion. Too often the elections become a plebiscite, with the voter having the opportunity of either endorsing the Longs or indicating no-confidence by casting a vote for one of several anti-Long men. The anti-Long men will kill one another off. This can happen, however, only in a first primary. If the majority of votes are anti-Long, a second primary will result. And in the second primary the issue is clear: Long versus anti-Long.

The poor have learned to depend upon the Long welfare state for their bread and butter and appendectomies. This has produced a splendid by-product: unusually good medical education. New Orleans can maintain two top-flight medical schools, Tulane and LSU, because the mammoth Charity Hospital presents such an abundance and variety of experience to fledgling doctors.

The middle- and upper-income groups pay their taxes with only the usual squawks, and otherwise accept the welfare state with reasonably good grace. For one thing, even the New Orleans country club set benefits from things like the sleek maroon Charity Hospital emergency ambulances which respond to accident calls with magnificent speed and equipment.

The Negroes owe and show a special gratitude to the Longs. For all the furor over public-school integration in the South, many Negro civic leaders think the salvation of their race is in the vote rather than in the court decree. In Louisiana the Negro has seen the power of the vote. In most Southern states the colored man has little choice of candidates, even when he can wriggle through the barriers to vote. One candidate tries to outprejudice the other in current political campaigns. But in Louisiana the Longs did give the Negroes a candidate in whom they could have faith. As mentioned earlier, the Negroes gave Earl Long the margin of first primary victory in 1956. Although the White Citizens Council purges of the voting rolls undoubtedly mean a temporary setback, the Negroes never again can be discounted politically in Louisiana.

Even Leander Perez recognized this when, speaking to a segregationist rally, he deplored the fact that "white politicians are now campaigning at Nigra fishfrys." Fast becoming political legend is the story of the candidate for sheriff in a southern parish who first addressed his formal announcement to "all the white voters of this parish," and then, having been defeated by the margin of the Negro vote, issued a new candidacy four years later to "all the voters of this parish, regardless of race, color or creed." He was defeated again, by the Negro vote again, and in the process learned that the Negro memory was equal to the white.

Despite the heavy taxation and class warfare promoted by the Longs, business has suffered none. New industries flocked to Louisiana even under Huey's dictatorship, and they have continued to increase. The Longs' bark has been far louder than their bite insofar as business is concerned. For all their promises to soak the rich, the Longs actually spread their high taxes very evenly over the entire population. Nothing and no one is exempt. Nothing and no one is bankrupted.

The courts have suffered most under Longism. Lawyers without the proper connections often don't fare very well no matter what the merits of their cases. One oil-company fixer openly boasts in New Orleans of the Cadillacs he has presented to some prominent jurists for Christmas. One state Supreme Court justice recently admitted he had not filed a federal income-tax return for several years.

Otherwise, the professions fare well. Because the charity hospitals have taught them the benefits of proper medical treatment, the people continue to seek it even when they begin footing their own bills. Educators also have profited from the Long emphasis on schooling. Both Huey and Earl drummed into the country folk the blessings of education, especially when it is free. And when the conservatives criticized Earl for overdoing things when he proposed free lunches for all school children, he came back with a sensible answer: "There's no point in providing free education if the children are going to school hungry." The Longs carried their free-education ideas up through the graduate schools of the university—which are not absolutely free, but as close to it as they can get at the moment. Earl did not tamper with academic freedom as did Huey, nor did Earl use the LSU football team and band and ROTC units as personal campaign trappings.

It was quite fashionable in the 1930's for magazine writers to depict Huey as a fascist or as a socialist. He was neither. He did realize the value of the parades and the staged rallies which Hitler and Mussolini utilized, and his Share-the-Wealth Plan certainly had socialist overtones. But Huey scoffed at the fascist and socialist labels. "Even if fascism or socialism comes to this country," he said, "it will come under a different name and be strictly American in type."

Huey was much more the pure American demagogue. But even in this respect he was unique. For one thing, he gave his people far greater rebates than the Georgians got from Talmadge or the Mississippians from Bilbo. Those states have yet to match even the road network that Huey left—and meanwhile Earl has improved upon this considerably. It was because of this that Richard Leche could remark in public:

"They're saying that Governor Allen and others stole millions. Suppose they did steal a few millions? Look what the people got."

The people got their roads and bridges. And they also got the state militia in the middle of the night. Must there have been both? Huey said Yes: to do things you must first get the power. But more learned students of government, blessed, it must be admitted, by the gift of hindsight, say otherwise. Huey had a great percentage of the people behind him anyway. He could have won any election honestly. His frequent use of the militia and of the Criminal Investigation Bureau was born of his impatience and his lust for power rather than of political necessity. Huey enjoyed this undue show of strength. This was his major failing and undoubtedly the cause of his early death.

It has become fashionable of late for political scientists to re-evaluate the administration of Huey Long and to grace him with praise from quarters where he rated only damnation while he lived.

Professor V. O. Key, Jr., of Johns Hopkins, made a study of Southern electoral processes under a Rockefeller Foundation grant and came up with this summation:

"He kept faith with his people and they with him. He gave them something and the corporations paid for it. He did not permit himself, in an oft-repeated pattern, to be hamstrung by a legislature dominated by old hands experienced in legislation and frequently under corporate retainer. He elected his own legislature and erected a structure of political power both totalitarian and terrifying.

"To the charge that he came to terms with the interests, the reply of the Long partisan is that the terms were Huey's. He is not to be dismissed as a mere rabble rouser or leader of a gang of boodlers. Nor can he be described by convenient label: fascist, communist. He brought to his career a stroke of genius, yet in his program and tactics he was as indigenous to Louisiana as pine trees and petroleum."

In the end, Huey's legacy was not the dictatorship but the

welfare program. It is an oversized program, to be sure. Going through the state-by-state lists of expenditures for various benefits, it is obvious that Louisiana does more than its share for its people. It is obvious also that too many individuals seem to qualify for the benefits only when Earl Long sits in the statehouse. But at the same time, Louisiana does have real need. It is a state with a rich port and with oil in its bowels. Yet the median income for whites is under $3,000 a year, and the median income for Negroes (who make up 33 per cent of the population) is scarcely over $1,000 a year.

One reason for this is the low incidence of organized labor. For all their devotion to the poor man, the Longs have not been outstanding friends of the unions. Earl did have the support of the unions, as much by default as by any favors he granted. The chairman of the state AFL-CIO became one of his closest friends. The Longs have remained aloof from the unions for two reasons: the comparatively low membership rolls and the danger that organized workers may transfer their gratitude from the Longs to the union as the benefits mount.

The war which the Longs waged against the newspapers for many years has claimed no noteworthy casualties. The only paper to die in the battle was the Long paper, the *Progress*, and this death can only be held a contribution to journalism. The papers which fought the Longs hardest have thrived most. Those which tended to shilly-shally died, but they did so as a result of economic attrition rather than of any reasons political. As a matter of fact, in most cases the shilly-shallying was the act of a financially sick newspaper hoping to get some state printing business from a Long administration.

The future of Longism rests today, of course, with Russell. It is possible that he will rise to a height never attained by his father and uncle. If, for example, Russell could succeed in his romance with New Orleans' "better people" and yet retain the old Long support because of his liberalism, he would emerge as the most powerful Long of all: he would have captured the enemy without the loss of a friend.

But should the country-club set fail to accept Russell, he still inherits a loyal and personal following. After the scandals disclosed the corruption and cynicism of the regime, the Gallup Poll went in to learn if the people still loved Huey. They did. The poll found that 55 per cent of the voters still thought Huey Long was "a good influence in the state." For all the side forays into the state treasury, he had led them where they yearned to be led. And, after all, as a seventeenth century English statesman said:

"A King is a thing men have made for their own sakes, for quietness' sake. Just as in a Family one man is appointed to buy the meat."

INDEX

Index